CHRISTIAN HERITAGE COLLEGE
2100 Greenfield Dr.
El Cajon, CA 92021

BLACK and CONSERVATIVE

BLACK AND CONSERVATIVE

THE AUTOBIOGRAPHY OF

GEORGE S. SCHUYLER

ARLINGTON HOUSE·PUBLISHERS
81 CENTRE AVENUE • NEW ROCHELLE, N. Y. 10801

To Josephine

Library of Congress Catalog Card Number 66-23140

BLACK and CONSERVATIVE

CHAPTER 1

A BLACK PERSON learns very early that his color is a disadvantage in a world of white folk. This being an unalterable circumstance, one also learns very early to make the best of it. So the lifetime endeavor of the intelligent Negro is how to be reasonably happy though colored. Certainly this requires considerable doing and, like all other people, the colored are not equally endowed with alertness, resourcefulness, ingenuity, and adaptability. Some have been unable to triumph over the vicissitudes of varying environments while others have. On the whole it is remarkable that the "race" has survived and prospered beyond the wildest imaginings of their forebears who stumbled ashore tethered by the Founding Fathers.

Contrary to the pundits on the Negro (or Caucasian!) problem who bewail the American racial facts of life, most of the colored brethren do not go about perpetually enveloped in gloom and despair despite the ululations and incitements of their professional agitators. Of course, not being insane, they are not always

1

happy and gay, as traditional "Southrons" have insisted for a century—but on the whole neither are the Caucasians of either high or low estate. It is ironical, however, that this fiction of eternal colored laughter has resulted in the Nordic adoption of the Negro minstrel grin as our national facial expression.

Puzzled head-waggers too often underestimate the human ability to adjust and adapt to environment and frequently to alter it to advantage.

The American Negro is a prime example of the survival of the fittest, and it is enlightening to contrast his position today with that of the Amerindian. He has been the outstanding example of American conservatism: adjustable, resourceful, adaptable, patient, restrained, and not given to gambling what advantages he has in quixotic adventures. This has been the despair of the reformers who have tried to lead him up on the mountain and who have promised him eternal salvation. Through the succeeding uproars and upheavals that have attended our national development, the Negro has adjusted himself to every change with the basic aim of survival and advancement. Had he taken the advice of the minority of firebrands in his midst, he would have risked extermination. The ability to conserve, consolidate, and change when expedient is the hallmark of individual and group intelligence. It is why the Negro will always be here. As the law, history, and literature show, no other element of the population has had a more profound effect on our national life. They have less reason than any others to harbor any feelings of inferiority, although naturally they suffer from frustration.

I learned very early in life that I was colored but from the beginning this fact of life did not distress, restrain, or overburden me. One takes things as they are, lives with them, and tries to turn them to one's advantage or seeks another locale where the opportunities are more favorable. This was the conservative viewpoint of my parents and family. It has been mine through life, not consistently but most of the time.

I was born in Providence, Rhode Island, on February 25, 1895, and reared in Syracuse, New York. If any of the family were ever slaves, it must have been before the Revolutionary War. On my father's side, they came from the Albany-Troy area. A great-grandfather fought under General Philip Schuyler and after the war became one of the first workers at the famed Watervliet Arsenal. My father, George Francis Schuyler, son of Anthony Schuyler, was born in Troy, New York, in 1842, and died on September 20, 1898.

My maternal great-grandmother came from Madagascar, was bound to service around Freehold, New Jersey, and married a sea captain named Liedendraugt from Saxe-Coburg. Interracial marriages were not uncommon in that time and area nor were color caste lines as firmly set as they became later. Many of Britain's Hessian mercenaries who had deserted to the New Jersey hills married escaped slaves or free colored girls. Malagasy maidens often have golden complexions, aquiline features, large eyes, and naturally wavy hair, thanks to Malayan mixture. One would easily find favor in any swain's eyes.

My grandmother, Helen Louisa Leidendraugt, was born in New York City on March 10, 1831, a time when colored people had the first free schools in the city and a wider diversity of employment than they had a century later. Many were seamen, both on merchant ships and naval vessels; there were several wealthy caterers, and much property was owned by them. The European immigration of the 1840's increasingly made Negro existence more parlous.

My grandmother married Philip Tod Fischer, and from this union came two daughters, Eliza Jane Fischer, my mother, and Amy Fischer, my aunt. My mother was born in New York City on February 28, 1860. Philip Tod Fischer was born in 1812 and died in 1876.

My grandmother told fascinating stories about the colored in New York of her time. In colonial days they originally settled just north of the wall they helped build that is now known as Wall Street. Later they centered in lower Greenwich Village around Minetta Lane and Bleecker Street.

I learned that some Amerindians were mixed up in the family, as was common along the Atlantic seaboard from earliest times. Indeed, it would be hard to find an old American family, colored or white, without Indian or African ancestry.

My folks boasted of having been free as far back as any of

them could or wanted to remember, and they haughtily looked down upon those who had been in servitude. They neither cherished nor sang slave songs. Such prejudices did not die among Northern Negroes until after World War I and the inrush of Southern migrants. Many regarded the latter as illiterate, ignorant, ill-bred, and amoral; as people with whom they neither had nor wanted anything to do. Like the European immigrants, most of the Southern Negro migrants naturally did not represent the better circumstanced or well mannered. The old Northern Negro families had the habits, traits, and outlook of the whites for whom they worked and whose prejudices they shared. They regarded the poor European immigrants, who were culturally on a par with the people from Dixie, as in the same class.

We lived in a two-story house on an unpaved, tree-shaded street with plank sidewalks a short distance from South Salina Street, the main thoroughfare in Syracuse, New York. Our family was the only colored one on the street. This was not unusual because there were fewer than one thousand Negroes in the total population of about 100,000, and they were scattered over the south and east sides of town. At one end of our block was a bicycle factory, alongside Onondaga Creek which flooded the factory's basement each spring. Across from it were the offices of a brewery and at the other end of the block, diagonally across from each other, were a German butcher shop and an Irish saloon.

Holy of Holies in our house was the large, carpeted parlor with its stiffly starched lace curtains, gleaming black square piano with a zither atop it, rose upholstered French chairs and sofa, a whatnot with curios from the Columbian Centennial Exposition of 1893 in Chicago, and a large green rug with a Saint Bernard dog depicted upon it. Two large potted palms almost reaching to the ceiling lent elegance to the scene, and between them on a small table was a large kerosene lamp with a hand-painted globe. The double doors of this room were kept closed and the window shades drawn except on special occasions or for cleaning.

Adjoining this shrine was a large sitting room with chairs and a reading table and a big coal stove with dozens of isinglass

4

windows through which in winter it was pleasant to watch the glowing red anthracite coals. It had nickel plated trim and sat on a zinc pad with a gleaming, well-filled scuttle of coal beside it. There the family gathered for evening Bible readings by my grandmother, a sage, crusty, and industrious matriarch, the repository of all knowledge, it seemed, and a mine of folklore. Any youthful dereliction was rewarded with a sharply pinched ear or the thumping of a bony knuckle against the side of the head.

This martinet presided over the huge coal-burning kitchen range, an impressive array of brass and iron pots well polished with ashes, a big ice refrigerator, and the kitchen floor almost white from sand polishing. She produced a steady stream of delectable culinary creations, bread, pies, and cookies which went into shelves and bins in the adjoining pantry, which also contained the chinaware, silver, flour, brown sugar, molasses, potatoes, onions, peas, and beans.

There was a dining room with a large oval table which could be extended with leaves when company was expected, six or eight chairs, a glass china closet for different kinds of tumblers and stemware, and on a wide wainscoting head high around the room were arranged large blue Dutch plates for decoration. The room was carpeted, and there were stiff lace curtains at both windows.

Downstairs there was a small sewing room with a foot-pedaled machine, baskets full of scraps of clothing, a dress form, and a sewing table. There was one small bedroom adjoining it, occupied by my grandmother. The other bedrooms were all on the second floor. All had large carved poster beds, marble-topped bureaus and washstands, flowered bowls, pitchers, and chamber pots, commodes for clothing, and a chair or two.

There was a rigid schedule of dusting, sweeping, mopping, scrubbing, laundering, ironing, soap-making, cooking, and baking. A little boy's job was to dust where the elders could not easily reach. Everybody had something to do and did it. There were a dozen kerosene lamps to be filled and cleaned, and have their wicks trimmed. There was kindling wood to be chopped and fetched. There was a front and back stoop to be swept or washed down. There were windows to be cleaned, and a dozen other chores to do. Order and discipline prevailed, and it was all very impressive. I was delighted to participate in maintaining the home. Here was something admirable to be preserved and improved. People are conservative when they feel that they have something to conserve.

Impressive, too, was the fact that all of the families on the block followed the same housekeeping routine. Without any calendar one could tell the day of the week by the activities going on: the boiling and washing of clothing; the sheets, pillowcases and clothing billowing on the clothes lines; the smell of waxed hot irons on starched garments; the odor of baking bread, cakes, and pies, with the latter arranged temptingly on window sills. There was housecleaning in the spring and canning in the fall, along with making a jug or two of wine. It took a lot of hands to do all the necessary chores in such large households, but there were many hands at home to do it. The employment of women was meager except as domestics. Men mostly held the clerical jobs and the factory work, too. Of course, every child had a chore to do, and woe upon him or her if that assignment was neglected! Punishment was swift, and frequently the young culprit was sent out to cut an appropriate switch for the inevitable spanking—he'd better not return with a fragile one!

The German butcher shop window was fascinating to behold with not only great haunches and ribs, but also sausages, rabbits, ducks, chickens, turkeys, and game birds—a staggering variety from which to choose. The butcher was a rotund and jovial fellow with a walrus mustache and a hearty laugh for all.

Diagonally across from the butcher shop was the corner saloon with the familiar swinging doors, the free lunch counter, and the comfortable family parlor with its paintings of pretty cherubim and bucolic scenes. Women and children, of course, were not permitted in barrooms. It was only out West, I later discovered, that women bellied to the bar and put their feet on the brass rail. When children were sent to the saloon with a large pail and a dime for beer, they entered the family room and then signaled to the bartender from the connecting doorway. He would come and take the well-greased pail and fill it up. The grease inside was to "kill the foam" and yield more solid brew. This trek to the saloon was called "rushing the growler" and was a family pastime. More affluent folk had cases of beer delivered at fifty cents per case. Downtown there were saloons where a 22-ounce goblet of beer cost five cents, and if a customer drank two in succession, he was given the third, along with a selection of whatever food was on the steam table. Nobody dared come in and try to eat unless he had bought a glass of beer. The retired prizefighters and ex-convicts who were hired as bouncers saw that the rule was obeyed.

Along with this dispensing of the Demon Rum went the Temperance movement, the occasional visits of Carrie Nation, and the wearing of the white Temperance ribbon in the lapels of men's coats. Evangelists came periodically to "save" the populace. They must have been effective, too, because there were successful drives against the brothels which flourished in every city from the Atlantic to the Pacific, and which soon officially disappeared save in the most hardened hell holes.

All of these developments were mentioned in the home, and little children have big ears, even if they may not understand what they are hearing. Of course, at that time they dared not ask; they had to figure it out themselves.

On our block, as perhaps on all others, every adult was the superior of every youngster. Boys tipped their hats to elders, and little girls curtsied. Any dereliction of conduct observed by an elder was corrected there and then with a tongue-lashing, a twisting of the ear, or even a spanking, depending on the severity of the offense. Worst of all, it was then reported to one's parents, and the punishment was repeated, possibly exceeded. The elder reporting the infraction was profusely thanked. It mattered not what color the parties were. Indeed, people thought of each other as individuals and families rather than as colors and races. They visited each other's homes and the children played together and, of course, went to school together.

All of these people were workers. They went to their jobs at seven or eight o'clock in the morning and returned around six o'clock in the evening. On construction jobs there were pauses for beer at ten o'clock, lunch from twelve to one, a beer pause at three, and on the whole the tempo was leisurely. Many workers came home for lunch as did the children. There was no such thing as school lunch.

There were at the time six lager breweries in town and one that made ale. Each brewery had in the foyer a large brass-bound barrel on a pedestal or rack of polished pipes from which a huge beaker of free brew was dispensed to all visitors, adults that is.

My grandmother had a night job cleaning the office of a brewery a block away. She would often take me with her. Ever and anon she would pause in her chores, draw a huge goblet of the cool beer, and drink it down with one extended swallow, after which she would exclaim blissfully, "Aye, it cuts the phlegm!" This spectacle entranced me, and I yearned to emulate her. Many years later when I was a soldier in Hawaii, I recall my triumph in acquiring the knack of drinking down a whole quart of beer, breathing the while, and yet never removing the neck of the bottle from my mouth.

I can very dimly recall my father as a balding brown man with a stately mustache. He was a chef in a local hotel, and they said he had traveled far and wide over the world as boss of many a ship's galley and told lively tales of his experiences. The women talked about him long after he died, and they related one of his favorite stories about the fierce, sexy girls of Valparaiso, Chile, an important coaling and supply station where ships stayed for several days. When a woman became enamored of one of the sailors, she would in all likelihood put her mark on his cheek with the jeweled dagger she wore in her hair in order to hold him in port and nurse him until his wound healed. I never had this confirmed by anybody who had visited Valparaiso, but I believed it.

A head chef was an aristocrat in the colored community, and so my father affected baronial living, insisted on a good table, and dressed well. His passing must have been a blow to the family, which was left without a provider. However, it was not

8

entirely as tragic a blow as it would have been to less self-reliant white women of their status. They simply took domestic jobs.

Aunt Amy, a rotund, light-brownskinned disciplinarian, insisted upon having her way and her say, and she had a very sharp tongue. Twice wed, she had a daughter by each union: Lila by her first husband, Watson, and Mary Louise by her second husband, a New York French hairdresser named Worré, recently deceased. Lila was dark brown and attractive; Louise was very light-skinned and very pretty, resembling a Sicilian or Andalusian.

When there was company for dinner, we three children ate in the kitchen, but generally we ate in the dining room with the adults. We spoke only when directly addressed, and our replies were monosyllabic.

The family ate well. I remember gleaming silver service, Haviland china, preserved fruit, and fresh fruit in season, with oranges at Thanksgiving and Christmas. It was a spectacle to see a huge silver platter of creamed codfish garnished with sliced boiled eggs and sprinkled with chopped parsley sitting in the center of the table.

Not a mouthful was eaten before a lengthy blessing, often preceded by a passage from the Bible. Dishes of food were not reached for but passed around by request. Decorum was invariable, and I cannot recall hearing a quarrel at the table. People of our class ate larger quantities and a greater variety of food than they do now, with meat and even pie for breakfast.

I heard that once the family had operated a hand laundry, but this must have been before my time. When my father died he was a chef in a local hotel. The recollection of the funeral is very faint, and it had no meaning to me then. What most impressed me at the time was being downtown with my grandmother one day when the first steam automobile came down the main street spouting white clouds of steam while an immense crowd watched.

I was a favorite with the men who hung around the nearby livery stable and blacksmith shop. They would give me candy and coppers, sometimes one of the two-cent pieces. I liked to

9

watch the sparks fly from the anvil, hear the ring of the hammer, and see the horses shod and curried, then hitched to gleaming carriages and hacks and driven away. Pleasant to the ear in winter was the chorus of sleigh bells ranging from the tinkling of the tiny ones on the one-horse sleighs to the loud bong-bong of those on the huge drays.

My mother had taught me the alphabet, forward and backward, and how to count. I could write one-syllable words on my slate, which was one of my proudest possessions. There was a kindergarten not far away, and it was there that I was taught to write my name. That was a proud day!

The first political event I recall was the assassination of President William McKinley at the Buffalo Exposition by the alien anarchist, Czolgosz. Great indignation was expressed by the adults. I was told that an anarchist was one of those foreigners who believed in no government at all. This seemed incredible. To me, government represented the genial cop on the corner, the jangling fire engines with their galloping horses, the even tenor of the way of life in our neighborhood. These were things one wanted to conserve.

Shortly afterward, my mother remarried. My stepfather was Joseph E. Brown, a stocky, light-colored man with wavy hair parted in the middle, and a false eye which I soon discovered he kept in a glass of water overnight. He came from Milledgeville, Georgia, and was an ambitious, industrious man of limited education who read only a newspaper, briefly. He belonged to a couple of the Negro fraternal organizations and cut quite a figure in his lodge uniform with plumed hat and gleaming sword. These Negro lodges played a much larger role in the colored community then than they do today.

After what I had heard the family say about Southern Negroes, the marriage surprised me, but I soon came to like him, and my mother seemed happy. She called him Gene. They contracted to buy a new fourteen-room house on the outskirts of the Brighton community on Wyman Avenue, a half-mile from the end of the streetcar line. The open-air streetcar ride out there with my mother was my first journey.

The new place was a revelation. Beside the two-story house loomed a huge oak tree that shaded half the roof, and alongside it was a large, fenced cornfield belonging to a neighbor. On our large lot was a cow shed, a chicken coop with a score of hens and a half dozen Chinese geese, some peach trees, a tiny vegetable garden, and the inevitable outdoor toilet.

The basement had a cement floor and a large cistern in one corner which served pumps on each floor. There was a coal bin and many shelves for storing preserves. Upstairs there was a parlor, dining room, sitting room, pantry, kitchen and two bedrooms. The second floor was similar. Above it was the attic reached by a ladder and one small room with a dormer window. There we later stored a ten-gallon jar of elderberry wine.

Our block was a long one, and there were not more than a half dozen houses on it. The street was unpaved, with plank sidewalks most of the way. After a heavy rain it was a quagmire. The last house at the end of the block was not far from tree-bordered Onondaga Creek. This popular swimming hole was a wide place screened by oaks, elms, and weeping willows. There the neighborhood kids cavorted, and there I was almost drowned.

Across the field from the rear of our land was a brickyard pond about a block long where toy boats were sailed and our half dozen Chinese geese swam.

In the summer one went picking wild strawberries and rasp-berries in the fields which were a riot of buttercups, goldenrod, daisies, clover, and sunflowers. Beyond them was the open country, a place of bucolic beauty, ever beckoning the youthful explorer, even in winter when snowshoes were necessary to skim the deep drifts.

Three Negro families lived on the block; one at each end and another next door. They were all Southerners recently moved to the city, and my mother did not associate with them. She felt that they were uncouth. They were never invited to our home. They had no standards, she charged, and didn't know how to act. On the other hand, she was quite friendly with a couple of white families that lived across the fields on another street. When she went to town, she would leave me with one of them until she returned. They did the same, leaving their children at our house for mother to look after and feed. These families were Yankees, and my mother said they were her kind of people.

Directly across the street lived a white Southerner with whom neither my mother nor my stepfather had anything to do. Relations were worsened by her charge that this man had given our half-bloodhound and half-bulldog some ground glass in his food. However, I was very friendly with their son who was about my age. We went berrying and frog-hunting together in the summer and built a big snowhouse together in the winter.

Not only was our neighbor a white Southerner and a suspected dog-poisoner, but even worse he was a Socialist whereas my people were Republicans. So were most Negroes at that time, not having forgotten the Civil War and those responsible for it. My grandmother and mother gave me my first lessons in Negro history by telling me of the draft riots in New York City in which white mobs hunted down Negroes like rabbits and burned down the colored orphan asylum and, before the war, of the dramatic story of the rescue of a Southern Negro slave in downton Syracuse by a crowd of Abolitionists and sympathizers from Southern police officers who had come up to reclaim him. Later on I saw the building downtown and its commemorative plaque.

However, there was surprisingly little talk in our home or in the town generally about the race problem. Prejudice on grounds of so-called race existed and one did not have to go far to find discrimination. There were people who did not want Negro neighbors, and there were fine restaurants and bars, I heard, where the patronage of colored people, no matter how well dressed and well behaved, was not encouraged. Reportedly, colored theatergoers could with difficulty buy seats in the orchestra section of the six theaters but were welcomed mostly in the back balcony and gallery. Of course, few Negroes in our town could afford orchestra seats. If a colored person wanted to rent a home, he might encounter difficulties in certain areas of town, and not due just to lack of money.

I asked my stepfather what a Socialist was, and he told me that the Socialists were people who wanted to divide up all the wealth other people had accumulated by industry and thrift. I couldn't see the sense in that, and I can't see it now, after having read much of the standard Socialist propaganda "literature" available. Indeed, it was reading Socialist tracts and apologetics that turned me definitely against all collectivism.

It was about this time that my mother took me to town to see a stock company play *Richard the Third* and *Macbeth* at the Weiting Opera House. Whether we sat in the balcony or gallery I do not remember, but I do know that Shakespeare won an ardent fan.

Whenever a colored show came to town, Negroes were freely admitted to the orchestra section, and most of them went. Almost all of the big Broadway hits eventually took to the road and all of them played Syracuse. This included the considerable number of all-colored shows such as Cole and Johnson's extravaganza, *The Red Moon,* and Williams and Walker's musical comedies. We could not attend the theater often because even in that day when tickets cost little we could not always afford it. Many circuses came to town in season and almost all of them, along with the medicine shows, carried a troupe of Negro entertainers and musicians. I enjoyed immensely these theater excursions.

It was during that period in Brighton on Wyman Avenue that my mother introduced me to the world of books. While she was a woman of modest schooling, not having gone beyond the eighth grade, she had a love of learning and literature and possessed a little library of perhaps one hundred books. She would read aloud to me the poetry of Whittier, Longfellow, Tennyson, and Kipling, and she read very well. When I was able to read better, I read our big, profusely illustrated copy of *The Black Phalanx* by Wilson, lying on our parlor rug and learning about Negro soldiers and sailors who had fought in all of our wars. This was a fascinating revelation, and no colored child could harbor any feeling of inferiority afterward. It was even more impressive to know that many such background books were written by colored people.

My mother was a religious woman, but she was not a regular churchgoer. We were officially Episcopalians and usually attended the little St. Philip's chapel located in the section of town where most Negroes lived. The better class attended it, although they also could attend the white Episcopal churches. I learned later that the family had been Roman Catholic but found the Episcopal church more to their liking. St. Philip's was supported by the diocese and had a colored priest. In addition, there were small Negro Baptist and Methodist churches, but their support must have been meager because the colored population was so sparse. The Episcopalians looked down upon them. Negroes were not barred from white churches, but they felt that they were just tolerated. The white Catholics were mainly people of alien European background, and there was prejudice against them.

Later, when we moved back into town from Wyman Avenue, my mother started attending a little Seventh Day Adventist church on Saturdays. The simple services and instruction appealed more to me than the Episcopal ritual. I liked their method of teaching the Bible, but I was even more intrigued by their dietary practices. They were pioneers in the food faddism which, like ragtime music, was sweeping the country. Those were the early days of corn flakes, shredded wheat biscuits, and grape nuts. The Seventh Day Adventists ground their own flour in little hand mills and made their own whole wheat bread which was most tasty.

Most people then also baked their own bread, cookies, cakes, and pies, but they generally used white flour, although whole wheat flour could be bought. On the other hand, brown sugar was far more generally used than it is today. Drippings from animal fat were saved in a large can and used in cooking and to make soft soap for laundering. There were canned foods for sale, but my grandmother had a deep prejudice against "old boughten stuff." This amounted to almost anything not put up by the family. Our family bought green coffee, roasted it in baking pans, and ground it in a kitchen mill fastened to the wall. The children were not permitted to drink it, being restricted to "cambric tea," which was just hot water mixed with sweetened milk. Although every drugstore had its soda fountain, the bottled soft-drink affliction was years away. The prejudice against coffee for children was almost as strong against tea, even though it was extremely popular. Another popular drink for all ages was apple cider. This was understandable in that great apple country where cider mills were located along all country roads. Each grocery store had two barrels available: a small one for hard cider and a large one for sweet cider. When I went across the fields to the store to get a quart or half gallon for the home, I would sometimes sit down under a big oak tree and take a sip of the cider. One day I was told to buy the cider from the small barrel. I did not know the difference between the contents of the two barrels and took the usual sip on the way home. My mother had to come out and get me because I had passed out. The usual whipping followed.

Canning time was a most happy occasion, what with all of the bustling, sorting, peeling, boiling, the pervasive odor of cooking fruit and vegetables, the sealing of Mason jars, the labeling, and the basement storage. Then, one could eat one's fill from bushel baskets heaped with apples, peaches, pears, and other good things during the process of preparation.

In Brighton there was much to engage one's attention, such as milking our cow. Each day the cream was skimmed off and placed in a jar until there was enough to make a little butter. Then there was the feeding of the chickens and geese, collecting eggs, and watching the bloody killing of chickens, their flopping around until dead, their immersion in a pail of scalding water, and their subsequent picking, cleaning, and evisceration. Another pastime was spearing big bullfrogs with a nail imbedded in the end of an old broomstick. The bullfrogs were plentiful in the pond and the creek. The meat market in Brighton bought all of the fat legs one could supply, and for these the price was very good. The money was taken home triumphantly to my mother. It was a welcome addition to a store of coins she kept in a large mug on the mantelpiece.

My stepfather drove a large delivery wagon at that time,

and I heard that he earned $10.50 weekly hauling building material. The winters were very cold, and then the work was more trying than during the rest of the year. When the dray drivers got very cold, they would stop in front of a saloon, feed the horses whose steaming blankets sent up a fog, and go to the bar for the favorite drink of hot rum.

Always eager to improve his lot, my stepfather later got a job as second cook on the New York Central dining cars. After that we began eating better than ever before, having delicacies only the rich could afford. Syracuse being a division point, the crews changed there and all food already prepared was thrown into the garbage. These steaks, chops, and other rich foods were wrapped in paper and towels, thrown nonchalantly into the big pails, and later stealthily retrieved to be brought to our table. It was dishonest, of course, but a widespread practice among hotel, restaurant, and dining-car cooks. Even the raffish hoboes who frequented the alleys behind hotels and restaurants had a ditty that went:

> Sink ye brick and rise ye muffin
> Come on meatskin, I ain't bluffin'.

Swarms of hoboes descended on the city, a division point on the main line of the New York Central and the Lackawanna railroads, and once arrived they knew where to go to get a feed and how to get it.

Aside from garnering their not inconsiderable tips, the Pullman porters often managed to make extra money selling sheets, towels, and pillowcases to rooming houses across the country. An apocryphal tale was told about a Frenchman who came to study Negro life across the country and for the purpose stayed in colored hotels and rooming houses. Seeing the lettering on the bed linen, he wondered why so many Negroes were named "Pullman."

CHAPTER 2

IT WAS now time for me to start to school regularly, and classes began at the nondescript Brighton Annex. There the discipline was stern. The instruction by a man teacher was excellent. We learned fast, and those that did not learn or were unruly were either ridiculed by being forced to wear a paper dunce cap and seated on a high stool facing the blackboard or were struck sharply with a long ruler on the palms of the hands. These measures had a very salutary effect. I was farther advanced than the other youngsters because I had been instructed at home.

The following term I was transferred to Brighton School, a large, red-brick, three-story building on the corner of South Salina and Colvin Streets which had a playground in front and a fire engine house on one side. The building is still there, although it must be close to a century old.

On the opening day of the term I registered three firsts: I was called "nigger," which had never happened to me before;

I had a fight with the offender, a pugnacious little Italian boy; and during the fisticuffs I had my nose bloodied. Being called "nigger" hurt me worst of all. I don't think I had ever heard the taunt before, and when I went home and asked my stepfather, he took me to the mirror and explained as well as he could. I had not thought of myself as different, even though I had heard the family mention colored and whites in their conversations about New York City, and I had pored over *The Black Phalanx*. I don't think it had occurred to me that there was this uncomplimentary slang synonym for colored. The word Negro was rarely used, and then more in the descriptive sense, as in Latin America. Certainly, I cannot recall any of our white neighbors using any other collective term than colored. My stepfather was an expert on the race question, as is almost every Negro in a short time. He pooh-poohed the whole thing as of no particular consequence, and I accepted this viewpoint. As I recall, my mother washed my face and comforted me, but otherwise she said nothing except that I was always to fight back when called names. We were as God made us; it was what was inside our heads and what we did with it that counted. There were great people among colored people as among whites. She mentioned such outstanding colored people as Bishop Alexander Crummel, Booker T. Washington, Frederick Douglass, who had once lived in Rochester, and Aunt Harriet Tubman, then living in Auburn, New York, who had led so many slaves from the South to freedom before the Civil War and then had served as a spy for the Union army. It made me feel a lot better. While aware that I was physically different in appearance from my white neighbors, I have never felt inferior. Indeed, I strongly question the view of many psychologists and sociologists that most colored people regard themselves as inferior. They simply are aware that their socio-economic position is inferior, which is a different thing.

There were no more fights. I got on very well with the other pupils and was delighted to learn new things every day. I loved going to school and was very friendly with the teachers who were uniformly kind and helpful. Among the several hundred children, only three or four were colored. Of course, there were no colored teachers, and there are probably very few, if any, now.

This is the unfortunate circumstance surrounding the colored child in these towns and cities with tiny, scattered non-white populations amidst an overwhelming majority of whites. He never sees anyone the same color as himself in any position of leadership or authority. However confident he may be of his inner worth, seeing no one of his kind who has accomplished anything and been rewarded, his confidence is apt to be shaken. This was especially so in the period of which I am writing because of the widespread downgrading of Negroes in newspapers, magazines, and books. Most space was given to accusations of rape and reports of lynchings. Streamer headlines were common in such instances. This was the sum total of the news about colored people.

The value of home instruction and training cannot be over-estimated. The superior scholars in all my classes were those who had had such instruction. To be taught to read and write, to know the numerals, and to speak properly is an excellent preliminary to formal schooling. Not to hear profanity and obscenity in the home but rather to hear regular Bible readings is a good start for any child. Readings of stories and poetry by parents or older children prepare the pre kindergarten child for grade school. In addition to our small home library, there was an illustrated book on physiology which I discovered in my explorations and which I was not forbidden to read. I did not understand everything in it, but it was informative enough so that I did not have to rely on what I heard from the boys in the streets for the facts of life. They could not tell me anything I did not already know. When I asked point-blank questions of my parents, they answered them as frankly as they could and did not reprove me.

When we moved to the suburbs, the rest of the family remained at the old home, but we visited each other except in winter. When I got a newspaper route for after-school delivery in and around the Brighton area, I began following current events closely. After delivering my papers, I would bring home the last one and go over it page after page while sitting on our front porch. Thus, the Russo-Japanese war and the news of its battles and sieges, the baseball and prizefight happenings, and the dispatches out of Washington were daily grist. On Saturdays I often sold papers downtown before serving my regular customers. Then I would stop by the old home for a little while and get a chance to sample some of grandmother's cookies.

It was thrilling to read about the Wright Brothers' triumph at Kitty Hawk, North Carolina; the heavyweight crown taken by Jack Johnson from Tommy Burns in Australia, the hunt for a "white hope," the global voyage of Teddy Roosevelt's Great White Fleet, and the discharge of an entire battalion of colored soldiers for alleged mutiny at Brownsville, Texas. Selling newspapers was a good way to make extra money, which I dutifully brought home to my mother.

Later on, when we moved from Brighton to Cedar Street, which was much closer to the center of the city, I got another newspaper route which included the houses in the red-light district along East Washington Street (popularly called Railroad Street because the New York Central Railroad tracks ran along it). It was the principal area of sin in the city but not the only one, and there I got the biggest tips from the generous inhabitants, most of them pretty young white girls, but some rather plain. The houses seemed palatial on the inside to me, no matter how dingy their exteriors. There were rich draperies, paintings of nudes, soft rugs, French furniture, and the perfume of voluptuous young women in diaphanous negligees. They always paid twice what a paper was worth. They hugged and kissed me and called me "cute," and many a matronly "madam" told the cook to give me ice cream. Most of the cooks and maids were colored women who knew my family. Colored men, of course, were barred from patronizing these houses. Democracy in the old Abolitionist center did not go that far.

Herbalism and witchcraft were widespread among the Dutch and Negroes in the Hudson Valley, Mohawk Valley, New Jersey, and eastern Pennsylvania. Most of the older women went to the woods and fields to seek medicinal herbs, my grandmother among them. I sometimes accompanied her when she set forth with a little basket over her forearm, and we would take a streetcar to the outskirts of town. She would go through the fields digging here and snipping there until the little basket was full. Upon returning, she would go to work concocting various medicines which were later used for draughts and poultices. On a couple of occasions I accompanied her to the woods on the drumlins south of the city where she collected certain roots and the bark of trees for similar purposes. I did not learn the properties of these herbs, roots, and barks, but I learned their uses because I had to take the nauseous doses afterward in order to keep me healthy, as I was told. At that time it was common to see warning signs tacked to the outside of houses announcing diphtheria, typhoid fever, scarlet fever, and other afflictions. One by-passed those houses even if one knew the people inside.

Necromancers and fortune-tellers then were as popular as psychiatrists are today, but they were much less expensive. Many Negro women made good livings reading tea leaves, coffee grounds, and ladies' palms to determine the future of their patrons. Or they would run the cards and tell the significance of various arrangements. There was quite a traffic in throwing on and off spells. My grandmother knew all about the business and hinted darkly that this or that person was a witch. When an individual became bewitched, it was necessary to hire a more powerful witch to throw off the spell. Such was the case when a noted witch from Albany, New York, had to be called to Syracuse to take the curse off a man who kept running around a tree on Fayette Street, urinating on the trunk like a dog and ambulating on all fours. The Albany witch went to work, and in a short time the victim was freed of his affliction.

There were demon fiddlers down in New Jersey who, according to my grandmother, caused people to dance all night until they fell exhausted. Other witches made concoctions which made old men potent or paralyzed those who stepped on the powder or brought all sorts of bad luck, ailments, or accidents which could not otherwise be explained. Some people just had a natural flair for the occult while others acquired the knowledge as apprentices of great witches and wizards.

My mother denounced all this talk of witchcraft as nonsense, the product of ignorance and superstition, saying that one had to actually believe in such things in order to be affected. My grandmother held stubbornly to her beliefs and cited an impressive list of apt anecdotes in support of them. My Aunt Amy sharply differed with Grandma about putting such notions in a child's head but, after all, the old lady was the family matriarch and brooked little contradiction. What she knew, she knew, and that was all there was to it. She charged mother with being little better than an infidel because of her iconoclastic views, while my mother chided her for believing in Christianity and occultism at one and the same time. An able Bible student, Grandma could cite the Good Book for belief in witches, and she could produce an apt quotation for almost everything else, pro or con. Her inspiration and that of the Seventh Day Adventists started me off on a project of reading the Bible from cover to cover, from Genesis to Revelations.

Actually, Grandma had plenty of company then in her belief in the occult, and would have plenty now. Superstition is widespread, and if it were not for the law, we would still be swamped with fortunetellers and witches openly practicing. They carry on surreptitiously as it is. In many parts of eastern Pennsylvania, hex signs adorn every barn. There are myriads who believe in conjuring and the evil eye. Astrologers have columns in every newspaper, and they are among some of the most affluent people in Washington, London, Paris, and other world capitals. It is a rare white person living in the African jungles who is not impressed by the powers of the black witch doctors.

Like my mother, I was a bit sceptical. For one thing, the people who knew most about these occult matters were invariably poor and lived in straitened circumstances. Why, if they had such great powers, I asked myself, were they not more affluent? Why couldn't they put a spell on the landlord and the banker, forcing them to do as told and line their coffers? Why did these witches and wizards get ill and die like everybody else if they possessed such powers as they claimed?

Grandma had encyclopedic reminiscences of New York City. She would talk endlessly about the period just prior to and after the Civil War, about the businesses owned by colored people, their fine homes and carriages, their expensive clothing and their churches. The big Negro center in those days was on Bleecker and neighboring streets where Negroes of power and importance were to be found. In later years my researches confirmed that colored people were more widely employed during that period than at any time afterward, because of the inrush of European immigrants and the economic competition that followed on even the lowest levels of employment.

In Syracuse with its scattering of colored people there was nothing to which a youngster could point with pride. Most Negroes were either laborers, janitors, messengers, butlers, maids, cooks, waiters, or bellhops, and they were in competition with whites. Thus, their employment was marginal and their income was low. There were no Negro clerks, city employees, policemen, or firemen, not even street cleaners. Nor were Negroes employed in any of the factories, department stores, banks, warehouses, or other enterprises. Discrimination was *de facto* rather than *de jure*, but it affected Negroes just as much nonetheless.

Labor unions were many and strong, especially in the skilled trades, and invariably drew the color line. Even if a shop was not unionized, there was a "white" union that made it the better part of wisdom for an employer to discriminate against a colored applicant for work. People are prone to forget that it was not until after World War II that Negroes began to make any important inroads into the ranks of organized labor, and in actuality they are widely discriminated against today. The older I grew, the more aware I became of this situation which was not altered by attending integrated schools and having on paper the same rights as others did.

These harsh facts of life began to make a profound impression on me. My cousin Lila Watson had good schooling according to the standards of the time. She had graduated from grammar school and was a good-looking girl with a cultured manner. Nevertheless, she could get no work except "in service" as a domestic. My cousin Mary Louise, who resembled a Sicilian countess, had graduated near the top of her class in high school and was a good organist and pianist and an extremely pretty girl. Because she was light-colored, she was able to secure employment in a dress factory where Italian girls were mostly employed. Being a smart and efficient worker, she did well until one day, when she was walking down the street with her mother, she met several of the girls from her shop. They realized immediately as they were introduced to her mother that she was colored. Shortly afterward the employer let her go.

These girls were well reared according to middle-class standards and were definitely above average. Seemingly, they would have been an asset to any business, but they could not get the kind of employment their education and training warranted. To be sure, the proportion of working girls at the time was much smaller than it is today, and a woman's place was supposed to be in the home; but allowing for all that, the unmarried colored girl's position was parlous. Well-mannered girls who were schooled in the bourgeois virtues were in a dilemma when it came to finding husbands of their class.

And there were definite classes in the tiny colored community. At the bottom were those associated with the underworld, an extensive midtown area. The town was wide open, what with it being a division point on the New York Central Railroad, a harbor on the Erie Canal, the central city of the state, with a large transient population with the expected contingent of pimps, gamblers, roustabouts, hoboes, and tramps. These types were taboo as prospective husbands. Moreover, they stayed in the "bad" section of town which decent people avoided, except men roving after dark.

Above this underworld class were the laborers and domestics who were poor but respectable, who had homes and families, but little schooling. Finally, there were the men who worked for wealthy families, who were chefs, butlers, coachmen, and

24

such; who had nice homes, well-reared families, and sought to maintain high cultural standards. They inspired their children to rise above the mired mass. We all knew these various categories of colored folk, and there were not enough eligible men around to encourage husband-hunting colored girls of the better class. So most of these girls went elsewhere and found husbands, or they remained spinsters. To be sure, there were a dozen or more racially intermarried couples in town (usually the husband being colored and the wife white), but I had heard of none where a white boy of local vintage was wed to a local colored girl. There were close neighborly relationships between colored and white families living in juxtaposition, but they rarely entertained or invited one another to parties. Since the better Negroes could not fraternize with the riff-raff, they were a socially in-bred group. This is true in many colored communities, but it was rather painful in a group of less than one thousand in a city of one hundred thousand.

It would be erroneous to think that Negroes were the only people against whom there was prejudice and discrimination. To a varying extent there were others who did not "belong," like Jews, Poles, and Irish.

From the time of their wholesale arrival after the potato famine in the Emerald Isle, the Irish in New York City suffered prejudice, discrimination, and ridicule. "Help Wanted" signs carried the phrase "No Irish Need Apply," and the same appeared on "For Rent" signs in many parts of town. Many of the Irish were squatters with their goats and chickens in the northern section of what is now Central Park. Throughout New York State and especially along the line of the Erie Canal, the prejudice against the Irish was increased by the fact that they were Roman Catholics. Many of the early arrivals from Poland were in virtual slavery to building contractors. However, the European immigrants slowly moved upward; the Negroes, all native Americans, remained as they were.

I never experienced that aversion to school which so many children reportedly have. I enjoyed school and was eager to learn all I could, never failed a class. One had to have an average of seventy-five in order to pass on to the next grade and no pupils were passed on in order to keep them in their age group. I was especially apt at arithmetic, spelling, and geography, and I found the latter the most entrancing. I got such high marks that the teacher used to have me help mark the class papers. There was no part of the world that I did not know, and I could reel off capitals, rivers, and products with great facility. I also read the newspaper daily, the *Popular Mechanics* magazine, and the books in our little library—to say nothing of the Bible. When I graduated from grammar school with an average of ninety-eight, the daughter of the colored Episcopal priest and I headed the class, which was otherwise all white children of classes ranging from the poorest to the richest. There were about ninety in the class, and all but three passed. It may be, as was later said, that in small classes of thirty or thirty-five students children learned faster and better, but I have not seen much evidence of it.

I could never sing much, but I could read music and for a time took piano lessons from my cousin Mary Louise, a brilliant piano and organ student who studied with an outstanding colored student at the Syracuse University College of Fine Arts. When I entered high school she was a great help to me with algebra and Latin. It was very disillusioning to find that neither she nor cousin Lila could get work commensurate with their education.

Many colored girls graduating from high school in the North obtained employment in Negro colleges in the South, I heard. In this sense separate colored schools were a boon economically, and those who went South to teach acquired a socio-economic status they could not have gained at home where they were usually domestics. Even in most large cities outside the South where there were large colored communities, there were separate Negro public schools. This was then true in Philadelphia, Harrisburg, Trenton, St. Louis, Kansas City, Gary, Chicago, Indianapolis, Atlantic City, Topeka, Columbus, Camden, Wilmington, Baltimore, Evansville, and so forth. The separate Negro school became the background of the colored middle class in an economy where colored workers were relegated to the outer fringes. In some non-Southern communities leading Negroes even asked for the establishment of separate racial schools so there would be jobs for middle-class girls as teachers. Save for working in the post office, the railway mail service, hotels, and restaurants, there was no other way to rise above the mired mass of common laborers and domestic workers. Municipal, county, and state jobs were almost exclusively for whites. Even New York with its large Negro population hired its first Negro policeman as late as 1909 and its first colored fireman a decade later.

The aristocrats of Negro labor at that time were the headwaiters, chefs, and head bellmen in fashionable resorts in Florida and along the Gulf Coast in the winter and in Saratoga Springs and other New England and Northern resorts in the summer. Often they carried their own crews with them. There were also many jobs on coastal, river, and lake steamers. Some of these men became moderately wealthy, owned homes, wore expensive clothes, Stetson hats, patent leather shoes, gold watches, fobs, cuff links, and diamond stickpins and sported gold-headed canes just like the aristocrats they served. We didn't see many of them in our town, but we heard about them from those great Negro news carriers, the Pullman porters and dining-car crewmen.

Then there were the Negro actors, entertainers, and musicians who were in their heydey from about 1895 until World War I and afterward. They could be found mainly in the big cities, but they were on all vaudeville circuits, around the country in road shows, and often had shows on Broadway. There were many more traveling circuses than there are now, and each of them had a side show in which Negro musicians and entertainers generally appeared, as they did in the many medicine shows that roamed the country. Some of the big Negro shows had their own special trains. Many of these people had good incomes and were no more profligate than their white counterparts.

Motion pictures, which first appeared in Syracuse about 1903, automobiles and airplanes sounded the death knell for these forms of entertainment and services. White competition eventu-

27

ally eliminated Negroes from many fields which they had dominated. We would hear of various celebrated hotels which had replaced a Negro crew with a white one, and we knew what that meant.

For odd jobs I ran errands for a midtown printer and helped my mother at one of the fine homes or chapter houses for which she cooked. One whole summer I worked as water boy on a construction job, and later I began running an elevator at the Yates Hotel while I was still going to high school.

It became increasingly clear to me that the Negro had his place in Syracuse, and it was nowhere near the top, nor would it be, no matter what his schooling. It was only later that I discovered this to be the case in most places. Actually, the farm owners and artisans in the South were the most stable Negroes of all. We were only marginal folk in the North and East, and that precarious position was continually threatened.

I never saw any colored person in any position of authority in Syracuse until the U.S. Army held maneuvers in the area around 1909, and several companies of Negro soldiers were camped in a large park where traveling circuses usually performed. The black infantrymen and cavalrymen were something else again. We were impressed by their superb order and discipline, their haughty and immaculate noncommissioned officers, and their obvious authority. The only colored men in uniform that we had seen were our fathers in the uniforms of the Knights of Pythias and the Odd Fellows, and they were simply ludicrous, representing nothing.

The soldiers, on the other hand, represented the power and authority of the United States. They were clean, upstanding, orderly, and polite. They talked of far-off places where they had served—the Philippines, Cuba, the Indian Territory, and the expanses of Texas, Arizona, and New Mexico. These were the inheritors of the tradition of conflict in the Revolutionary War, the War of 1812, the Civil War, and the Indian wars in the West. How they contrasted with our uninviting lot in Syracuse!

Legally we were free, but actually we were social pariahs. We created our own social life with our little churches, our fraternal societies, our house parties, and our formal dances. Our city's Abolitionism had considerably declined since the Jerry Rescue days. While the colored people lost no sleep over this and seldom discussed it, the awareness was there.

Our tiny community was so fragmented by class divisions that any group unity was out of the question. There were several Negro fraternal organizations, and they all met in the same rented hall. They could never get together to build a meeting place of their own. There was no colored spokesman because of the jealousies that rent the group. At the same time, Negroes were not invited to join various local social, political, and economic groups. It was readily apparent to any intelligent youngster that he was living in a society quite as closed as that in Dixie.

At that time there were no high school fraternities, no school dances, no social affairs; but if there had been, a colored student would not have been invited—and if so, with whom would he have danced except a colored girl? There were two colored girls in the entire high school, and I only knew them casually.

With our immediate white neighbors I remained friendly, often chummy, but I was not invited to their house parties as were white youths from across town. So it was to the tiny Negro world one had to turn for socializing, and there parents frowned upon certain youngsters whose families were not highly regarded, sometimes with reason. For instance, there were two families named Brown. One was called the "Many" Browns; the other, the "Dirty" Browns. The former were clean, respectable, industrious, and thrifty; the latter were just the opposite. The "Many" Browns had two attractive teen-age daughters who were all one would expect from such a family. The "Dirty" Browns had two teen-age daughters also, both ravishingly beautiful but definite slum types with whom a teen-age boy could easily get into "trouble." Their mother had lived with a succession of men and had a police record. I was warned against associating with them or their family.

There were several interracially married couples scattered over the city. Contrary to the widespread but generally unsupported belief, these were among the most respectable families in the community, except for two who were living in a common-law relationship. The children of these black-white marriages were neat, polite, and well-mannered, as well as attractive. This is quite usual as I later found out while researching the subject. Generally, these mixed couples are above-the-average Americans.

Most colored people lived in the east central part of the city, either on or not far from Washington Street, along which the New York Central Railroad ran and many underworld denizens were congregated. Rents were cheap, the houses were dingy and unpainted and, what with the smoke and cinders, there were no lawns or flowers. At the eastern end of the street was a big tube factory where periodically there were artillerylike explosions as the white-hot steel tubes were plunged into water. Several families lived around it and soon became accustomed to the noise, but visitors never did. Understandably, the rents were cheap. The children from those homes rarely rose above their environment and dropped out of school at fourteen when they got their working papers. This was true of both colored and white.

After my stepfather left the dining cars and got a job as custodian of the office building and laboratories of the Crucible Steel Company at the other end of town, I used to cycle out to assist him on occasion. The people living nearby were mostly Slavs of the working class employed in the mills. Jews and Italians were grouped largely in the central and southern parts of town, with Germans on the north side. They all had their own churches, fraternities, and social clubs, and there was little fraternization off the job. It was voluntary segregation even though families of different ethnic groups might live on the same block. I observed that while there was much talk about a melting pot, what we had was religious and national-istic groupings which associated and married with their own in the main. As I traveled about later, I observed the same phe-nomenon in other towns and cities. The ostracism of the colored people was only exceptional in its extremity. Many years after-ward, Edna Porter, the actress, who had traveled the theatrical circuit all over the country, told me that whenever she visited a new town she would ask, "Well, who do you hate here?"

There was even then a "tipping point" in residence, although that sociological term had not yet been invented. If "too many" Negroes moved on a block, whites began to move out. This could not occur too frequently because there were too few Negroes to speed the trend, but it happened. Of course, low wages restricted the Negroes' choice of housing, but even if that had not been the case, there were areas that landlords and rental agents would have conspired to keep Negroes out of. The residential covenant only lost its legality in the courts in 1949, but it is still widely effective in all parts of the country. Two young Negro men who were printers in a downtown shop, and another who was a clerk in the post office, would have had difficulty renting or buying a house in certain neighborhoods even though their income was adequate.

There were never more than two or three colored students attending Syracuse University at that time. None lived in dormitories or fraternity chapter houses. Indeed, they could not be long to any of the all-white fraternities or sororities. There were none for Negro students. They roomed with Negro families and worked their way through school as bellhops, waiters, and elevator operators. Even fair Harvard permitted no Negroes in its dormitories until the late 1920's and none could matriculate at Princeton. Progress has been made, but it was not always observable then.

I became convinced that there was no future for me in my home town. The colored people seemed to be in a rut, and I did not want to stay down there with them. So what should I do? Where should I go? The United States Army seemed to be the best choice. What I had seen of it three years back had started me thinking, and I expressed those thoughts to my mother. To my delight and surprise, she agreed, and although I was only seventeen, she signed the papers saying I was a year older. She thought the Army would "make a man of me."

Perhaps I should have stayed in school, but it must be remembered that the time was 1912, and no spirit of hopefulness pervaded the colored community. Opportunities were very slim, not only in Syracuse, but just about everywhere. In the Army I could see the world I wanted to see and have a chance to advance myself. At any rate, I would be away from my home town!

I have never regretted my decision. I waved at the crowd of friends and playmates who were waiting at Walnut and Washington streets when my train passed by picking up speed, but I did not shed a tear.

It seems to me to be a mistake to remain in one place or situation when there appears to be a better one. Individuals and groups have been seeking better places since the beginning of time, and rarely if ever do they migrate consciously to a worse one. This has motivated all of the pioneers everywhere and at all times. I had thought this move pretty well through for some time, and now I was making it. A teen-ager can get into all sorts of mischief through escapades, innocent and otherwise, and many of my acquaintances had. There would be little such temptation in the United States Army.

CHAPTER 3

FORT SLOCUM, the large recruiting depot on David's Island off New Rochelle, New York, was spacious and pleasant, somewhat resembling a college campus. It had an immense parade ground and a large red brick barracks, opposite which were the officers' residences, with headquarters building at one end and a vast mess hall seating about fifteen hundred men at the other. An Army ferry traversed the short distance from the island to the mainland. However, since the recruits lacked money, and could not get passes, the depot might as well have been in the mid-Atlantic. One had to be at the station some time to get a pass.

The colored recruits were assigned to the Second Recruit Company and stayed in one barracks. Like the other quarters, it was immaculate and the noncommissioned officers, all white, were insistent about it being kept that way. Printed instructions were handed to each newcomer to "observe and obey." In this booklet we were told that "Prompt obedience is the first military virtue . . . Be neat and clean in all respects . . . Bathe at least twice a week. Keep your hair cut short. Wear clean gloves and polished shoes . . . Whenever you leave the depot, wear your best clothing . . . Don't spit on the floor or sidewalks. Always use spitoons if possible . . . Don't use profane or obscene language . . . Don't get drunk. Don't enter saloons in your uniform. Remember the respect you owe the uniform . . . Don't gamble." Recruits were admonished to eat slowly, there being plenty for all. They must remain at table "at least 15 minutes" at breakfast and supper; "at dinner at least 20 minutes." One had to eat all one took on one's plate, or it would be saved for one's next meal!

There was the traditional close-order drill, calisthenics, work assignments, and guard duty. The fatigue duty ran the gamut from kitchen police and waiting on tables to shoveling coal and mowing the vast parade ground.

We were also handed a *Soldier's Handbook* on how to carry out our orders and assignments. Discipline was strict, but it was as we had expected; the noncommissioned officers were fair and just, but could be stern and withering. I never heard one of them curse, although they could be cuttingly sarcastic.

There were daily inspections of quarters and persons. The company commander would wipe on top of shelves and under radiators and sharply criticize the first sergeant if his white gloves showed a single smudge on them. Youngsters, most of whom had never shaved in their lives, had been issued straight razors they did not know how to use. They were denounced as if they were as bearded as Rip Van Winkle if there was noticeable fuzz on their faces. Whether it was needed or not, one shaved. Any spots on the barack room floor had to be scratched up with pieces of glass. Mess hall stools were scrubbed daily with sand at a big pile behind the mess hall. Any infractions were punished by assigning the culprit to scrub a number of these stools. Not a piece of scrap paper nor a match stem was to be seen anywhere. None of this seemed onerous to me because of my training since infancy in order, obedience, personal hygiene, and punctuality. What I did not like was the communal sleeping. I had always had my own room.

Some of the colored boys had been at the depot several days when the bulk of us, about twenty, were sworn in on July 18, 1912. They came from many distant points, as far south as Savannah, Georgia, and as far north as Boston, Massachusetts. They were all literate, although some of them barely so. It was so difficult for me to understand the two from Savannah, who spoke a Geechee dialect, that I thought at first they were Filipinos! All were fine physical specimens because the Army would accept no other kind. The minimum height was then 64 inches, and no exceptions were made for physical defects.

I wrote almost immediately to Mother reassuring her that all was well, because I knew that she had been saddened by my going away. I told her truthfully that I was happy, but I did not think that she was. We had been very close, especially after my grandmother died in 1908.

We learned our drill and duties rather quickly, and none of the boys got into any trouble. We knew very soon how to assemble, handle, and clean our rifles and equipment. We rose and retired early, ate well, and could not, of course, dissipate. Nobody beefed because we all knew we were in the Army for three years, and there was no way out, no matter how homesick one became. I was never homesick.

After three weeks of intensive training, word came that we were being assigned to the 1st Battalion, Twenty-fifth U.S. Infantry, which was stationed, with headquarters, at Fort Lawton, Washington, and we would leave shortly. It was a thrilling prospect—going entirely across the vast country, seeing many of the places I had read about, glimpsing territory that was mostly unknown less than a century before.

Loaded down with our barrack bags and feeling very blithe, we boarded the government ferry which skirted Manhattan and its skyscrapers, passed under the famed Brooklyn Bridge, and saw the Statue of Liberty. Next we went to Hoboken for the train west. There were about twenty of us, and we had a special car, including facilities for cooking our meals. A couple of white noncommissioned officers were in charge. Although we had not yet been paid, I seem to recall that we were given some travel expense money. However, we did not have a chance to spend anything except in Chicago, where we changed trains and stayed overnight. We found our way to South State Street, and it was an eye-opener to see the sights.

Taking the Chicago, Milwaukee, and Puget Sound Railroad, we continued through Wisconsin, Minnesota, North Dakota, Montana, Idaho, and Washington to Seattle, enjoying every bit of the way and getting off at certain points to exercise. We knew now that the recruiting appeal to join the Army and travel was much more than a slogan. In 1912, what other way could a score of poor Negro teen-agers within so short a time after leaving their homes see so much of the continent-wide country they were sworn to defend? I wrote postcards home daily.

Perhaps the biggest thrill of all was when we arrived at the railroad station in Seattle. When we got off our car with our barrack bags, a fine, upstanding Negro battalion sergeant major took command from the white sergeant in charge on the long journey. We had seen only white noncommissioned officers at Fort Slocum, but we knew there would be many Negro noncoms where we were going. Now, here was the first, and he was not a corporal or sergeant but a battalion sergeant major! It made us all feel very proud.

Fort Lawton, an old, comfortable post on a peninsula that jutted out into Puget Sound, was surrounded by a big stand of Douglas fir trees reaching the sky. It was arranged like all Army posts with officers' residences on one side of the long parade ground and the two-story wooden barracks on the other. In great timber country, all of the buildings were wooden, excellently appointed and, of course, immaculate; and they were heated by great wood-burning furnaces taking logs four feet long. Even the highway into Seattle was a corduroy road that sometimes caused difficulties for loaded Army wagons because ruts developed early in that excessively rainy country. When a wagon wheel sank in one of those holes it was a big job getting it out, and sometimes the wagon had first to be unloaded. Passengers between the Fort and Seattle used an interurban electric streetcar line.

There were four companies of infantry, a machine gun platoon, and other auxiliaries stationed at Fort Lawton. The other two battalions were at Fort George Wright at Spokane, Washington. The latter, we learned, was an inferior post for Negro soldiers because there was more color prejudice shown by the populace and there were fewer Negro civilians. Seattle, we heard, was very cosmopolitan and liberal on the color question, with many more places of amusement.

We were quickly assigned to companies A, B, C, or D and to squads according to stature. I was picked for Company B and assigned to the last squad because I was only 65 inches tall, while the men in the first squad were between six and seven feet tall. The barrack rooms were smaller than those at Fort Slocum, but everything was as neat, clean, and orderly. They were much like college dormitories, except more quiet and orderly, with no commotion, loud talk, obscenities, or fights. In the basement were toilets, showers, and bathtubs. Laundry cost $1.50 monthly, which left us $13.50 of our pay to spend. That seems very little, but in 1912 it went a long way, when carfare was five cents, a burlesque show twenty cents, a restaurant meal thirty cents, beer ten cents, and a full quart of the best rye whiskey eighty-five cents. Women were available at comparable prices.

The Twenty-fifth U.S. Infantry was an old and distinguished regiment organized by act of Congress in 1867. Its men were recruited from Civil War colored regiments that had fought for freedom on a dozen battlefields. It had been in the Indian wars and "pacification" from Montana to Arizona and Texas. In the Spanish-American War it participated in all important battles and had fought in the Philippine Insurrection. There were a lot of silver battle rings on its regimental standard.

It was a crack regiment and had the *élan* and *esprit de corps* of all distinguished fighting units and was so well trained and disciplined that the white officers had very little to do except supervise the routine and sign papers. The sergeants major, warrant officers, and first sergeants were so capable that they could have run the show. Most of them had long service in the same companies. This was due to the fact that the Negro soldiers could serve only in the two colored regiments of infantry (Twenty-fourth and Twenty-fifth) and the two regiments of cavalry (Ninth and Tenth). There were very few in the Hospital Corps, Ordnance Department, Quartermaster Department, and Commissary Department. No colored men were enlisted in the Signal Corps, Engineer Corps, Coast Artillery, Field Artillery, or any special branches. White soldiers might transfer to any branch of the military, but Negroes were permitted to transfer only to the other of the two black regiments in infantry or cavalry. In the Navy, where Negroes had once constituted a fourth of the enlisted personnel, they were fast being eliminated and in a few years would be restricted to the category of mess attendants.

Because of the noted restrictions, most noncoms in the regiment were men of long service. In B Company there was no corporal in his first enlistment; most were in their second or third, while sergeants were in their fourth, fifth, and sixth. William Blaney, our first sergeant, was a veteran of Indian "pacification," the Spanish-American War, and the Philippine Insurrection. He was also the only man of the 1st Battalion not dishonorably discharged by President Theodore Roosevelt as a result of the Brownsville Affair, when the Twenty-fifth Infantry men, goaded by the white citizens of Brownsville, Texas, in 1907, had shot up the town. Blaney was on furlough at the time.

The B Company commander was a potbellied German in his mid-forties, with walrus mustache, named Captain W. G. Fleischauer. The first lieutenant, C. A. Meales, a slender, businesslike man in his mid-thirties, was second in command. The battalion commander, Major Butts, was a squarely built, tanned athletic type who had perfected the Butts manual of rifle calisthenics. The regimental commander was Colonel L. W. V. Kennon, a stately, white-bearded aristocratic soldier resembling General Robert E. Lee. The men loved and respected him. He was an impressive figure on full dress parades or at any other time. These officers were advanced in age for their ranks because promotion was slow in the peacetime professional Army. A second lieutenant might serve ten years before being promoted.

The only colored officer was Chaplain O. J. W. Scott, who

attended to the spiritual needs of the men, if any, and preached at the post chapel. The famous Twenty-fifth Infantry Band was led by Leslie King, a Negro warrant officer, the highest noncommissioned rank, a well-trained musician and composer. Most spectacular, of course, was the drum major, a very tall brown man who entranced everyone with his gymnastics just prior to passing the reviewing stand. After twirling the stick around his body and neck, he would hurl it yards straight up in the air, then catch it nonchalantly and salute the commanding officer. Many civilians would come out from town to see and hear the monthly review in full dress uniform: blue, with light blue piping, trouser stripes for noncommissioned and commissioned officers, black shoes and white gloves, and gold ornaments. The officers, sergeant majors, and first sergeants wore swords. The regimental and battalion staffs were mounted.

None of the young recruits had been to Seattle on pass although we were all impatient to go, so pay day was more than welcome. We had pay coming from the date of enlistment on July 18, but we did not get paid until the end of August, so we were due quite a lot. Our comrades and corporals who knew the town briefed us on where to go, what to do, and how much to pay for what.

First Sergeant Blaney called the new men to the orderly room and warned us what *not* to do. He was a slender, brown-skinned man with a well trimmed but thick black mustache, unusually erect posture, and clipped speech. I never heard him curse or even lift his voice unnecessarily. His eyes were piercing and his manner brusque. When recruits first met him and sought grinningly to ingratiate themselves, he would say, "Don't show me you're teeth. I'm no dentist!"

When we were finally paid, the men put in for passes, and the gambling tables were set up in the basements. This was probably against regulations, but nobody in authority interfered unless the crap shooters got too loud or the stud poker players got to quarreling. The mere appearance of a noncommissioned officer put an end to that. The first sergeant never showed up during these seances, but he knew all that was going on. So, undoubtedly, did the officers, one of whom later pontificated that he didn't want any man in his company who didn't smoke, drink, gamble, and whore! But woe to a man who staggered into line Monday morning "with a head full of crackskull."

The only gambling I had ever done was to pitch pennies and match coins, but I decided to try my luck at craps to augment the little money that was burning my pocket. So I went to the basement where the old-timers were waiting for unsophisticated recruits with gold and silver in their pockets. I had twenty-odd dollars and a sudden urge told me to risk it all. A couple of the men got enough together to cover me. I shot the dice across the pool table and, with the traditional beginner's luck, threw seven! I was astonished and delighted. The fellow who had covered my bet was angry and disappointed as I raked in the coin. Everybody importuned me to shoot again, that the dice were still mine, that it was the fair thing to give the loser a chance to win back his money. This was exactly what I did not want him to do. It was not the sporting thing, but I obdurately shoved the gold and silver (there was no other currency out West at that time) into my pocket and raced to the orderly room for my pass to town, with the imprecations of the disgruntled following me.

Two fellow recruits and I grabbed the first interurban car. Our initial stop was a place called Interbay where the focal point was the IXL Café. It was not so much that its cuisine was above average, which it was; nor that its liquor business boomed so that there were several bartenders busily dispensing whiskey and the excellent Tumwater beer, but that there was a bevy of pretty, young waitresses ready to serve in the half-dozen booths that lined one side of the café across from the long bar. Each booth had two benches with a table in between. One went into a booth, followed immediately by one of the waitresses who took one's order (including a drink for herself) and pointedly inquired if there was anything else wanted. When she brought back the order, she would lock the booth from the inside. Around paydays these bosomy babies did a land-office business.

Negroes were not plentiful in Seattle, and while race relations were better than in most places on the Pacific Coast, it was no Negro heaven. This became clear when we shortly discovered that there were saloons which did not want colored patronage. One would walk into such a bar, and after taking some time to do it, the bartender would saunter up and ask what was wanted. When drink had been served and consumed, the bartender would take the empty glass and deliberately smash it on the floor. This was shocking and humiliating.

One of my Savannah buddies who had prospered at the gaming tables decided that we should do something about it. We went to a fine looking saloon and each of the five ordered whiskey. The bartender surveyed us coldly and leisurely waited on a white customer who had come in behind us. Finally, the bartender turned to us and asked sharply, "Are you lookin' fer Sam?"

"Who's Sam?" my buddy asked.

"Sam's the porter," replied the gentleman in the white jacket, winking at the customer he had just served, "an' he's just gone home fer th' day."

"Well, he might come back," I suggested, "so we'll all have a drink while we're waiting."

The bartender grimly sat the drinks in front of us. We drank. Then he took the five empty glasses and one by one smashed them on the floor, as we watched with mounting rage.

"That's what we do with our glasses when you kind of people drink outta 'm," he explained.

"A'right," said the Savannah boy, with one of his infrequent smiles, "we'll have another round. We don't care what you do with your glasses."

Five more whiskey glasses were filled, drained, returned to the bar, and deliberately smashed on the floor.

"Now give us five beers," I ordered grimly. "The beer glasses cost more."

The beer was served and the big goblets were drained, to be as promptly smashed; but the bartender was plainly tiring of the game.

"Why don't you fellers go where yer wanted?" he asked.

"If we only went where we was wanted," observed one of the boys, "we wouldn't go nowheres."

"Well, I don' care," defended the bartender, now red with rage. "We don' serve colored. That's th' boss' orders."

"But we're American soldiers in uniform," the Savannah boy objected.

"Don' make no difference, yer colored," was the ultimatum.

"All right," I said. "We'll go, but we'll be back."

We filed out and assembled around the corner. Each of us sensed our next step. We went four blocks down the street to a Negro saloon full of 1st Battalion soldiers, most of them broke and thirsty. We explained the situation and our strategy. Forty of them joined us and we retraced our steps to the offending bar. We lined up and put our feet on the brass rail. The bartender was thunderstruck.

"What do you people want?" he asked weakly.

"Beer all around," I ordered grandly, ringing a five-dollar gold piece on the bar.

The bartender scratched his head and grinned sheepishly and drew the foaming brew. We tossed it off, slammed the goblets down on the bar, and waited.

"You boys win," the bartender conceded. "Have one on the house!"

I thought of the pertinence of Rudyard Kipling's *Tommy:*

> I went into a public 'ouse to get a pint o'beer.
> The publican he up an' sez, "We serve no red-coats here."
> The girls be'ind the bar they laughed an' giggled fit to die,
> I outs into the street again an' to myself sez I:
> > O it's "Tommy this, an' Tommy that, an' Tommy go
> > away";
> > But it's "Thank you Mister Atkins," when the band
> > begins to play—
> > The band begins to play, my boys, the band begins to
> > play.
> > O it's "Thank you Mister Atkins," when the band begins
> > to play.

This had been one of my favorite Kipling ballads, but it had not occurred to me before that I would be in the same position as Tommy Atkins. And I speculated as to why the plight of the professional soldier in peacetime civilian life was the same in so many parts of the world. It was not only a matter of color, for the Tommy Atkinses were white, and even white American soldiers were not exactly received with open arms by their own civilian countrymen.

Older soldiers reported that so far as colored were concerned, the state of Washington outside Seattle and Tacoma was little different from Mississippi in race relations. They knew because they had recently been down there on maneuvers.

At any rate we had staged the first stand-in and won.

CHAPTER 4

BACK AT the post a school was operated afternoons for those soldiers whose schooling had been retarded or even nonexistent. While all could read and write, the education of many had not gone beyond that. So after I had been at the station several weeks, I found myself teaching English and geography to a score of grown pupils. It was pleasant and also enabled me to make something extra. Another source of extra money was chopping cord wood for the quartermaster. Wood was the most plentiful thing around there. We were in the midst of a thick fir forest, and huge trees were already cut down and trimmed by lumberjacks and sawed into manageable logs. These had to be split, then chopped into four-foot lengths and piled four-feet high and eight-feet long. It was by far the most lucrative extra work one could get around the post, but it was no child's play, even for young men.

One might also become a striker or dog-robber, that is to say, an officer's servant; but such pursuits were not to my liking, and never have been. So I taught in the post school and occasionally

45

chopped some wood. Between military duties and these pursuits, I had little leisure to play pool and cards.

I enjoyed listening to the veterans relate their experiences in the frigid posts in Montana and Nebraska, the tours in Mexican border areas, sojourns in such places as Iloilo, Zamboanga, Camp Statsenberg, Camp Bumpus on Leyte, and elsewhere in the Philippines. It had been rough service there, chasing the elusive rebels and risking one's neck on sentry duty where soldiers walked in pairs, and even then both might be neatly beheaded by Filipinos or Moros who spent all of their daylight hours sharpening bolos to the keenness of well-honed razors.

Quartermaster Sergeant Henry Bell was the oldest man in the company and also one of the shortest. He was a bespectacled, brown, wiry fellow with a large, graying mustache. He was the best shot in the regiment, an expert rifleman since his first enlistment back in the late 1880's, as could be seen from the added bars on his rifle medal. His accuracy was uncanny. At the 1,000-yard range he would curl up in his extended gun sling, and using a sandbag rest, would make bullseye after bullseye with monotonous regularity. This required iron control. It was an education to hear him tell of his experiences in posts on the old frontier, of range wars, Indian uprisings, and protection of settlers from outlaws, red and white. He would chuckle sardonically when he reflected that some towns he had helped protect in their infancy would not now give a colored traveler any sort of accommodation.

Seattle, some men said who knew it years before, was deteriorating interracially. What they called the Southern influence was becoming more apparent with the growth of population. In the early days, most of the white pioneers fraternized with the Indians and either lived with or married Indian girls. The shortage of white women was then remedied by a canny San Francisco entrepreneur who sent up a boatload of prostitutes off the Frisco docks. But now, the city which had been so carefree and amoral had developed a reform movement whose aim was to clean up the town. Admittedly, this would be a tough job, what with seamen, miners, lumbermen, prospectors, fishermen, and railroad workers gravitating from the East, California, and Alaska. However, cities all over the country were being inundated by the wave of reform aimed at the red-light districts, sparked by the feminist and suffragette movements. Eventually, they would win, too, even in hell holes like San Frisco, Chicago, and New Orleans. In 1912, however, Seattle was manfully holding out. This made it an enviable place for the soldier. On that all were agreed.

It was therefore a big shock to everybody when the news was headlined that a white woman near Interbay had been raped by a Negro soldier. Nobody doubted that it might have happened, but everybody wondered why, since intimate association between white women and colored men, both civilian and military, was common in the community.

What shocked and outraged all of the soldiers was that the next morning the entire garrison was assembled by units in front of their respective barracks to be inspected by the aggrieved white woman in the hope that she might recognize her assailant. It was most humiliating to the men to be peered at in this manner, and for this reason. However, the ordeal was soon over, and the culprit was never found; but we never forgot it.

All in all, Fort Lawton was a pleasant post. The duties were not arduous, and passes to town were much more readily obtainable than the money to spend on such excursions. Many of the soldiers had civilian friends, and those who were married had their wives in town. Much was to be learned about the surrounding country through practice marches and field exercises.

One afternoon in mid-October I received a telegram from my stepfather telling me that my mother had died. That was a shock. I was nearly 3,000 miles from Syracuse, and the journey would have taken five days, even if I had the transportation money. So I cried it out alone with no one to console me. Through the night the past paraded before me, and I took myself to task for my selfishness in leaving home. She had lived less than three months after I went into the Army.

A woman of nobility, integrity, intelligence, curiosity, and a healthy scepticism about this world, she played a decisive role in molding my thinking, my manners, and my outlook on the society in which I lived. A true conservative, she was an apostle of the possible, a strong believer in preserving the values of society, and a firm advocate of reasonable change. From the beginning she imbued me with a taste for reading the best in books and for the amenities of gracious living. She taught me early that there were several sides to every question, and we should consider them all before making decisions. She believed in principles and standards as guides to personal conduct and that one should adhere to them whether others agreed or one was alone. Nor did the fact of being alone impair the validity and rectitude of one's position. I had a happy and fruitful childhood because of her.

I now felt completely alone. My mother, father, grandmother, and Aunt Amy were all dead. Only my two cousins, Lila and Mary Louise, remained. My stepfather and I had very little in common. We did not even correspond after my mother passed away, and I only heard from the two girls occasionally. I exchanged letters fitfully with two girls of my age and a youngster who was a good friend and who later joined the 9th Cavalry. Otherwise, I was cut off from Syracuse, and I preferred it that way. I never felt homesick because almost all of those who were close to me were gone.

Company B now became my first home rather than Syracuse, and my friendships and allegiances were there. It was very much like a family itself. The strict discipline was beneficial to all concerned, preventing the impositions which so often marked familial associations. Nobody took advantage of anybody, nor did authority deal unfairly. If one thought so, one could get a hearing. Few complained, not even about the food, which indicates that everything was satisfactory. An exception were the two boys from Savannah who could never get accustomed to rice pudding. One of them noisily complained: "Mon, you sweetum rice, spoilum rice!" They were accustomed to rice as a vegetable, not a dessert.

To almost everyone's surprise, orders were issued soon after Thanksgiving that the Twenty-fifth Infantry was to be transferred at the end of the year to Schofield Barracks, Territory of Hawaii. This involved a train trip to San Francisco and a boat trip of more than 2,000 miles to Honolulu. It was an exciting prospect except to the old soldiers who had female attachments in Seattle. Some had been to Hawaii, but none had served there. Schofield Barracks, twenty-six miles from Honolulu, was reportedly the largest American military post. There the entire Twenty-fifth Infantry would be assembled for the first time in years.

There was another big feast at Christmas and then, with the customary military dispatch, we left with arms and barrack bags on the special train going south. Happily, we were paid just before the train's departure, so we would have money when we hit San Francisco the following day, which was New Year's.

From the train, ferried across from Oakland, we went immediately to the Army transport *Logan* berthed at the foot of Mason Street where all was in readiness for us. In no time at all we were assigned to three-tiered bunks below, and after mess, passes were issued wholesale and we were off to the Barbary Coast on Pacific Street which was quite properly nicknamed.

On the streetcar, one heard the Barbary Coast many blocks before one reached it. Ragtime and jazz music smote the ears from afar, and the street was crowded and ablaze with lights. It was the perfect soldier and tourist trap, and everybody was delighted to be trapped.

The reform wave had not yet struck San Francisco. The town was wide open with all that implies. Pandemonium reigned nightly and into the wee small hours. Black boys pounded out the jungle beat for boozy shufflers, a beat which was later to become world famous. Dance halls were side by side, with bands ranging from three to nine pieces, depending on whether it was the All Nations Bar with its drummer, pianist, and cornetist on a platform under the ceiling or The Ivy with its large stage and more elaborate decor. In none of the places was any sheet music used; everybody played by ear.

Two flights down in the cellar of one place was allegedly the biggest game of craps in the district, and it had the dubious distinction of being run by a tall, cream-colored, pleasingly plump colored woman with full red lips and a mouth full of gold teeth. This was Gold Tooth Mame who could cut a craps game with the best of them. Wearing a John B. Stetson hat and a box back coat that only touched her on the shoulders, she presided over the game like a veteran, calling the dice in a deep voice.

"Th' ma–an th' owed eight! Eighty-eight, eighty-eight! Take yo' money tuh Sistuh Kate! Brutha, yoh point is eight! Let th' dice roll, goddam you soul!"

To reinforce her decisions, Mame had a .45 revolver parked near her right hand, but nobody disputed her. The room was crammed with as nondescript a crowd of ruffians as one could assemble, but she maintained order like a martinet and watched the gold and silver with an eagle eye. When a player threw craps, she would bellow, "Shoot, nigger! You ain't los' nuthin' but yoh money!"

Not even "Rough House" Reed, a wiry, black fellow out of the slums of Chicago who was acknowledged to be the toughest man in the battalion, was able to faze her. When he familiarly put his hand on her shoulder, she turned in a flash and snarled, "You gittin' ready tuh shave with one han' foh th' rest o' yoh life!"

We had four nights of the Barbary Coast and its multiracial denizens and then the *Logan* steamed through the Golden Gate toward the South Seas. The men were broke but happy and had hangovers which were not helped by the storm that struck us as soon as we got out into the ocean. Scores were ill, but Army discipline and routine continued as if all were in perfect shape. It was my ill fortune to be on guard duty that first night, and even Mothersill's seasick remedy helped very little.

The *Logan* was the oldest and worst transport in the service, having been commissioned about 1880. It wallowed like a tub and the storm outside was the worst in years. When it careened on one side it seemed as if it would never straighten up, and it creaked and groaned as if in misery. Most men strapped themselves in their bunks to keep from being thrown to the deck.

It was at this time that "Rough House" Reed chose to start a craps game on a blanket, and the click of the dice attracted a group of soldiers still physically fit. Hatches were battened down and the air below was foul. Rifles rattled in their racks, haversacks scuffed about, here and there a man vomited, and the great seas battered the aged transport. It seemed that every lurch would be its last.

There was a morose, rabbit-toothed fellow whose piety had won him the cognomen of "Reverend" Jackson. His Bible was well worn, and he quoted from it on every occasion. He was one of the two men in the company who regularly attended church services. As the craps game progressed he muttered dire warnings, urging God to forgive the poor sinners and not send them to the bottom of the Pacific. As the old boat sank far over to one side and the propeller raced, "Reverend" Jackson bellowed like a mastiff, "We's sho gonna die, Jesus, in uh watery grave!"

"Shut up that goddam noise, nigger!" yelled "Rough House" Reed, with one dice laden fist poised in mid-air and glaring malevolently at the preacher. "I'm gonna make this six if I hasta do it on th' bottom of the mammy-rapin' ocean. Ain' no use o' you niggers prayin' tuh God 'cause yer too damned black tuh go tuh He'ben . . . Ah! Six, dice! Jimmy Hicks!"

Awed and silenced by such blasphemy, "Reverend" Jackson and the others watched transfixed as "Rough House" Reed made his point with the deck slanted at thirty degrees.

The next day the storm had abated, and for the next week we skimmed across painted seas, watching the porpoises, the flying fish, and occasional whales, with nothing else to do but eat and go through setting-up exercises once daily.

It was during this pleasant period that I had many occasions to chat with Corporal Jesse Coleman, company clerk and the outfit's intellectual. He was a plump, brown-skinned chap of about forty who had been in the army some twenty years and once was first sergeant of a company while serving in the Philippines. He was well read, had a beautiful Spencerian handwriting, and was an amazingly dexterous typist. It was he who had recommended me to teach in the post school. It was apparent that he could have held any noncommissioned rank, and I believe that he did end his military career as a warrant officer. There were several such men in the regiment. Like the intelligent and well-schooled Negroes in civilian life at that time, it was not easy for them to get the positions they were capable of holding.

My best friend in B Company was John Hudson, one of the Geechees from Savannah whom at first I had difficulty under-

51

standing. He was a year older than I, and we had had the same kind of upbringing and schooling, although his had been strictly segregated. Indeed, one of the first things he wanted to know on the day we enlisted was how it felt to go to school with white children.

Hudson was a very black youth, with smooth skin and perfect teeth, but he must have pleased First Sergeant Blaney because he never showed them. Always aloof and serious, he quickly acquired the nickname of Rain-in-the-Face. He was extremely race conscious, supersensitive, contentious, a good speaker and debater, and prone to agitate against presumed wrongs and injustices. He was not as well informed on Negro history and personalities as I was but was eager to learn. On the other hand, I learned much about the problems of growing up in a city like Savannah where, of course, the color line was maintained, but allegedly in a softer way than in other Georgia cities.

Years later when I traveled intensively in the South I found in going from place to place that differences in race relations were so great that one could not generalize about the area nor even about the same state because local customs so varied, as did the people.

About the middle of January, 1913, we landed at Honolulu. It was a strikingly beautiful scene which I shall never forget. The deep blue harbor waters skimmed by dozens of fishing boats with varicolored sails, the wall of green palisades seemingly close enough to reach out and touch, the fleecy clouds crowning the summits, the sprawling white and pastel buildings climbing the hillsides and spreading along the shore, the majestic Diamond Head in whose crater the great artillery mortars lurked, and the vast surf of the world-famed Waikiki Beach. Testifying to its modernity, however, were the Ford cars on the docks and the open-air streetcars on the thoroughfares. Seeing this lovely panorama of tropical magnificence justified the Army's recruiting propaganda, and I felt superior to the young friends I had left back in Syracuse, New York.

What struck us all was that in marching through the narrow streets not one cheer or wave came from the crowded balconies, and this seemed odd. White people were far in the minority, much more so than now. There were swarms of Japanese, Chinese, Filipinos and other Orientals sprinkled with Portuguese, some Russians, and a few Hawaiians. We did not know what significance to attach to this silence until we got our first pay, went to town in search of pleasure, discovered the sprawling Iwilei district of brothels, and learned of the anti-Negro propaganda which had been circulated by our white comrades of the other regiments and services. As a result, the populace was dubious, if not frightened, about fraternization.

We had ample opportunity to stretch our sea legs and see the strange countryside of Oahu In the long march from Honolulu to the immense expanse of Schofield Barracks. The road was metaled and rose steadily as we left the city. It was a long hike, up from the parklike Fort Shafter where the 2nd Infantry was stationed, then between cane fields and vast pineapple plantations; with the Waianae 4,000-foot mountain range on one side and the longer Koolau range on the other, the scene was dramatic. There were deep gulches in the red volcanic soil, with large trees growing in them and vast gold-dappled fields of wild guavas.

Habitations were scarce until we approached the village of Wahiawa at the edge of the military reservation which was marked by concrete posts and strands of stout wire. Near the entrance was Castner, the lower barracks, where the 1st Infantry was stationed. These buildings were of cement and quite modern three-story structures. Then there was a dusty hike of a couple of bush-covered miles to the ranchlike headquarters of the commanding general of the brigade, on the edge of the cantonment the Twenty-fifth Infantry was to occupy. The barracks there were one-storied and wooden, with a wide veranda on each side and well-clipped grassy lawns between them. At the other end of the reservation were the cantonments of the First and Fourth Cavalry regiments, the First and Ninth Field Artillery, and auxiliary units similarly housed.

Schofield Barracks was said to be the largest U.S. military reservation. It was located on a high plateau at the foot of the

53

Waianae Mountains between two great gulches. In addition to the various regimental parade grounds with their rows of barracks on one side and officers' quarters on the other, there was an immense plain where the entire First Hawaiian Brigade could be assembled and paraded. The reviews there were quite spectacular, what with the regimental and brigade mounted staffs, the marching infantry, the trotting cavalry units, the rolling artillery, the hospital and machine gun units, the engineers, and the signal corps, with guidons, regimental colors, and the national flag flapping in the breeze while the bands, mounted and foot, played martial music.

About ten miles across the central plateau loomed the long, dark green mass of the Koolau Mountains, like a vast wall stretching the entire length of the island of Oahu from Diamond Head to Kuhuku Head to the north, their summits usually wreathed in clouds. A paved road ran the length of the central valley, ending at the lovely northern beach of Haliewa and the pretty little settlement of that name. At the other end of the valley was Pearl Harbor, on which work was just getting under way.

We came to know Oahu well, what with practice marches and maneuvers in every part of it. Outside Honolulu the island was sparsely settled. Here and there were settlements of agricultural workers, mostly Japanese and Filipinos who did the back-breaking stoop labor on the pineapple fields which extended for miles in all directions in the drier areas in the uplands. In the lower regions were large sugar cane fields in which the glaring white mills were centered amid the waving greenery with the little narrow gauge plantation railroads leading to them.

Our barrack was 200 feet long with wide verandas on each side shaded by shelving, over-hanging roofs. At intervals were benches. At one end was the orderly room and the domain of the company artificer, at the other end the barber shop. There was a central partition, largely an open framework to which were attached shelves to accommodate personal belongings. At the foot of each bunk was the soldier's foot locker and hanging behind the head of the bed was the barrack bag. Mosquito bars were hung from stanchions inserted at the head and foot, and let down at bedtime. The vast room was clean and orderly at all times, but especially at Saturday morning inspection, when all was immaculate. Each trunk had to be open and arranged in a specified manner without exception. Each shelf had to be arranged a certain way. The beds and trunks were exactly aligned from one end of the barracks to the other. The men standing alongside their foot lockers were also aligned, and woe be to the man who was not. There was never any variation.

At one end of the barrack and separated a few feet from it was the building set transversely like the bar on the T. It was the mess hall and recreation room with the kitchen adjoining the eating place. These, too, were always well-scrubbed. The men stood at their places at the tables and were seated on command, and, hungry or not, decorum prevailed. There was a corporal or two at each table to see to that. The sergeants had their own separate table. This was frankly a caste society and one did not, could not, and better not, forget it. The men filed out in as orderly a manner as they entered. The eagle-eyed mess sergeant watched to see that no man wasted food by leaving much on his plate. If so, the offender might be served it at the next meal.

In the adjoining recreation room were two pool tables, a piano (some companies had player pianos), card tables, and a rack of newspapers and magazines. Officially there was no gambling but in practice there were big stud poker, blackjack, craps, and three-card monte games operated after payday. They did not last long because in a few days almost everybody was broke again, what with having allotments deducted and going to town, paying the barber for haircuts and the tailor for having khaki suits processed.

At the other end of the barrack were the latrines. Since there was at first no modern sanitation, we used dry earth toilets. Underneath the seats were cans into which one sprinkled dirt from a nearby box when finished. Around two o'clock in the morning, Japanese workers driving wheeled kettles emptied the cans, scraped them out, sprinkled them with crude oil and then burned them out. These kettles were emptied in cesspools miles away. These cesspools, fourteen feet square and fourteen feet deep, were dug by guardhouse prisoners, as punishment, under the rifles of guards. It was hard work that everybody detested. It went on interminably, and each regimental guardhouse sent its contingent. The huge mounds of red, volcanic dirt piled neatly alongside each cesspool, were progressively shoveled back in as the pool filled. Considerable bantering went on between the military prisoners and their guards, and the latter would urge them sadistically to try to run in order to give guards a chance to try out their rifles without being punished for it!

Next to the latrines were the showers, with a boiler for hot water. The facilities were adequate and the premises clean. There was a continual emphasis on personal hygiene, as is more necessary in the tropics than elsewhere. Recalcitrants were disciplined by their comrades. Once a month there were physical inspections, mainly to detect any cases of venereal disease. These were dubbed shortarm inspections. Every man had to have bathed that day, and each was nude on passing the lynx-eyed medical officers.

Those medical officers were largely instrumental in keeping down the number of sick. There was sick call every day, and a soldier could malinger with scant success. For his complaint he was given either a small bottle of liniment or an ounce of castor oil, the latter consumed on the spot under the eye of the attendant watchful to spot attempts to spit it out. When a man was actually ill or crippled by some accident, he was sent or taken to the hospital. There were rarely more than a dozen men on sick call from the entire regiment as a result of these rugged measures.

Once during field exercises I fell on my left knee. It soon stiffened and could not be bent, so I was hospitalized for a week. The living was easy there and I left reluctantly. As I grew older that knee has increasingly bothered me when the weather changed, but it did not interfere with the strenuous life of drilling, marching, field exercises and wall-climbing; nor did it hamper me in field sports such as dashes, distance runs and running broad jumps.

The regiment prided itself on its proficiency in military exercises and sports, in which it customarily outdid its rivals. The racial element entered here because all of the other regiments were white, and winning over them in track meets or baseball games was extremely relished. A high degree of discipline and skill was attained in the black regiment because men served longer in one outfit and there was less turnover. From 1913 to the spring of 1915, we scarcely received a recruit. This made for a machinelike efficiency in which the men took great pride.

For example, the regiment was noted for its marksmanship, and men trained like athletes for target practice, giving up smoking and drinking for the period, and getting much sleep. They went out on the target range rested, sharp-eyed and iron-nerved. This was necessary in order to insure high scores in slow and rapid fire at 200, 300 and 500 yards, kneeling, sitting and prone; and for the longer distances of 800 and 1,000 yards where the slightest tremor of the muscles or lack of breath control would put one entirely off the target. There was much studying of wind direction and adjustment of sights accordingly, depending upon whether the day was sunny or dull. Almost all of the men in B Company were either expert riflemen, sharp-shooters or marksmen and wore the appropriate silver medals, which respectively added five, three or two dollars to their monthly pay. When the company passed in review the silver medals made a long flash in the sun. Some of the best riflemen were sent to the musketry school at the Presidio of Monterey, and returned Distinguished Marksmen. At the longer ranges during target practice, we got instruction firing with Maxim silencers and telescopic sights. It was uncanny to see a line of riflemen firing with silencers and not to hear anything more than a hissing sound.

Aside from the chaplains of the four Negro regiments, there were only three colored commissioned officers in the entire Army, and none at all in the Navy. The Army's colored officers were 1st Lieutenants John E. Green and Benjamin O. Davis, and Major Charles Young. The latter two were in the cavalry, while Green was an infantryman. The two lieutenants had been commissioned from the ranks, while Major Young was graduated from the United States Military Academy in 1889, after four years in which nobody conversed with him! Although Negroes had constituted a disproportionate percentage of the Navy enlisted personnel from the birth of the Republic and in many instances had attained high noncommissioned rank, none had ever been regularly commissioned.

When Lieutenant John E. Green was assigned to the Twenty-fifth Infantry, it caused a certain strain, much to the delight of the black soldiers. Mr. Green was high-ranking among the first lieutenants and this entitled him to a house, whereas lower ranking men and second lieutenants had to settle for pyramidal tents, wooden-floored and -walled, until more officers' quarters could be erected.

Lieutenant Green was a tall, dark man with an erect figure, finely chiseled features, flashing teeth and an austere manner. The other officers would have preferred that he not attend the officers' club, although automatically a member, but Lieutenant Green was frequently there, although he neither drank nor smoked. Instead of merely leaving his card at the homes of newly arrived officers, he would actually call. Like the men, many of the officers gambled heavily and were often in debt because of money borrowed to pay for their losses. Lieutenant Green did not gamble, was not married, and so was frequently solicited for loans, which he gave. It did not add to his popularity when he was taken up socially by the Hawaiian royalty, and would bring some of the lovely princesses out to the post in his Packard car and entertain them at the officers' club.

A young white second lieutenant came to the regiment. He had a charming young wife. There being insufficient quarters available, he had to be quartered in one of the modernized pyramidal tents. It was hinted to Lieutenant Green that he give up his house to the young couple and move into the pyramidal tent they would vacate. There was and could be no order to that effect because rank is rank, and adhered to with almost religious fervor. So it was just hinted. Since everything that happened on the officers' line was immediately known to the rank and file (because all of the servants in the homes and the club were regimental enlisted men), everybody waited to see what Lieutenant

Green would do. To the men's delight, he ignored the hint and did nothing.

On another occasion, a payday, companies, troops and batteries from all of the regiments were marched to the paymaster's large tent fly. This was pitched with its long tables loaded with stacks of gold and silver coins in front of the headquarters of the Twenty-fifth Infantry, it being centrally located. It was all so organized that there were never more than three or four outfits waiting to be called and paid. The company, troop and battery commanders, armed with their respective payrolls, sat with the paymaster and indicated how much each man was to be paid.

Along the quadrangle lounged a battery of the First Field Artillery with its first sergeant, smoking and chatting. Along came Lieutenant John E. Green in shirt sleeves but insignia prominent, carrying a canvas bag of company funds. He passed by the reclining battery. Nobody paid him the slightest attention.

"Get up!" he shouted, drawing himself up to his full stature, "Get up! Don't you recognize an officer!"

The red-faced first sergeant jumped to his feet, shouted "Attention!" and the men stood erect as the head noncom broke off a snappy salute, which the officer returned. Then Green commanded in a loud voice, "Rest!"

Our company which was also awaiting payment was close to the little drama, and the men beat each other's backs and shoulders in delight. It endeared the crusty Negro officer to them and was the main topic of conversation that day in every barrack and recreation room.

Years later when Green had retired as lieutenant-colonel and was in New York City for a small dinner at Frank's Restaurant celebrating the graduation of his son from West Point, I reminded him of the incident, and we chuckled over it. He took occasion at the time to comment on the pressures to which he was subjected and the subtle and not-so-subtle discriminations he suffered as a lone black officer who deported himself as a white officer would.

Two odd characters in our company were a Major Woods and a Mister Wright. These first names had been given for a purpose. In the South everybody of importance was either Captain, Major, Colonel or General; so to make sure that their son would always have an honorific, the Woods parents named their son Major. Similarly, the Wrights, knowing that Southern white people would rather call a Negro "General," "Field Marshall," "Admiral," "Professor" or "Reverend" than call him Mister, decided to give that first name to their offspring.

Mister Wright often laughed over the embarrassment he had caused white people who customarily called a Negro by his first name, even if they had never seen him before. So they would ask, "What's your name, boy?" and he would reply "Mister Wright." Then they would warn, "Don't get smart with me, nigger! What's your first name?" He would reply, "Mister," and hurriedly explain that that was really his given name. Many compromised by simply calling him Wright.

Major Woods was a thin-faced, very black, trim, precise fellow who had remained private through two enlistments because he was so often drunk despite his meager wages. In the latter half of the month when everybody else was broke and therefore sober, Major Woods would show up three sheets to the wind and smelling like a distillery. It was a mystery.

His great distinction was that he was acknowledged to be the greatest orderly bucker in the outfit. When a man was assigned to guard duty, he tried to present the neatest appearance at Guard Mount so that he might be chosen as orderly to the commanding officer, the colonel. He then sat around headquarters and carried messages for the colonel. This beat walking post. So the competition for orderly was called orderly bucking.

The tendency to be Beau Brummel was general in the company. For important parades, the men would go to extra expense to have their uniforms processed. In the marching ranks they looked like grey steel in motion, and with their medals and polished rifles, they were quite extraordinary. Significantly, the white troops did not take such pains with their appearance, or such pride in their regiments.

CHAPTER 5

WHEN WORLD War I began we were having field exercises at Red Hill on the heights above Honolulu, marching deep into the jungles of the Koolau mountains from our encampment. From our position we could see in the distance the city and harbor. During this period a Japanese battle cruiser chased a much smaller German warship to a position just outside the three mile limit. It was a most uneven contest, so after an exchange of cannon fire the smaller vessel in self-preservation entered Honolulu harbor and was interned. The larger ship then departed, presumably to clear the ocean of other German vessels. The crew of the interned cruiser was shortly afterward moved to a stockaded camp at Schofield Barracks not far from our cantonment and a contingent of the Twenty-fifth Infantry was assigned to guard them. It was quite a comedown for these erstwhile colonial masters of their possessions on the Shantung peninsula, where they had lorded it over the Chinese for many years. In a short time the Japanese had taken all of the German

Pacific Island possessions, which they retained until the Americans took them during the years after World War II started.

We were at the time excited by the prospect of entering the world conflict but the United States was then neutral. The Japanese were not the allies they later became nor were the Germans enemies, but there was a general feeling that had been long existent in military circles that the Japanese were our natural enemies. This was undoubtedly the reason for the big military build-up in the Hawaiian Islands beginning even prior to our regiment's arrival at Schofield Barracks. The island of Oahu was a veritable fortress where all arms of the service were assembled, both Army and Navy. Their supply was facilitated by the opening that year of the Panama Canal. Pearl Harbor was not yet completed and of course military airplanes were in their infancy and there were none in Hawaii.

There was much to see and do during spare time for the more interested and adventurous soldiers. The highest mountains behind the post, in the Waianae range, reached to 3,000 and 4,000 feet. I climbed both, alone and with companions. The lower one with its sheer razorback ridges sometimes no more than a foot wide was the more difficult, with a summit not more than twenty feet wide. The taller one, Mount Koala, was more heavily forested, although with similar razorback ridges, but in case one slipped and fell there were bushes and low trees to break the fall and to hold on to. At the summit was a large swamp filling the ancient crater and almost always wreathed in clouds.

Between the two mountains was Kole Kole pass to the Waianae coast where there was a fairly good beach and a small town with its inevitable wholesale liquor store. I walked there several times with a comrade on a two- or three-day pass, camping in the forested western slope of the mountains and on the edges of canefields. The inhabitants were friendly and affable. Few soldiers made this journey or climbed these mountains, and I never encountered any of the white boys en route.

One of the men in my squad, a slightly older fellow than I, named McSpaden, was an experienced gambler, and we went into partnership together. In the afternoons between paydays, we would sit opposite each other and deal cards, perfecting the art of dealing seconds and from the bottom of the deck, palming cards, and trying to find flaws in these acquired skills. Honest gamblers rarely make money.

From a house in Chicago we bought a dozen packs of marked cards at a time. These were always accompanied by a half card, usually a face card, which one studied closely to find the mark. This card was then compared with the other aces and face cards until the mark was detected on each. Then we drilled each other in determining the various marks swiftly and accurately. As we dealt the cards, we knew what each player had in the hole whether in poker, blackjack or three-card monte. This method was not foolproof but in the course of the sessions it assured winnings.

The military reservation was so vast and the gulches were so deep and tortuous that some gamblers built little shacks a distance from all barracks, and sometimes a short way outside the fence, where games could be played without interference. There were no patrols and the regimental guards walked post around government property. After taps we would slip out to these rendezvous and sometimes gamble until reveille. Since this occurred for only a few nights after payday when the men had money, we did not lose too much sleep. Moreover, that did not matter much because we were all young, and one could catch up on lost sleep in the afternoons after mess.

McSpaden and I became more ambitious as our winnings grew. So we branched out by buying an electric demountable craps table and loaded dice which would make seven when we pressed one leg of the table with a knee. The batteries then charged the wires in the table and the dice would register seven when they stopped rolling. It was phenomenal and the winnings were fast and fantastic.

Then came tragedy. One big gambler from a Third Battalion company who had cleaned up in a Georgia Skin game (the fastest of all games, and the most likely to cause mayhem because only the most nimble-witted could keep track of the bets) came to our shack in the gulch and began plunging at the craps table. He won several hundred dollars from other players, and then McSpaden took over, and through his judicious use of the electric current the other man steadily lost until he had only a few silver dollars left. My partner had a stack of five, ten and twenty dollar gold pieces piled in front of him. Fortunately, as was our wont, he would occasionally slip several tens or twenties for me to pocket.

When the man was cleaned out, enraged by his losses, but attributing them only to his ill-fortune, he kicked the table hard and it collapsed amid spirals of electric wires, scattering McSpaden's loot over the dirt floor. I immediately doused the lantern, and pandemonium reigned as the gamblers fought their way outside and in the melee scattered to their barracks. The irate gambler went in hot pursuit of the fleet McSpaden while I wisely stayed behind, lying on the floor. When they had all gone, I used up a box of matches retrieving the gold and silver coins, returning to the barracks by a circuitous route—after sprinkling kerosene from the lantern and igniting it. The blaze destroyed both the shack and the incriminating evidence.

That ended the craps table adventure, but that afternoon while we were enjoying two big T-bone steaks with sliced onions and tomatoes in the restaurant of the post exchange, who should happen in but the fleeced gambler of the night before! He spotted us, came over to our table with blood in his eye, and demanded to know, "What're youse guys puttin' down?"

Here was crisis. Losing no time, I asked innocently, "What do you mean? You break up our game and then ask what *we're* doing!"

He was bigger than either of us and his lip was trembling. I didn't think he realized the enormity of our offense; didn't know the crap table had been wired, probably had not seen the incriminating wires. So trying to use psychology, I placated him with an invitation to join us in a steak and, hungry like all soldiers, he accepted, to our enormous relief. Then, knowing that he was broke, McSpaden generously offered him a twenty-dollar stake. A man who has lost several hundred dollars is not easily mollified, but this fellow actually believed that *he* was at fault for breaking up the game!

Happily, we each got a weekend pass and were off to Honolulu to adjoining rooms in a Chinese hotel, two comely Chinese-Hawaiian girls, a washtub with a 100-pound cake of ice surrounded by bottles of beer, and a classic Chinese dinner with sparkling burgundy. We lived it up that weekend and actually returned with money enough for another weekend foray. The only wages of sin in this instance were enormous headaches.

Most soldiers on pass headed for the notorious but glamorous Iwilei district where red lights were over every doorway. It was cosmopolitan and interracial with a sliding scale of prices. The armed forces had thoughtfully provided a clinic near the entrance to the district for the soldiers' and sailors' protection after returning from the brothels. A record was kept, and if one of the men contracted a venereal disease and it was disclosed that he had *not* gone to the clinic, he was court-martialed and lost pay. At that time, too, each enlisted man was provided with preventive kits.

The district was a source of friction between the colored and white men, the latter disliking to patronize the same girls as the former. Of the twelve or fifteen thousand armed men on the island, fewer than two thousand were colored. To discourage the women from soliciting or accommodating the Negroes, rumors had been circulated prior to our arrival ranging from habitual disease to warnings that Negroes were so enormously endowed physically that they would permanently harm the women. This propaganda was effective for about one payday. The women found out that the colored men were more prone to invest in the pleasures of the perfumed garden than the whites, and returned more often.

Nevertheless there were conflicts and clashes, culminating in a full scale riot in 1915 when the Ninth Cavalry (colored) came through from the Philippines en route to the States. A big blow-out was given for them by the Twenty-fifth Infantry at the National Guard armory. A large contingent of soldiers from our regiment went to town to fraternize with their colored brethren.

I did not go because I anticipated trouble. But it happened that my boyhood friend from Syracuse, Ray Banks, was in the cavalry regiment and telephoned my company's office where I was doing some chore for Sergeant Jesse Coleman. I was delighted to hear his voice and promised to meet him at the Oahu Railway station when the 2:45 p.m. train from Leilehua arrived at 3:59. We met as agreed, went the rounds of several of the sixteen bars in town, and I staked him to dinner at my favorite Chinese restaurant. I had money and a 24-hour pass.

Ray was his usual gay self. He was a little taller and more robust, thanks to his cavalry experience. He had enlisted not long after I had, and we had quite a time exchanging reminiscences. It also brought back memories of Syracuse, of which I had been thinking very little of late. Save for a very infrequent letter, I did not think of the place. Hawaii was much more interesting to me.

When darkness came, Ray wanted to see the notorious Iwilei district whose reputation, it seemed, was known throughout the Orient, like similar districts in Hong Kong, Shanghai, Manila and Yokohama. I had some apprehensions about going because, as Kipling wrote, "Single men in barracks don't grow into plaster saints," and the cavalrymen had been three weeks at sea without women or liquor.

My doubts were increased by the knowledge that many strange white women from San Francisco (who had been chased out by the police in preparation for the Panama-Pacific Exposition) had been arriving in Honolulu and were ensconced in Iwilei. Unfamiliar with the free and easy mores of Hawaii, they had been accused of refusing Negro patronage. Incidentally, Somerset Maugham visited the city about that time, and I have always felt that his famous story "Rain" was based on the trans-Pacific trek of one of these Frisco trollops escaping arrest and seeking a safer and more lucrative set-up.

By the time we reached Iwilei, my worst fears were being realized. Pandemonium reigned. Because many of the cavalrymen had been haughtily refused by these alien white girls, several of these girls had been beaten, chased out of their pads in

66

flowing negligees, and their houses fired. It looked like one of the more rabid scenes in *The Birth of a Nation,* or the worst exaggerations of the more extreme professional Southerners.

Black soldiers were milling about the narrow streets, tearing palings from the fence along the entrance road, cursing the terrified women, defying the local police and threatening the firemen attempting to extinguish the several blazes. I remembered all I had been told about the Brownsville incident and what resulted from it.

"Come on, Ray," I importuned, "let's get the hell out of here!"

We turned and retraced our steps. I advised him to get back to the troop transport as soon as he could, while I went immediately to the Oahu Railway station, bought a first class ticket (eighty cents) and sat down to await the departure of the 11:30 train to Leilehua and the sanctuary of Schofield Barracks.

I had arrived at the station none too soon. Looking up the avenue I saw what appeared to be a battalion of the Second Infantry with fixed bayonets marching double time toward Iwilei. The bayonets flashed in the light of the street lamps. There was a temptation to see what would happen but it was a very transient one. When the interminable wait ended and the 11:30 train of the narrow-gauge railway finally pulled out, I heaved a sigh of relief.

My worst imaginings were confirmed. Scores of colored soldiers, cavalrymen and infantrymen, were arrested all over the city, not only in Iwilei and environs. There followed an intensive investigation. The transient soldiers were held aboard their transport and the Twenty-fifth Infantrymen involved were confined to quarters, there being insufficient space in the guard house.

The officers investigating the riot knew very well what was the cause of it. As a clerk in the orderly room, I heard our captain admit as much in a conversation with the first sergeant. The investigators therefore were sympathetic. Nobody was punished.

Ray Banks had wisely followed my advice, had returned to

the transport and was thus in the clear, as he told me in a letter sent before the ship's departure. As there were several members of Company B involved, I knew that adverse notations were made on their records, and I assumed on those of all the other offending infantrymen.

One by-product of this serious affair was the strengthening of the antagonism of the powerful missionary element (that had dominated the islands for decades) toward the Iwilei district, as a breeder of crime and disease that sullied the fair reputation of Oahu. This feeling was echoed by the forces of organized tourism that each year promoted the Mid-Pacific Carnival. There seemed to be little appreciation of the fact that Iwilei was one of Honolulu's main attractions, and that 12,000 young and virile bachelors needed it, as did the even greater number of Oriental plantation workers without women, and the transient seamen who swarmed there as soon as their ships tied up to the docks. The protestations of the military powers fell on deaf ears.

The forces of goodness and purity won out, and with a great reformistic flourish the Iwilei district was closed down. Of course the result could easily be predicted. First, the amount of homosexuality in the barracks increased to the extent that the lights were ordered to be kept on all night, and twosomes to the neighboring gulches became far more frequent than at any time in the past. Second, the denizens of Iwilei followed the usual practice in the circumstances, and scattered all over town. So there were residential areas where in the past soldiers and sailors had never been seen but which now saw them frequently, often drunk and disorderly, to the annoyance of respectable citizens. Third, the military men seeking romance began frequenting pads in the Camp No. 1 and Camp No. 2 districts and the Aala Park area where the slum proletariat and criminal element of the lowest type vegetated. These two camps were quadrangles of multi-storied galleried tenements with only one entrance-egress to the area. Unlike in Iwilei, there was no police protection and no military clinic to protect the uniformed patrons from robbery and disease on their post-payday excursions. The Aala Park area was an unpaved few blocks of two-story houses with upper balconies where the lowest type of criminals, and the murderous Aala Park gang, roamed, ranged, and robbed. The police were conspicuous by their absence most of the time. The Chinese-Hawaiian hoodlums that infested the area selected lone soldiers and sailors as their prey, and armed with clubs and cane knives, they were a formidable crew. Many a man whom they lured into the district on promise of supplying girls ended up in the hospital. However, the physical needs of the men and the closing of Iwilei drove to these dangerous districts those who did not know the location of the scattered pads elsewhere in town whence the regulated prostitutes had fled. Apparently these effects of this misplaced zeal did not disturb the slumber of the reformers who had wives and respectable homes.

The case of Pap Echols confirms the fact that every cloud has a silver lining. The recruiting officer who enlisted Pap Echols must have been drunk. The fellow was forty if he was a day. He was short, dark brown and bowlegged, and he walked and looked much like a gorilla. His head was shaped like an over-size nutmeg and he seemingly had no neck; his little red popped eyes were close together; his nose rambled over his face; his ears were cauliflowered; his chin rudimentary and his lips like frankfurters. His shoulders were very broad and his arms long and apelike. His shambling gait had been acquired in a chain-gang. It was a gait which defied all the efforts of the company's ablest drillmasters.

It was amply evident that Pap Echols was well nigh hopeless soldier material. Dredged out of the slums of Cincinnati, he was inured to liquor, vice and crime, and the constant threat of military prison did not cause him to mend his ways. When in his cups he would snarl to all and sundry: "Ah'm th' goddamdest baddest niggah that evah come tuh this goddam Army. Ah don't give uh damn 'bout nobody er nuthin'. Bettah not *nobody* fool wi' me. Ah'll cutcha yo goddam hea't out an' stuff hit down yo goddam th'oat. . . . Ah've spent mo goddam time on th' chain-gang 'n mos' o' you nigguhs has bin in the worl'."

The entire company was impressed. A couple of men who had known Pap in civilian life spoke respectfully of his prowess with knife, razor and gun. When he got two or three drinks under his belt, Pap was quite a raconteur. He would sit astride his bunk, talking out of the corner of his mouth, exposing anon a row of tobacco-stained snaggle teeth in a hideous grin when he said anything he deemed humorous in his inexhaustible string of anecdotes. Very good at pantomime and armed with a mess kit knife, he would regale the boys by the hour with graphic accounts of the robberies and homicides he had committed.

He claimed to have beheaded a man one night in a Columbus dive and kicked his head under the bar rail. He swore he had shot one white man in Arkansas and stabbed another to death in Cairo. Once, while doing a year on a North Carolina chaingang, he had, he said, brained the guard with a pickaxe and escaped. He declared that he had slaughtered so many Negroes, men and women, that he had quite lost count.

One sceptic, nicknamed Bear, often sneered at Pap's tales and insinuated that he was only a blowhard. One payday night at a crap game in a nearby gulch, he called Pap a liar. The older man's eyes narrowed, and rising quickly, he seized the box on which he had been seated and crashed it down on Bear's head. Then, as his tormenter lay helpless on the floor of the shack, he kicked him in the face with his size twelve shoes. Only the concerted effort of the witnesses kept Pap from doing the boy permanent injury.

This enhanced Pap's reputation as a toughie. The men gave him a wider berth and even some of the noncoms did not bellow so loudly at Pap as they did at others. Except for a couple of bits in the guardhouse for drunkenness and insolence, he pretty much had his way.

When the battalion went to town to drill and parade at the Carnival, Pap fell in quite logically with the hoodlums of the Aala Park gang. He had a ball the first night, and came back to camp, drunk and happy, announcing that "Me'n 'em damn Japs is jush like that," holding up two crooked black fingers.

Men who knew the Honolulu score warned Pap to stay away from these dubious companions but he ignored the advice.

Next night he went back, bought a couple of demijohns of dago red, was cordially greeted and invited to join the guzzlers in a second floor flat that looked out on a narrow, dusty lane.

They hit the jugs hard, swapped stories of crime and became increasingly inebriated. Pap jeered at the accounts of their modest misdeeds, and made the error of loudly declaring that the "damn Chinks can't be bad . . . ain't got th' guts." A fight was narrowly averted at that juncture.

Then Sarah came in. She was an ultra-tough Chinese-Hawaiian whore who was rather pretty until she opened her mouth and you saw how few teeth she had. Immediately Pap began making overtures to her, consisting of gorillalike pawing. Unknown to Echols, her pimp was present, so Sarah shook off the Negro's efforts to massage her breasts and thighs. When Pap persisted, her pimp intervened. Pap swung a punch at the man, missed, and fell sprawling among the others. The gang piled on him with fists and clubs, beat him unmercifully, and then threw him off the balcony to the hard-packed ground below.

Shortly after reveille next morning I spotted old Pap shambling sidewise down the camp street shaking his bloody head and talking to himself. His campaign hat was as battered as his head, one eye was closed, his nose was trickling blood and his uniform, rent in a dozen places, was gray with the coral dust of the road.

"What's the matter, Pap?" I asked. "Did you meet somebody badder than you?"

"Yoah damn right, boy," groaned Echols through puffed lips. "Th' whole Japanese Army musta' jumped on me back tha'!"

"Going back to clean them out?" I presumed.

"Like hell I am," he groaned, shuffling painfully into his tent.

The silver lining in the cloud of gloom caused by the closing of Iwilei, was the reformation of Pap Echols. Thenceforward he came as near being a model soldier as was possible, what with the shattering of the myth of his invincibility, and the resultant loss of face.

Honolulu was not all rum and roistering. I took streetcar

rides to the outskirts of town, went up to the Nuana Pali and glimpsed the breath-taking panorama of the fifty miles of green palisades with waving canefields at their base, and visited the Bishop Museum with John Hudson who also appreciated such things. There was a post library at Castner, the lower cantonment in Schofield Barracks, and there I borrowed many books like Machiavelli's *The Prince,* Creasy's *Fifteen Decisive Battles of the World,* von Clausewitz' *On War,* Admiral Mahan's classics on sea power, and works on the psychology of fire. I followed assiduously the progress of the war. Unfortunately, the barrack atmosphere was not conducive to intellectualism. Such conversation as there was tended to be visceral and for this reason one's choice of close friends was limited.

There was a large recreation hall close to the Twenty-fifth Infantry cantonment and patronized by the entire garrison. There were frequent shows there, vaudeville and musical comedy, amateur and professional, and these were quite a diversion. I remember seeing there the popular Negro vaudeville team of Tim and Gertie Moore leading a small troupe. They were among the best in the business and had recently had a big success in Australia. They were just one of a number of Negro acts that came to Schofield Barracks and lightened the boredom of military routine.

CHAPTER 6

THE END of my enlistment was now approaching. The three years had been immensely instructive, and I had seen and experienced more than I had ever dreamed of before I left home. But I was eager to try civilian life again and have some privacy. I was now past twenty, but had no desire to return to Syracuse because I was sure that nothing there had changed. Nor was I eager to even return to the mainland. Honolulu was quite to my liking, and I did not think any place under the "Stars and Stripes" could be better for a young colored man. So I decided to remain after I was discharged on July 17, 1915.

I went immediately to my favorite Chinese hotel, bought a couple of suits of clothes, shirts and accessories, and was on my own. I soon discovered that there were available jobs only at Pearl Harbor, and they were common labor. Plantation jobs were only for those who knew the work, mainly Orientals. The pay was meager and living conditions far inferior to the Army. Moreover, there could be little companionship because few of the workers knew more than rudimentary English and I had nothing in common with them if I should take a plantation job. Language and customs are tremendous barriers to meaningful association.

The only people with whom I could establish rapport were Americans, and there were really only a handful of them, mostly in administrative capacities. Work such as I could do, clerical and typing, was monopolized by Orientals, mainly Chinese, and they were a very clannish people. If they knew of a vacancy for a job, they saw that one of their own got it, usually a relative. Negroes were not hired as clerks either in Hawaii or on the mainland at that time, and those who owned the big stores and other businesses were of the old white families or the Chinese.

So I went to work at Pearl Harbor. It was hard outdoor work in the broiling sun and not to my liking but I stuck it out for a couple of weeks. The pay was pretty good and if I had stayed there I might have gotten a better job, like watchman or caretaker. I knew none of the skills like plumbing or electric wiring which were in demand. There had been no opportunity to learn them while in the service.

At this juncture fate intervened in the person of an older man who soldiered in B Company and had a little money. Together we bought a secondhand Packard touring car, and arranged with Quartermaster Sergeant Henry C. Bell to chauffeur soldiers to town under his direction, and on credit when they did not have sufficient money. Sergeant Bell made the collections on payday and then paid us, after taking his commission. I was to be the driver, take the boys to town and get them back to the post in time for reveille. There was a flat rate for the car regardless of the number of passengers up to six or even eight. The Oahu Railway was cheaper but the first morning train on weekdays did not leave Honolulu until six o'clock, arriving at ten past seven, which was too late for reveille. There was no train at all to Leilehua on Sunday. An automobile solved those problems.

I knew nothing about driving a car, but I soon learned. On August 9, 1915, I got my chauffeur's certificate #3782 from the Honolulu Police Department, and the fee of three dollars was

74

paid to the examiner. It was an easy life and much to my liking. It was far better than toiling at Pearl Harbor.

There were only about three or four round trips a week, and the rest of the time I had to myself. I already knew the topography of the island very well, and all of the entertainment facilities of Honolulu. A car was helpful in the girl department, and Honolulu was a female flower garden. Also I had considerable money, which as everywhere is the "Open Sesame" to youthful pleasures. I took pretty girls frequently for beach parties at Waikiki or Haleiwa. It was not necessary to make a trip to Schofield Barracks to find out if there was any job for the evening; it was only necessary to telephone Sergeant Bell. Once I brought a carload of boys to Honolulu, I did not have to chaperone them but only to know where to pick them up early in the morning for the return trip, when usually everybody but the driver was drunk.

Toward the end of September I began to get restless. I wanted to see the Panama-Pacific Exposition before it closed down, and I found that I could get free passage on a transport as an ex-soldier, unemployed. This was government policy to keep down the number of what were called tropical tramps or beach bums. I had employment and some money. So without ado and to the surprise and chagrin of my partner and Sergeant Bell, I collected what was due me after the September payday and boarded the next transport for the mainland and the fair. I did not like Honolulu any less but I was eager to see the big show.

It was a grueling, stormy trip, taking twelve days instead of the usual eight, and there was nothing to do but eat and sleep, smoke cigars and chat with the few discharged soldiers aboard.

The exposition was beautiful and the city was lively, but the Barbary Coast had yielded to reform. Oakland had a flavor of its own and I savored it. I found the available work to be red capping, portering, or working on the railroads as waiter or Pullman porter. I wanted none of these servile occupations. The Pacific coast Negro population was quite sparse and economic opportunities seemed no greater than in the East. It was about the same story from San Diego to Seattle: a few thousand Negroes in an ocean of whites, hanging on to the economic fringes of society, too few to make any impact, even if sufficiently united to do so. The Army, after all, seemed a better bet. So in November, 1915, I re-enlisted. In retrospect it seems to have been the best thing to do.

After a short time at the recruiting station on Angel Island, I was again en route back to Hawaii and the old regiment, but I went this time to H Company instead of B Company, and for four years instead of three. I settled back into the routine of garrison duty. But military companies are like families, all different. The first sergeant puts his imprint on a company, as a father does on his family. Officers come and go, but the top soldier remains. This was especially so in companies and troops of the Negro regiments for reasons previously stated. The man who molded H Company was First Sergeant William Glass.

"Ah want you people to understan' that Ah'm First Sergeant of H Company," I heard him say to the men at midday mess, the first day I ate with the company. I heard it daily for the rest of my service with the outfit. So did everybody else because there was no way of avoiding it.

Depending upon the first sergeant, a company is happy-go-lucky or it is tough. It was said all over the regiment that if you could make the time in H Company, you could do so anywhere. Such companies have a certain fascination. They put a fellow on his mettle. It is something of an adventure, this business of seeing how long you can stay out of the guardhouse. In B Company it was much easier than in H.

Sergeant Glass was a veteran of the Spanish-American War and the Philippine Insurrection, and had been a noncommissioned officer for nearly twenty years. Woof, as the men nicknamed him for obvious reasons, was a chocolate-colored Kentuckian of medium height, stocky, with powerful shoulders and arms, and short sturdy legs. He had a square head, determined jaw and little, piggish eyes that smouldered under heavy brows and corrugated forehead, while his close-cropped mustache hid a stern mouth.

As a clerk in the orderly room, I came to know him very

well. He was rather widely hated because of his insistence on rigid discipline, yet he was feared and respected. He knew his duty thoroughly, and what was worse, he knew the duty of everybody else. He could and interminably did tell everybody what his particular duty was. There was just one way to do anything, and that was according to the Army regulations and the Infantry Drill regulations; that is to say, "The Book." Thus, there was never any debate about what was right. In all differences or disputes, he would firmly inquire, "What do the regulations say?"

Rapport was quickly established between us in the orderly room when he discovered that I was also a close student of "The Book." I studied the regulations assiduously, and even challenged him on a couple of occasions, which was dangerous license in H Company unless you really knew your stuff. But at twenty-one years of age one is brash.

In most companies the departure of the officers from the vicinity of the barracks was the signal for a letup in tension and a certain tolerance toward minor infractions; but not so in *that* company. As long as Woof was about—and he always *was* about —it was just the same as if the colonel, the major, the captain or the lieutenants were about. Any infractions or violations, no matter how slight, were religiously and accurately reported to the company commander. After an arduous field exercise in the tropic sun, with the red, volcanic dust caked on the face by perspiration, it was usual for some "ragtime" companies to simply break for the gun racks after a perfunctory "dismissed" from the top soldiers who were as weary as the men. None of that for Woof! He followed regulations. "Company, attention! Squads right, march! Compan-e-e, halt! Port, arms! Inspection, arms! Now you people . . . dismissed!"

It was H Company that was the best drilled. It was H Company that had the largest number of expert riflemen, sharpshooters and marksmen. It was H Company that had the quietest and most orderly mess hall, recreation room and barracks. It was H Company that held the straightest line on parades; that had the largest number of men depositing part of their pay monthly; that had the cleanest equipment; that won tent pitching contests; and that had the smallest number of drunks the morning after payday. You couldn't gamble there and you'd better not be caught with liquor in the building. As the big, red-faced captain from Tennessee (nicknamed Sniff-Snuff because of his catarrh) was wont to say, it was a company run "according to Hoyle."

Woof was as exacting on himself as on his men. He was ever smoothshaven, immaculate, and his room next to the office was always ready for inspection. He tolerated no mistakes in his reports and duty rosters; was never late or absent for a formation, and, as was quite fitting, he was an expert rifleman and the best pistol shot in the battalion.

And yet this military perfection was not appreciated by the men. They hated him. None would say a good word for him. Once some of the rougher element plotted to place a bomb under his bedroom. At another time an undiscovered enemy fired a ball cartridge at him during the annual maneuvers. The most delightful pastime of some privates was to lie on their bunks after drill and mess, and talk of what they would do to Woof if they ever caught him "on the outside." The punishments they proposed ran the gamut from blackjacking to decapitation.

Once, a tall, black, evil-looking Negro from northern Florida, goaded to desperation by the rigid discipline, sat down and wrote a long anonymous and scurrilous letter to the Secretary of War protesting against the "tyranny" existing. Inevitably the letter was returned to the company commander through the usual military channels, decorated with a dozen endorsements.

Woof was furious and his little eyes flashed. "Ah'm gonna find out who it is if it takes a year," he confided to me. An uncanny judge of men, he pondered only a short time before he reduced the suspects to three, all of them fairly well schooled, and this included the man from Florida. Two or three days afterward he casually invited the trio to the orderly room. He artfully informed them that the company commander had decided to have a man in training to take my place as company clerk in case of sickness, death or dismissal; that he had chosen them as the three most likely candidates. It would, of course, be necessary for them first to submit samples of their handwriting to the Captain. He instructed me to give them examples in arithmetic and to write sample letters and reports. They had scarcely gone out of the door before he unlocked his desk drawer and compared the handwriting on the troublesome anonymous letter with that on the samples.

Soon he emitted a chortle of triumph, grabbed the telephone, and requested the captain to come to the office as soon as he could. The company commander came from the Officers' Club immediately, and the two pored over the material. I typed out the charges against the offending Floridian whom they were convinced was the culprit. He was promptly court-martialed by Old Tremble, the summary court officer, and given a stiff sentence in the guardhouse.

He preceded Woof from the Summary Court room and as that worthy came along to deliver his usual midday lecture in the mess hall, the man leaped at him with a drawn knife. With great agility Woof hurdled a low wire fence around the company's lawn, sped across the grass pursued by the enraged private, leaped up on the porch, wrenched a fire axe from the barrack wall, and promptly turned the tables. Instead of serving a couple of months in the guardhouse, the man got a general court-martial and went to the military prison on Alcatraz for years. I never saw Woof in such excellent spirits. He actually hummed.

Sergeant Glass was a man who would brook no rivalry. Probable aspirants for his job were either squelched or got rid of in some Machiavellian manner. If some sergeant had better schooling than Woof, which was not infrequently the case, he was viewed with suspicion, even if he gave no evidence of being ambitious for promotion.

It happened once that a very light-colored college graduate nicknamed Lily-White by the men, who had been a corporal and former company clerk, was suddenly promoted and appointed supply sergeant to Woof's surprise and consternation. The position was an important one, and next in line to the first sergeant.

Woof did not like it at all, and since he apparently had no other confidant, he mumbled his troubles to me. Even worse, the new sergeant was a "high yallah nigger" and thus *persona non grata* to a top soldier whose other noncoms were as dark complexioned as he. From the time Lily-White was appointed, Woof waged continuous warfare against him, and seldom above-board. The relations between the two became so strained that Sniff-Snuff noticed it and sought vainly to patch things up. A darker man was groomed for the job. By a fortuitous circumstance, in which Sniff-Snuff must have played a part, Lily-White was promoted to battalion sergeant major, and Woof breathed freely again.

Sergeant Glass then arranged my appointment as corporal to fill the resulting vacancy. Curiously, he seemed not to resent my superior schooling, and indeed, was quite amiable and friendly with me; but I had seen enough to be cautious and not to trust him. I did not lower my guard because we were in daily proximity with adjoining desks.

Woof was always taking the joy out of life. There was the incident, for example, at Waianae whence we had hiked by a circuitous route around the end of the mountain range rather than across Kole Kole Pass, a distance of only nine miles. The troops had marched more than twenty miles through dusty pineapple plantations, vast seas of sugar cane, and up the coast to the little town of Waianae where I had spent some pleasant times on pass when in B Company. There had been no trees en route to shade the hikers burdened with full field equipment, caked with dust, drenched with perspiration and terribly weary. They had started at sunrise and the golden orb was sinking into the Pacific when they trudged into camp.

In many companies after such an arduous day, the buying of a little strong drink at the nearby liquor store would have been winked at by their superiors. Not so in Company H! Despite his weariness, Woof was alert. This evening several of the company's "liquorterians," including Big Fairy, Whiskey, Bear, Squareface and Dip (for Diplomat), chipped in enough money to purchase a big demijohn of dago red and a squareface quart of the appropriately named Elephant Gin. Knowing Woof, they did not bring their alcoholic cargo through the gate of the pasture in which the company was camped, but smuggled it in through the waving sugar cane in the rear. However, they reckoned without the ingenious first sergeant and a couple of other noncoms who confiscated the booze. With a chuckle of triumph, Woof retired for the night.

What annoyed the men more than anything else was that there was seemingly no way to "get anything" on Woof. He did not drink, smoke, gamble or run after women, although his well-supported wife was far away in Kentucky. He was not addicted to any of the sexual vices to which so many single men in barracks fall victim, and he read his Bible nightly. Dip observed dolefully, "How can you get anything on a black sonofabitch like that? He ain't human!"

Only once did Woof stray from the straight and narrow path, and only the Captain's "dog robber" (servant) and I knew anything about it. This "dog robber" was appropriately nicknamed Handsome. He was quite a Lothario, and among his stable of lady friends there was a Portuguese charmer named Marie. Thinking to make himself solid with the first sergeant, he conceived the brilliant idea of arranging a liaison between the two. At first Woof was indifferent to these blandishments, but after considerable urging from both of us, coupled with a glowing description of the Iberian maid's youth, beauty and voluptuousness, he decided to make a visit to Honolulu. As he almost never went on pass, his going occasioned company-wide comment and surmise. Handsome went along with him to make the introduction, although Woof took a dim view of such fraternization between himself and one of his men.

After the weekend in town, he returned, radiant and enthusiastic, and confided to me the satisfactory result of his mission. Knowing the teen-age Marie, I knew it could not be otherwise, and was happy for him.

In other outfits "dog robbers" got special privileges such as exemptions from certain formations and often from guard duty; but not in Company H. It was the desire to win some of those privileges that had impelled Handsome to play the John Alden role. Accordingly, the Monday morning following Woof's romantic adventure, Handsome absented himself from reveille. He suffered bitter and immediate disillusionment. After calling the roll, Woof turned to the Officer of the Day and snapped, "H Company, one private absent!"

Not even the closest friendship stood between Woof and his duty. As his company clerk and confidant, I gained the impression that he might overlook a minor infraction of the rules in my case. The company artificer, Bob Thomas, a good friend of mine, who did not have to do either guard or fatigue duty, went to Honolulu on pass. He returned on the 12:40 a.m. train, bringing along a fifth of Johnny Walker Red disguised as a potted plant, for our mutual consumption. When he arrived, he tiptoed to my bunk and nudged me awake. I dressed hurriedly, slipped out of the building, and we made our way across the reservation fence and over to the brink of the neighboring gulch. There we sat smoking, talking and consuming the scotch. We killed about half of it, saving the rest for later. Since the company would be absent on guard duty and fatigue, and I was noncommissioned officer in charge of quarters, the chances of detection were virtually nil.

After morning mess, Bob came to my bunk and we finished off the bottle. I glided to one of the open windows, looked carefully up and down the veranda and thrust the "dead soldier" into a handy trash box. Unknown to me, Sergeant Glass was standing in the doorway of the orderly room and had seen the move. When I went into the office to do some work, there was the empty Johnny Walker bottle on his desk and a triumphant gleam in his little eyes. My heart sank but I said nothing.

When Sniff-Snuff came in, Woof related the story with great relish and some histrionic ability; dwelling with great emphasis on the fact that I had "eased" the bottle into the trash box instead of nonchalantly tossing it in as an innocent man would have done. He accompanied his description with pantomime of the action.

I glibly lied out of it with the explanation that I had simply found the bottle on the gun rack and tossed it into the trash. The old man seemed satisfied, but Woof was disgusted. Several times afterward when he thought I was off guard, Woof would inquire, with a deceptive attempt to be jocular, "Now didn't you really have that bottle of liquor that day?"

To have confessed would have inevitably invited demotion.

If Woof was a martinet, he was no coward. If he had been, perhaps the men would have hated him less, because it is only human to fear. One Saturday morning when the men were busily cleaning rifles, brushing equipment, aligning beds, arranging trunks, folding blankets, and shining shoes for the weekly inspection, a man went insane. He had concealed about him a clip of ball cartridges. These he shoved into the magazine of his Springfield and began firing indiscriminately in the crowded barracks.

At the first shot everybody started in alarm. At the second shot they all deserted the building via windows and doors for the security afforded by the space underneath. Then Woof came on the scene, one side of his face lathered, his little eyes red with anger, his lips drawn back in Rooseveltian style, yelling as he ran down the veranda, "Why don't some of you people stop that man?" From under the barracks somebody yelled, "Why don't *you* stop him?"

Woof did. Leaping through the door nearest to the lunatic who with foaming mouth was ready to fire another shot, Woof snatched the rifle from his hands and knocked him unconscious with the butt. His hands and feet were bound by willing aides, and the ambulance was summoned.

After the still unconscious lunatic was taken to the post hospital, Woof yelled down through the barracks, "All right, all right; you people hurry up and get ready for inspection!"

Being a corporal meant that I was now eligible to join the Noncommissioned Officers' Mess of the Twenty-fifth Infantry. It had its own building and was a replica of the Officers' Club. There was a restaurant and bar. No non-member noncom could purchase anything, and of course no privates were admitted. It was run by a Board of Governors, all noncoms, who hired a steward and assistant under the supervision of the Board's secretary.

Dances were held weekly, and most of the women attending were the wives of noncommissioned officers who lived in a section removed from the cantonment which was dubbed the Fourth Battalion (there being three battalions in the regiment). Both colored and white noncommissioned officers had nondescript quarters there, but none of the whites were ever in attendance at any of our social affairs. Neither were any loose women invited. Everybody knew who they were, whether they came from nearby Wahiawa or the Iwilei district in Honolulu. Some members knew respectable women and girls, and sometimes they came as guests, usually by car, but not often, because of the distance. There were no accommodations for overnight guests, although some female guests stayed in the Fourth Battalion.

As 1917 approached, we sensed that war was coming closer. General Leonard Wood conceived the experiment of training green recruits in ninety days, and it was first tried out at Schofield Barracks with Negro youngsters fresh from the mainland and drilled by experts from among our regiment's noncommissioned officers. When the ninety-day period was over, the graduates were assigned to regular companies.

It was during 1916 that I began writing satirical skits for *The Service,* a weekly magazine edited by civilians for military consumption. These pieces were rather popular among the Schofield Barracks readers and the editors kept asking for more. Local incidents were satirized under such titles as "The Fable of the Self-Opinionated Chieftain," "The 16th Decisive Battle of the World" and "Waianae Waftings." I also did a couple of pieces for the morning paper, the *Honolulu Commercial Advertiser.* To amuse the company I did a typed newspaper which was tacked on the bulletin board. Having access to a typewriter, I was able to do this writing and continued it until I left the islands.

During Wilson's 1916 re-election campaign when the slogan was "Peace At Any Price" and the Democratic crowds were singing "I Didn't Raise My Boy to be a Soldier," it was evident to a cynical minority among us that we would soon be in the war against the Central Powers, what with America's "Armed Neutrality."

In March 1917, H Company spent a pleasant week on the island of Hawaii, camped in a barrack on the rim of the Kilauea volcano. We traveled by inter-island steamer to Hilo, then by wide-gauge railroad to the railhead at the foot of Mauna Loa mountain, the twin of Mauna Kea, and from thence we hiked up to the 4,000-foot plateau where the fiery crater of Haleamaumau was inside the Kilauea volcano. We passed through the fantastic fern forest, saw the gardens where Russians raised strawberries as large as crab apples in steamheated soil, visited the petrified forests and went over the whole volcanic area. We journeyed through the Devil's Throat connecting two small volcanoes, scrambled the 900 feet to the bottom of the old crater Kilauea-Iki, which was as flat as a tennis court, sweated in Pele's Bathhouse, a deep cave in which volcanic steam rose every fifteen or twenty minutes. We were supervised by the Virginia-born mulatto guide, Alex, who had been at the national park for twenty years, and knew the volcano in all of its various moods. Alex could predict accurately what was going to happen fifteen minutes before it happened.

The crater of Haleamaumau (House of Everlasting Fire) was, and probably still is, a lake of fire some 1200 feet in diameter with a crag mass in the center around which flows a stream of lava varying in temperature and flowing around with a black scum filming the surface which periodically parts to expose the orange-red underneath. A half dozen of us dared the descent and stood a few feet from the boiling torrent oxidizing nickels in the cracks of the hardened lava. Alex warned us when it was time to go because a section of the crater wall was about to crash. We climbed out, and sure enough the section fell with a resounding crash, causing immense thermal activity and pyrotechnic displays.

It rained in the area every day, sometimes twice. There were at least a dozen slight earthquakes daily; and as we would walk down the road the ground would shuffle under our feet. All water for drinking, bathing, and cooking came from big redwood tanks kept filled by the heavy rains cascading down the roofs and gutters. This water was remarkable in its purity since there were no pollutants in the air. Near our barracks was a half-mile, 100-foot high ridge of pure sulphur. A short distance from the habitations were many steam pots, holes in the rock which would hold a man's body and from which steam issued every few minutes. It was very invigorating to the bather.

We were returned to Schofield Barracks just a few days before war was declared against the Central Powers. Almost immediately the companies were successively assigned to guard duty at Pearl Harbor, sleeping in warehouses and plants of various kinds.

The most historic development, however, was the selection of some eighty noncommissioned officers from the Twenty-fifth Infantry to be sent to the separate Negro officers' training camp being established at Fort Des Moines, Iowa. Young men from many parts of the country, mostly college-trained, assembled there in late June and we noncoms were the cadre to train them under the supervision of white army officers. Our trip from Honolulu to Des Moines was pleasant and uneventful except for an entirely unexpected meeting with Lieutenant Colonel Charles D. Young on a street car in Oakland. Several of the noncommissioned officers were ex-cavalrymen and had served under him, and he remembered them.

He talked freely, and what we learned from him is a part of American history and also a measure of what the Negro army officer was up against at that time. He had been ordered from command of his regiment on the Mexican border to the Letterman General Hospital in San Francisco, allegedly because of a heart condition which the doctors were unable to discover. He seemed in robust health and he said he was feeling fine.

His ailment was not physical but military. He had been given instructions to pursue and capture the Mexican bandit, Pancho Villa, and his cavalry regiment proceeded diligently to this arduous and difficult task. Other U.S. regiments did likewise. Young's regiment chased Villa into a long valley and he urged the commander of another regiment to close the other end of the valley so the Mexican forces would be bottled up. This the other colonel failed to do, with the result that the elusive Villa and his men escaped. Colonel Young indignantly reported this failure to his superior.

What he did not know and what he had not been told was that instructions had been quietly given to the other commanders that Pancho Villa was to be pursued but not captured; that the real American intention was to follow Villa as deeply into Mexico as possible.

Thus, Colonel Charles D. Young, the only Negro West Point graduate (Class of 1889), was removed from the scene, a sacrifice on the altar of political expediency, a thorn in the side of the military hierarchy. He was retired for alleged physical reasons, which he later disproved by riding horseback from Xenia, Ohio, to Washington, D.C., to the embarrassment of the Wilson Administration. Had he remained on active duty, the War Department would have certainly been confronted with the painful task of eventually promoting him to brigadier general, as were so many officers with whom he ranked, and he might have left the Army a major general, a division commander. His story did not leave any of us with a good feeling.

The Officers' Training School opened on July 1, 1917. In ninety days the young men were supposed to receive instruction for commissions as infantry, cavalry, artillery and engineer officers, to be dubbed later as "ninety-day wonders." The first month was devoted to infantry training, and it seemed to me that a good job was done. I was regarded as an exceptional drill master and the Twelfth Company was one of the best prepared.

The noncoms became suspicious when none of the rest of the prescribed courses of study given at other (white) camps were given to the colored candidates at Fort Des Moines. Nor were they ever given. This had every appearance of sabotage. Worse, the training was not ended after three months, as elsewhere, but was extended another month, as if the Army was racked by indecision. I personally lost interest after the first month when I saw the trend, and so did many of the other noncoms drawn from the four colored regiments. There was really nothing else to do but continue what we had been doing, and spend as many evenings in town as we could afford. Many of the officer candidates also sensed that we were just marking time for some high-echelon purpose; and the officers assigned as instructors displayed little enthusiasm after that first month. A succession of Negro leaders like Robert R. Moton of Tuskegee, Dr. Kelly Miller of Howard University, Dr. Emmett J. Scott, who was civilian assistant to the Secretary of War and had been Booker T. Washington's secretary, came out as morale builders. Even Colonel Young visited the twelve colored companies, now virtually stranded in the midst of the training program.

There were diversions to take the war off my mind. There was, for example, Sergeant "Tush" Morgan. In the vocabulary of the Southern upland folk, a tush is a real tough fellow, the name being taken from the tusks of the boor hog. A ranking duty sergeant of F Company, he was assigned to the Twelfth Company of Des Moines. He was about forty-five years old, stood six feet four inches in his socks and was dark brown in color with an unblemished set of teeth. He wore a fierce mustache that pointed upward in the Prussian manner, and his pugnacious jaw, piano box shoulders, hamlike fists and bull voice added emphasis to his nickname. His first ten years of service had been spent winning all of the heavyweight boxing events in the Army, and his last ten years had been spent boasting about it. He challenged anybody who expressed the slightest doubt of it. He was the model for all recruits who wanted to appear tough, for had he not fought in Cuba and the Philippines, and was he not an expert rifleman? They repeated his choice epithets and affected his belligerent swagger.

I had not known him well when he and an Irish cavalry sergeant were detailed to maintain order at the Blue Goose (nicknamed Bucket of Blood) beer garden a few yards outside the reservation fence at Schofield Barracks. Each payday it was beseiged by 8,000 thirsty soldiers. At the first sign of disturbance, he would grab the combatants by the scruff of the neck and either shake them or bang their heads together, bellowing, "You damn savages, stop that!" or, "Cut that out or I'll crush your jaw!"

Betimes he and his Irish colleague (who was equally handy with his fists) sat opposite each other and killed as many quarts of Schlitz (only twenty-five cents then) as the admiring audience would buy. Disdaining a glass as effeminate, "Tush" would turn up a quart bottle after decapping it with his teeth and drain it without lowering it from his mouth. Then, nonchalantly tossing the "dead soldier" over his shoulder and wiping his mustache, he would remark to his buddy with a wink, "Aye, God, I'm as thirsty as a damn camel." Then he would further astound the boys by drinking another quart as if he had drunk nothing for a fortnight.

We became eating and drinking companions at Fort Des Moines. There was a restaurant outside the post where we often went to relieve the monotony of Army chow. An ordinary meal for "Tush" was an extra large T-bone steak with two orders each of sliced raw onions, french fried potatoes, sliced tomatoes and apple pie a la mode, washed down with three or four cups of coffee. The waitresses stood aghast. Here was a Gargantua for true! Watching him clean up a table full of food reminded me of Rabelais' *Discourse of the Drinkers*. It was an ordinary thing for "Tush" to "kill" a half pint of bourbon in a couple of swigs. He loudly deplored wartime prohibition, and he greeted the prospect of training soldiers, let alone officers, in ninety days with ribald derision.

I shall always be indebted to "Tush" Morgan because he persuaded me to go with him to his favorite pad in Des Moines where in the course of a bibulous evening I met a girl named Jack Patterson. We danced to the then popular Shimmy Sha Wabble. I fell like a battleship's anchor for this most glamorous girl I had ever seen—and I had seen many.

Jack Patterson was an optional Negro: that is, she could "pass" for whatever "race" she chose. She was my height, with long, wavy brown hair, blue-green eyes, a babyish face that would have enthralled a Hollywood casting director, a bosom

89

menacing her chin, a slender waist, and limbs that would have enchanted Rodin. She spoke and walked like a lady, and dressed like a Paris mannequin. She had come up from Omaha, and I presumed that she had not journeyed to Des Moines to play checkers. She was smart enough to wear a minimum of make-up. She was also canny enough not to try to put the bite on a man at first meeting, a tactic that has driven away more good men than the bubonic plague.

That Jack Patterson had been traveling in the big time was evidenced by her possession of a low-slung red roadster which she drove with the nonchalance of a taxicab driver. Afterward it gave me a big lift when around evening mess time she would swirl up to the barrack of the Twelfth Company with her hair blowing, and after the wolf whistles had subsided, ask somebody to call Corporal Schuyler. Sometimes I would wait until the lads called two or three times before I would saunter out, hop in beside her, carelessly drape my left arm across her shoulder, and we would take off in a cloud of dust. We would dine at the nearby restaurant and probably take in a picture or go to her place. Whatever noncom was in charge would cover me at taps, knowing that the pillow stuffed under my sheet was not me. The early morning interurban car enabled me to make reveille.

Like Kipling's old soldier I soon admitted that "I learned about women from 'er." Jack was almost completely corrupt and was rapidly approaching the nadir of amorality, but despite this she was a woman endowed with kindness and generosity. When sober she was a delightful companion; but she did not stay sober very long. She was so beautiful that it seemed a pity she was an alcoholic. Worse, she insisted on driving when she was high, and I had no intention of becoming an auto fatality, just when the future looked so bright.

This was just as well, because within five or six weeks I had become so fascinated that there was no telling in what I might get involved. Virile young men of twenty-two are apt to do foolish things. So when commissioning approached, and Jack wanted me to take her East with me, I saw that wouldn't work at all. We parted as good friends but with a bitter-sweet ending. With a big war going on, and she a camp follower de luxe, I did not figure she would miss me long, if at all.

Finally, on October 15, 1917, near the end of the fourth month, 639 of the 1,200 candidates were commissioned—106 captains, 325 first lieutenants, and 204 second lieutenants. I was one of the first lieutenants. I proudly donned the new officer's uniform with silver bars, and traveled on leave to Syracuse and Boston before reporting to Camp Dix.

It was a happy homecoming, indeed, after five years' absence. I met all the boys and girls I had known, colored and white, and was generally lionized. One very wealthy woman for whom my mother had cooked gave an afternoon tea for me to which all of her class was invited, and where more liquor than tea was served. Several parties were given by colored and white families I knew. I stayed with my two cousins, Mary Louise and Lila, who had their own flat, now that they were the last of the family on my mother's side.

The local girls were extremely attentive, especially a lovely *café au lait* daughter of an interracial couple. I had corresponded with her throughout my enlisted service. I met again another ravishingly beautiful quadroon who had greatly attracted me before I enlisted, when she was but thirteen years old. She was now married and had a baby, but we made notes for the future.

The other Syracuse girl with whom I had exchanged letters now lived in Boston, which is why I headed there. She was a dark girl with Indian features, of good family, upright and engaging, a high school graduate. She met me at the South Station and we taxied to her home in a nice neighborhood where her mother provided me with a room. Those few days were an idyllic period. We went everywhere about town, attending all of the dances and parties we could. At twenty-two years old and with an Army salary of $181 monthly, I began thinking seriously of marriage, and this intelligent girl seemed to be ideal. We even talked about it, and her mother approved of it.

It was soon time to report to Camp Dix, New Jersey. It was nice to be saluted there and en route. From childhood I had always wanted to be somebody, and now I was. The camp, however, was in a state of disorder with many buildings unfinished and unfurnished. Many streets were quagmires in November, with thousands of draftees milling about, but always recognizing an officer.

Quarters were assigned to the Negro officers, identical with but separated from those of the white officers. We had our mess, our service staff for the kitchen and cleaning, but our suspicions were aroused by having nothing to do. We were not assigned to companies because there were no men to command. As a result we were off to Philadelphia nightly "to keep the home fires burning," which was no big chore considering the women's wartime mood. The town was full of Southern migrants working in the various industries, military installations and on the railroads. It was astonishing to pass big, stalwart black women wearing men's shoes, coats, and hats, and smoking big black cigars as they strode along South Street guffawing loudly and exchanging obscene pleasantries. I had never seen such people before, as I had never been South.

Weeks went by. An artillery regiment was being formed and the colonel commanding this paper organization was seeking Negro officers for it. I was ordered to his office and he tried to persuade me to transfer to this colored regiment but I flatly refused. I knew absolutely nothing about artillery or horses, had never handled or fired an artillery piece. I was strictly an infantryman, and I thought a good one, but I would not join a branch of the service for which I was not trained, but would yet be expected to train others. It was ridiculous and smacked of a plot to discredit Negro officers as incompetent.

Others refused, too, having arrived at the same conclusion. So it was back to the "Battle of Philadelphia." This was continued well into February 1918, when we were finally ordered to the 368th Infantry at Camp Meade, Maryland. There were plenty of men there, scores of thousands of them. There were 250 men to a company, 1,000 to a battalion, 3,600 to the regiment, what with auxiliary troops. I was in my element drilling the raw levies and whipping them into shape. Indeed, I guess I was too good because after a short service with a company, I was detached exclusively for that work with new recruits who, after a period of initial training, were assigned to companies. I did this for months, long after the 368th had gone, in Camp Meade and at other camps. When the war finally ended in November, I was among the first to be discharged.

During those months several important things had happened in my personal life. The girl in Boston whom I had planned to marry had died suddenly that winter. The young quadroon from Syracuse had left her husband and was going to New York City to live, so what better place was there for me to go?

Fortunately, a former company commander, Captain John E. Hunt, had been promoted to colonel and assigned to command the Atlantic Branch United States Disciplinary Barracks on Governor's Island where military prisoners were housed in ancient Castle William. I learned of this and wrote him to ask if there was any employment available there. He wrote back encouragingly and I went there one day for an interview. He was a slender, tall, cadaverous, hawk-faced man who had always liked me from the time I joined H Company of the Twenty-Fifth Infantry and began doing clerical work in the orderly room.

As it happened, with war's end hundreds of military prisoners were being brought back from prison camps abroad, and the job of processing them from ship to cell was a growing one and help was needed. Colonel Hunt gave me a temporary civil service job as chief clerk in the office of Colonel Humphrey, the executive officer. There, with a staff sergeant named Dikenja and an old corporal, we processed scores of prisoners daily. I was back in civilian life and with a good job.

CHAPTER 7

LIFE WAS wonderful! New York in the spring! Central Park in a riot of greenery! The calm and order of Governor's Island contrasting with the teeming, boisterous city, only a short ferry ride away. The gloom of the red stone fort with its ancient cannon and the hundreds of numbered prisoners inside waiting for whatever fate, in the form of Uncle Sam, had in store for them. Some few were serving life sentences while others were burdened with varying numbers of years. They were a cross-section of America, of all colors, and classes. I recall one of the more notorious inmates was Jack "Legs" Diamond, the later gangster who won the dubious distinction of being shot more times than anybody else in the underworld until some gorilla finished the job.

I was happy in the work and even more happy in Harlem where I had a sunny two-room apartment at the back of a private house on Fifth Avenue just north of 131st Street. I was living with the lovely nineteen-year-old Myrtle from Syracuse, a quadroon beauty, laughing and voluptuous, who had first startled me at an Episcopal Church social just before I joined the Army. In the interim she had made a bad youthful marriage and was now separated from her husband. We hit it off immediately when I visited Syracuse on my furlough, carried on a flaming correspondence while I was at Camp Dix, and when I was about to be discharged, she came to New York where I soon joined her.

For a while the situation was ideal. She was vivacious, accommodating, loyal, and the type of gorgeous female a young man delights to be seen with strolling on the avenue or in a night club or restaurant. She had a tapering face, large brown eyes, a swanlike neck and a wealth of wavy hair. She was exceptionally well formed and walked with grace. What she lacked was education and anything concerned with it. She was made for dancing, drinking and partying until the wee sma' hours—"having a ball" as she put it. She was a pretty picture at a ball, too, with her full bosom, slender waist, long legs, and agile feet negotiating the intricacies of the Charleston or Walking the Dog.

I liked that sort of life, too, but there was another side which it did not satisfy. Myrtle read nothing except the comics while I was reading about the stirring events taking place in the world of 1919 in the *New York Times,* the *Nation,* the *New Republic,* and the Socialist newspaper, *The Call.* The editorializing, the features, the cartoons, the revolutionary occurrences in Russia, China, Ireland, the Near East and Siberia, the Peace Conference in Paris, and the race riots in Chicago, Washington, D.C. and other places all created an intellectual tension which the ebullient Myrtle did not share. When I yearned to discuss these things, the only response was an embarrassing silence or a shrug of indifference. It was disturbing, even disconcerting. Perhaps she was wiser than I, but it was annoying.

I had assiduously followed the fortunes of war and peace and revolution, especially the latter. Day by day in the newspapers, long before I was discharged, I read everything I could find about Russia from the deposition of the Czar to the rise of Kerensky and the violent overthrow of the legitimate government eight months later by the Bolshevist riffraff. Although I had had a lifelong interest in geography from the time when places like Romelia and Bokhara appeared on the maps, I knew nothing about Russia, its history or economy. I wanted to know more of the background in order to better understand the lurid dispatches in the press. I had always thought dangerously, believing there should be no limit to thought, that the mind should be free. I could entertain any idea without accepting it. Anarchism, feudalism, communism, republicanism, monarchy, vegetarianism, cannibalism, monogamy and polyandry—all had their points. But with whom could I discuss these things? Certainly not with my daily associates at Castle William, nor the denizens of Leroy's, nor the crowd that went to Edmund's basement place at 131st Street and Fifth Avenue where Ethel Waters sang.

The Harlem of 1919 was a small community amid a sea of whites. It extended from 130th Street to 143rd Street, from Seventh to Madison Avenue, with some blocks extending to Eighth Avenue. Lenox Avenue was much more attractive than it is now, with more trees and fewer people. There were more private houses and fewer store-front churches, less loitering and more decorum, and the people were well-dressed in contrast to the shabbiness one sees today. It had a state assemblyman, an alderman, two weekly newspapers, and a number of impressive churches, a YMCA and a YWCA.

The trouble with me was that I had no friends or acquaintances in Harlem as yet with whom I could discuss matters that were uppermost in my mind; and being busy from nine to five every day left little time to cultivate anyone outside the gay circle in which Myrtle had involved us, and which up to a point I enjoyed. There were such people there but I did not meet any of them until long afterward. Whom one associates with is extremely important to one's development. Sometimes companions are thrust upon one, rather than sought, or they just accumulate by coincidence. To a large extent we are fate's children. The one man I should have cultivated at the time was Warrant Officer John Waller, a soldier of long experience, who handled transportation for the Department of the East headquartered on Governor's Island. I had a nodding acquaintance by passing him almost daily en route to Castle William. Years later we became fast friends. A handsome brown man of medium height whose father had been U.S. consul at Tananarive, Madagascar, he was well-known and popular in Harlem.

I read as much as I could, and curiously I never had any of the prevalent enthusiasm for the murderous Soviet regime. I saw it as a combined Asiatic Tammany and Mafia, less democratic than Czarism had been. Many I encountered saw the Communists as the heralds of freedom, but to me they were a murderous gang, and I hoped they would be suppressed. I had never liked disorder locally or nationally, and I could not approve of it in Russia just because that country was far away.

Although I had been reading newspapers from childhood, I was still naïve enough to believe that no correspondents would deliberately distort life, and that no desk editors would callously color and slant stories in accordance with editorial prejudices. I had great respect for the press, and I believed what the newspapers presented as truth. Then, as I began to read several papers daily, I noticed how differently reporters and correspondents reported the same stories from the same places, with their stories from abroad going through the same censors. I began to note the attributions from unnamed sources which could be no more than a newsman's hunch or unsupported opinion, or, it could be, fear of the censor. In any event it was nothing to swear by. So I read less widely and more deeply in order to get to the kernel of truth buried somewhere in each dispatch.

We were living a happy, carefree life in our neat little apartment. We went out almost nightly to a motion picture, vaudeville show, or night spot that we regarded as good fun. Myrtle was ebullient and tireless, pretty, lissome and wore her clothes well. She was really something to stroll with down Lenox or Seventh Avenue, or sit with at Leroy's. Men turned to admire her, and that always makes a fellow feel pretty good. We were not saving any money, but that did not seem too important at that age and time. Those were prodigal days.

However, I began to be aware that my temporary civil service job was not perpetual. The U.S. Army was running out of prisoners from abroad. There were fewer on each transport, fewer to process, fewer to assign to cells, fewer to transfer to Leavenworth or Alcatraz.

I could see that it would be wise to look around for some other way to make a living. Thus when I learned of a Federal civil service examination for first class clerks, I sent in an application and took the test in downtown Manhattan. I passed with a mark above 90, and I was jubilant. In fact we felt so good about it that we had a night on the town, drinking and dancing until quite late.

In due course I received a notice to apply to an office of the U.S. Shipping Board in Hoboken at a certain day and time. Buoyantly I boarded the ferry going across the Hudson and was soon striding through the vast offices to that of the person in authority. I can remember neither his name nor how he looked. I can only recall that he looked at my papers, and then after some hesitation, told me to return home and await word from him as to when I should return to go to work. I was extremely elated. The fact that among the scores of clerks I did not discern a single colored person caused me no concern. After all I was probably the first Negro to pass this first class examination. In any event I was sure of employment because I was high on the list.

Next day I returned happily to Castle William and told my colleagues of my good fortune. Soon I would have a permanent job that paid more than I was getting; a lifetime job, and that was really something for a Negro at that time.

I waited anxiously for several days, but there was actually no reason to feel uncertain. One just had to be patient with the Government. There was no need to worry, for after all I was high on the list; must have been to be called so soon after passing the examination.

Finally the notice came. It was very blunt and to the point. It read, "In view of the fact that you refused the position offered, your name has been removed from the list." There was nothing more except a signature. Telephoning to the Shipping Board on

Broadway and writing to the Civil Service did no good. The case was closed, according to Uncle Sam.

I should have been more wary. Once before I had taken a clerk-carrier examination at Leilehua, Hawaii, the postoffice that served Schofield Barracks. It happened fifty years ago and I have forgotten the details but I do remember that I made the highest mark and was number one on the list but by some hanky-panky the job went to the number two man, who just happened to be white. I seem to recall that the choice could be made among the three highest on the list. It was a convenient provision for excluding the unwanted.

A few months later in early 1920 the anticipated blow fell. The end of my temporary civil service appointment came and I was through as clerk in the executive office of the Atlantic Branch U.S. Disciplinary Barracks. I had to find another job, fast, and there were few to be had during the mild depression we were experiencing throughout the country. The days of wine and roses were ended.

With our income sharply curtailed, we had to move to a less attractive, cheaper, two room apartment around the corner on Madison Avenue. It was a dingy house and the landlady was careless in her housekeeping; but it was the best that we could afford under the circumstances.

After an initial try as porter in an uptown Broadway drug store, I got a better job at The Sun Press, a small plant on East 84th Street near Third Avenue run by two Polish Jews. It did not pay much more than portering in the drug store, but there was a chance to learn more about printing. However, most of my time was spent delivering packages, collecting bills, picking up job linotyping, commercial cuts and colored paper stock from paper houses. This required a lot of traveling about town from the lower East Side to the Bronx, and I became expert on the city's transportation system, and at what points to transfer in order to save a nickel, which was then the fare. The system was then privately owned and the five-cent fare was a big political football, with every aspirant for office swearing that he would defend the five-cent fare to the bitter end. With the price of everything else going up, it was foregone that the fare would have to be raised or the companies go bankrupt. They did, the city bought them and it was a big step in the march toward municipal socialism, another burden on the taxpayers.

Myrtle had willingly taken a job to help out, and was running an elevator in an apartment house on Amsterdam Avenue, which was then a lily-white area. Between the two of us we just kept our heads above water, but there was no time or money for "having a ball," as she put it. She was a good-natured, cheerful, adaptable girl, who had much of that fatalism and slight cynicism that has sustained colored women of the domestic class in our urban areas for generations. They could get work more readily than could colored men, excluded from all of the good jobs in the "liberal" North and East. This explained the "shift-lessness" of the Negro men, who had tough competition for even unskilled work. The Socialist and labor papers had no remedy for that (as they did for everything else) except to talk about "Black and White, Unite and Fight." But they set no example.

In search of better-paying work, I quit the print shop. I did so with reluctance because by riding around town daily I had been able to read all of the newspapers discarded by other passengers, as well as occasional copies of the *Nation,* the *New Republic* and other magazines. There were many more New York newspapers then, and even the Socialists and the Communists had dailies. However, I had found it extremely difficult to find time to read the basic books I knew I should. Most people who chide the manual workers for not doing more reading do not understand the difficulties and problems of the ordinary people who must work hard all day and have so little leisure and so few of the amenities that provide the necessary relaxation for reading in depth. Without the background knowledge, how are they to understand and properly appraise the significance of the news they run through in the daily newspapers to and from work in crowded and swaying subway cars and buses? To be sure, columnists and editors are supposed to make up for this deprivation of the ordinary reader, but it is hazardous to take them on faith because few are actually objective.

People who have been to school ten or fifteen years and have enjoyed some leisure and are employed in largely nonphysical "soft" jobs in offices (and think of themselves as "intellectuals") generally read more if so inclined. Working on the dock or on a demolition job takes just about all a man has. He is more ready to absorb propaganda than knowledge, if either. Nor is hard domestic work with its continual demands, laborious tasks and long hours likely to incline a woman toward heavy reading when she gets home to husband and children in the evening and prepares the meal. When there is time for reading, it is likely to be some literary froth whose chief merit is entertainment.

Looking back over a lifetime of reading thousands of books, articles, columns, and essays, I would conclude that reading contributes much to one's knowledge but not necessarily to wisdom. The awe in which the lowly poor hold the "intellectuals" is mostly unwarranted. They are more often than not insufferable snobs who preen themselves for the literary upmanship that puts them six or eight books ahead of their fellow men. They talk glibly, using phrases culled from the works of others with whom they pretend familiarity and association, although knowing little more about them than the window cleaner or the scrubwoman knows. During my time I have rubbed shoulders with hundreds of the best-known "intellectuals" in America and abroad, conversed with them, read their writings and juggled their theories, and in retrospect it is appalling how downright wrong so many have been and still are. At least the poor whom they chide for not reading more have led nobody astray!

When I think of all the nonsense I have read in the literature on socialism, communism, history, the so-called social sciences, much of economics, psychoanalysis and the rest of it, I feel less than reverence for the written word. At least the illiterates have less to be forgiven for and to forget, which is probably why I feel companionable with many of them. They have not pretended to omniscience in print.

There was a job vacancy at a brass factory on East 28th Street off Lexington Avenue, and since the work paid more and the hours were from 7:30 a.m. until 4:30 p.m., I went to work there. There was a mixed racial crew which got on well together. However, it was the noisiest place I had ever been in. There was a routine of putting ingots of brass in furnaces until they were cherry red, then trucking them to sunken acid baths, then removing them and trucking them to rollers where they were successively reduced in thickness. What started out as an inch-thick, three-foot ingot was by this process finally made about a 32nd of an inch thick and many feet long. I operated one of these rollers which were aligned across the width of the factory. Just above one's head was a long stick by which one could switch off one's machine without disturbing the others. As the strip of brass came through the rollers it curled up and fell out behind the machine. This was then piled on a truck as it came by and was sent for an acid bath before being sent to another machine which would reduce its thickness still more.

The screeches and screams of the machines, the overhead pulleys, cables and belts, the roaring of the furnaces, the rumbling of the iron-wheeled hand trucks on the iron floor, the hissing of the acid tanks, combined to create a horrendous crescendo that was deafening and defeated all attempts at normal conversation. To give any orders or directions it was necesary to speak in a falsetto voice that somehow seemed to pierce the din.

Then at noon the whistle sounded and as the huge flywheel stopped, a weird silence settled over the plant as the men sat down to eat their lunch and smoke. For a minute or two after the unearthly machine chorus stopped, men still talked in falsetto voices, grinning sheepishly at the sound of their voices in the temporary quietude. Then, again at the sound of the whistle, the infernal noise resumed, men jumped to their machines, and quiet was banished until half-past four.

There were very few accidents while I worked there. The machines were protected by metal guards and men rolled up the sleeves of their overall jackets to avoid catching them between the rollers. One day a green worker got a raggedy sleeve caught in his rollers but did not think to switch off his machine. He was inexorably pulled toward the rollers and his hand was crushed before his predicament was noted and all of the current was shut off. He had screamed but was not heard above the din. In the ensuing silence his mashed hand was removed from the rollers and he received emergency treatment before being rushed to the hospital.

In a short while the shaken crew returned to the various machines, the whistle blew and the pandemonium proceeded as before, another man taking the place of the unfortunate neophyte. This was not callousness on anybody's part. Every job has its risks, even where the workers are protected most elaborately. Some workers are smarter, quicker, more observant and agile than others. Even the most efficient have their off days, sometimes the result of a hard night with the grog, a slight illness insufficient to keep them from work, or perhaps family troubles. A slight dizziness at the wrong time caused one man to stagger into a tank of acid, and he was disfigured for life before he could be pulled out. Of course there is Workmen's Compensation and insurance, but that is small recompense for the loss of a limb or lifetime disfigurement. Such work is a far cry from sitting in an office all day.

There seemed to be virtually no future at the brass plant; so I gave up the job there and took a job as night dishwasher at a restaurant on Broadway in the Eighties. It paid a most attractive wage for those days, and one could eat whatever one desired of the rich foods available, especially since there was no one present from midnight onward except the dishwasher and the cook. The latter was a plump, amiable, brown-skinned man, full of reminiscences and anecdotes, and endowed with a gargantuan appetite and a roof-shaking gift of laughter.

One needed more than a gift of laughter to work there. The hours were from eight at night until eight in the morning. After the dishwashing stopped right after midnight, there began the job of cleaning up. The chairs had to be placed on the tables and the entire tile floor mopped. The kitchen had to be cleaned from end to end, the basement had to be swept and the food properly arranged and stacked, the garbage-filled cans put out on the sidewalk to be picked up by the private carting firm. The only thing I did not do was to clean the windows. One worked seven days a week. There was no such thing as a day off. By the time one returned home, bathed off the pervasive odor of the kitchen and got to bed, it was nine o'clock. Whenever we would go to a moving picture, it had to be around four or five o'clock, so I could get to work on time, and Myrtle had only one day off herself.

This was dangerously close to slavery, so I looked around for another job less taxing, and I found one nearby at 96th Street and Broadway. After the fortnight at the other place, the new job seemed almost like going on vacation. The hours were still twelve, from six o'clock in the morning until six at night, with one day off a week, and no scrubbing, cleaning and taking out garbage, but it was a much larger-scale operation. I was at first the only Negro employed there. The busboys were mostly Puerto Ricans, the cooks were Polish and Russians, the countermen were Irish. The patrons were a conglomeration of U.S. sailors, policemen, sanitation men, small business people, taximen, and clerks, and we fed as many as 2,000 for lunch, sometimes more, and hundreds for breakfast.

So it was a workhouse, too. The rush was so great that I needed an assistant just to scrape dishes and stack them up before washing and rinsing. There was no time to wipe dishes. They were just piled on slanting shelves to drain and dry. A half-barrel of soft soap was used during the day, and when it became necessary to change the water in the twin tubs, dirty dishes stacked up mountain high during the brief interval of draining the tubs and refilling them. This was the period when we most often got stuck, and the manager, who was able from long experience to fit in anywhere, would pile in himself and assist the dish scraper. The latter was a slight old fellow of German extraction, with thin gray hair and sallow skin. During the tremendous rush hours he was wont to exclaim, "Easy on the whip, it's a hired horse!"

One after one the busboys would march in with their deep trays piled with dishes and dump them on the shelves of the extended sink until it seemed that dirty dishes were scraping the ceiling. The dishscraper would fight like mad to reduce the pile by scraping them into the waiting garbage cans, as I furiously washed, rinsed and stacked. Some idea of the volume of trade in this hash factory may be gathered from the fact that another man spent all of his time just washing the silver. Three cans of garbage were taken out after each meal. Six countermen labored feverishly in front and six men toiled in the little fifteen-by-six kitchen with its enormous cooking range, its huge hot water tank, its dishscraping trough, its washing tubs and its duck-board floor.

Three or four cauldrons of soup were sold for lunch, four crates of eggs and several hams disappeared during breakfast hours, along with scores of loaves of bread, baskets of hard rolls, four huge urns of coffee, great pans of fish and meat, gallons of stew and goulash, huge cans of potatoes and other vegetables during the day.

One grew sick of seeing and smelling so much food in that hot cubicle, mingled with the odor of sweating bodies, soft soap, garbage, greasy pots and wet sawdust. In summer time the place was almost insufferable. When lunch slacked off and we went to eat at about two o'clock, we would go out into a tiny courtyard behind the kitchen, since we could not go into the dining room with our odoriferous garb.

I immortalized this place in an article I wrote ten years later for *The American Mercury* entitled "Memoirs of a Pearl Diver" in April 1931.

The place was a miniature League of Nations and just about as successful. Schwartz, the scraper, was a German whose Prussian patriotism had not been dimmed by thirty years in the United States; Carl, the Polish chef, bubbled with enthusiasm over the new Republic of Paderewski and Pilsudski; Nick, the vegetable man, was a little Russian whose God was Lenin; George, the silver-and-glass man, was a British West Indian from Jamaica who shouted the praises of Marcus Garvey; Clarence, the adenoidal short-order cook, was a Limehouse cockney who vociferously lauded the supposed excellence of everything British; Juan and Jose, two of the busboys, were Colombian mestizos, the four others being Puerto Ricans; Eddie, the head counterman, like his assistants, was Irish. Sam Karlin, the manager, was a jovial Jew.

Schwartz, the dish scraper, hated just about everybody, and he confided that enmity to me during the rare intervals when we were not working like mad. He hated Clarence because he was English, Carl because he sang the praises of the new Poland created partially at the expense of Germany, the two Colombians and the four Puerto Ricans because they were "spiggoty people." This was conveyed to me in low tones out of the corner of his mouth with baleful glances at the white-coated workers as they came within his ken. "Ah," he would comment, "dese damn spiggoty peeble. Dey tink dey're as goot as a vite man!"

He never expressed his opinion of the three Negroes working on the shift, doubtless because I was one, and they could understand better than the Caribbean folk what he said. He always readily agreed with George, the Jamaican, when the latter denounced Great Britain for handicapping the work of Marcus Garvey. Although proudly admitting that he was a British subject, he was always referring to "Awfricah, the blawck mawn's nawtionawl home." The two Britishers, Clarence and George, white and black, nearly came to blows one day when the Limey sneered that "This Gawrvey fellow 'asn't an 'arf pint o' sense."

It was between Carl, the Polish chef, and Nick, the Russian vegetable man, that there was the greatest conflict, quarreling over the respective merits of their native lands which neither had seen in many years. Voluble and quick-witted, Nick constantly extolled the dictatorship of the proletariat, the Soviets, Lenin and the New Economic Policy, and mourned the loss of so much territory the Soviet Union would have had but for the intervention of the French and British. Somewhat dull and slower of speech, Carl would stand over the meat block, his sleeves rolled up, cutting and chopping furiously and more savagely as his anger grew. Suddenly he would brandish his cleaver, curse all the foes of Poland, particularly the Bolsheviks, whereupon Nick would dub him counter-revolutionary or reactionary. Everybody who disagreed with Nick was a tool of the capitalists. One day the argument in the shed grew so heated that Carl threw his cleaver at the little Russian, then grabbed a formidable butcher knife and chased him out into the kitchen, through the dining room and onto Broadway where the Russian lost himself in the crowd.

Sam Karlin placated the irate chef, and when the Russian finally returned, the Jew consoled them, reminded them that neither one actually knew what was going on abroad and would be well advised to forget it. They ended up shaking hands, but everybody knew it would be an uneasy truce. Sure enough, when the Polish armies ignominiously routed the Bolshevik hordes, Carl's joy was so loud and he gloated so offensively over Nick that the war in the shed was on again.

Eddie, the Irish counterman, continued against Clarence, the Briton, the civil war then going on in Ireland. Clarence was no match for the witty Irishman. By the time he had thought up a reply to the last Gaelic shaft, two more penetrated his hide. A dozen times a day misunderstandings arose that ended in mutual exchanges of insults, with Eddie always the winner, to the vast amusement of both customers and crew.

Eddie's wit found its highest expression in devising new nicknames for the dishes he ordered through the window. When Navy ships were in port, ham and eggs became "Sailors Delight." At the time when the newspapers were full of accounts of the fight at the Lamb's Club between McGraw, the baseball manager, and a club member, a lamb stew became "One McGraw." A New England boiled dinner was a "Yankee Feast." An order to "Clean Up the Kitchen" meant hamburger steak. Pork and beans became "Musical Fruit." Milk toast was "Graveyard Stew." An order of pig's feet was shouted "Walk One" while pig tails was translated to "Snatch One." Shredded Wheat Biscuit was a "Bale o'Hay." Chicken was "Harlem Special." Porterhouse steak was "Burn Up a Bull."

All of the wisecrackers and jokesters in the neighborhood flocked into the place, recognizing in Eddie a kindred soul, a man of wit who could be always counted on to clown. All the latest quips and jokes were bandied about first over his counter, as taximen, cops, firemen, sailors and hustlers sauntered in. For stories, mostly blue, the cafeteria outdid a Pullman smoking room.

It was curbstone humor, but we were all on the curbstone. It helped to enliven the frenzied pace of the hash factory where we dishwashers and bus boys toiled for $22.50 a week, with all we could eat. With a mild depression on, that was not too bad.

To be sure, we never got fully rested after twelve hours on our feet. My hands were spongelike from constant immersion in hot, soapy water. It was also a good place to develop flat feet. My feet were awfully tired at the end of the day and the busboys were even worse off walking back and forth with heavy loads of dishes on the unyielding tile floor. We in the kitchen and behind the counter at least had duck boards to walk on.

With one day off a week, Myrtle and I at least had that time to ourselves since she arranged to get her day off at the same time. But I was less and less satisfied with my life. Aside from newspapers there was little time for reading anything. Considering the time it took to get to and from work, there was a period of only about ten hours of actual rest, including sleeping. Aside from an occasional movie or a dance which I did not particularly enjoy after standing all day over a steaming dishtub, I went nowhere, and my association with Myrtle was not intellectually stimulating. She was beautiful, gay, and earthy but not interested or concerned with what was going on outside her tiny environment. And having tried in vain to elicit her interest, I gave up trying.

It became increasingly clear that Myrtle and I had nothing much in common except the normal activities of people of our age, and we even had little time for them. It was a rat race just existing. She was a companion any young man would desire: gay, vivacious, very pretty, shapely, graceful and sexy, a swell dancer and blessed with the gift of laughter, but completely lost in any serious conversation. She was an unpolished diamond but I surmised that it would take a lifetime of polishing to bring out all of her facets. Many people who are fine as they are often suffer from efforts at improvement. It is better to leave some people as they are lest they develop all sorts of unpleasant complexes and fruitless aspirations.

If I had had other more sophisticated acquaintances, I might have better tolerated her mental dullness, but I had not had the time to develop them. On the rare occasions when we went out socially to visit with people she had come to know, her lack of knowledge of the amenities was painfully apparent. These people were just ordinary folk like us, but urban living had polished off the rough edges. They knew what *not* to say and do. I had started with a romantic fixation on Myrtle because she embodied the dream of the girl every youth wants; but romance is based on illusion, and its staying qualities are limited. Something else is needed to hold people together in the cold gray dawn after the night before. It is possible that she sensed that we had little in common.

I would have married Myrtle when we first settled in New York, and perhaps that would have made some difference; but she was already married, her husband was very much alive in Syracuse. They were permanently separated but neither had any inclination to make it legal; and I didn't have money enough to make it all respectable. Indeed, we were lucky to pay our bills and clothe ourselves.

At any rate I was becoming more and more disgusted with my circumstances and myself. We began to snap at each other and I guess I said sarcastic, hurtful things that I would not have dreamed of saying before. We coasted closer and closer to the reefs of disaster. The seams of our imitation matrimony came apart and sensibly, I believe, we agreed that perhaps we had better try going separate courses. I think it was a painful decision for both of us. I know it was for me, and her tears told me that it was for her, too. Although we had grown up in the same environment, we had not grown up in the same class.

So we separated and I quit my job, and went to Syracuse. I was definitely fed up with New York City, though my home town never had any attraction for me since I gratefully left it in 1912. But my family, such as it now was, Lila and Mary Louise, resided there, and I guess at that juncture I needed the consolation of their relationship. So I quit the fetid world of steam, odors, dirty dishes, and twelve-hour days, went back to the familiar streets and faces of nine years before, to try to start all over.

CHAPTER 8

LILA AND Mary Louise were delighted to see and have me. Each had a small flat on Franklin Street opposite the Lackawanna Railroad station, and each was working; Lila in some kind of domestic work and Mary Louise in a dress factory. As Louise had a roomer (whom she later married), I stayed with Lila. It was an inauspicious time. Economic conditions were bad and jobs were scarce. People I knew warned that there was really nothing for Negroes to do in the city, and they wondered why I had come back at such a time.

I figured there had to be some kind of work. There must be families that wanted various things done around the house or yard, and while they could employ nobody regularly, they could afford to pay for two or three hours or a half day's work. So I went to the post office, bought seventy-five cents worth of postcards, and adopting a standard text, I typed them out on Louise's typewriter, picking names indiscriminately from the telephone book of people in middle class and upper class neighborhoods.

I did not have to wait long. Within a couple of days Louise's telephone was ringing every evening after six o'clock (the stipulated time). There were all sorts of things people wanted done: kitchen floors scrubbed, rugs cleaned, gardens attended, windows cleaned, furniture moved, and so forth. Never was seventy-five cents invested more successfully.

It was a new venture and I went about it with considerable verve. By the week's end I had enough customers to keep me busy the following week. Mostly it was inside from attics to cellars; sweeping, dusting, scrubbing, polishing, all of the things I knew well how to do. After a couple of weeks I happened to run across a book of formulas from which I learned how to recondition brass beds and chandeliers. They were much in use at that time and with long use they became dark and discolored. The process was first to remove the lacquer, then use a certain acid to clean the brass to its pristine brightness, and finally to freshly lacquer. I practiced on a brass bed at home and was delighted with the result. There were not many customers, but those I secured were highly pleased and willingly paid what was charged.

I traveled from one end of town to the other on the street cars. This was time consuming and cut into my income on a number of short jobs but made little difference when I would work several hours at one place. Soon the orders increased to the extent that I could not fill them all, and had to find somebody to assist me. This posed a problem because the person had to be willing, versatile, and trustworthy. People would sometimes leave their homes to go to a store or downtown and leave me there alone to finish the job I was doing. I never stole anything but I could not be sure about whoever was helping me. After a couple of experiments, I decided to turn down some of the customers in order to do all of the work myself and run no risks. Moreover, the Negro community was very small and there were not many trustworthy youngsters that I knew, since I had not lived in the town in ten years. For a while I tried a white fellow I came to know.

The customers varied from middle to upper class, and most of them were middle-aged housewives. Some were stolid and businesslike, some were very vivacious and friendly, others strained the aloofness I sought to maintain. The first time I went to a place everything was very proper but on the second and third occasions the housewife became more familiar, even confidential. It is astonishing how familiar some people will get on very short acquaintance. Many were lonesome and wanted to talk to somebody. Husbands were away at work and children were away at school. The relationship of worker and employer, colored and white, man and woman became dimmer, and soon they were treating me as if I were a close relative. This produced unexpected dividends, not anticipated and unsolicited.

But I did not relish that way of life. I had enough regular jobs not to need to go to one house any more frequently than necessary, and to avoid becoming involved, I quit going to some altogether.

Meanwhile, I had the leisure to read what I wanted. Syracuse had an excellent library, and my work was not so arduous that I had no inclination to read, as had been the case in New York on those twelve-hour jobs. Now I quit around four or four-thirty and was through dinner after six. I read Plato's *Republic*, books on astronomy and geology, socialist books by Marx, Engels, Plechanov, Kautsky, Hyndman, Bellamy, Wells, and the works of some of the anarchists. I found the writings of the socialists on the whole very tedious, and most of Marx was guaranteed to cure insomnia. It was quite an ordeal to wade through the three volumes of Karl Marx's *Capital*, but I did.

The most active group around town, intellectually, was the Socialists, and it was not long before I began meeting with them in their forum and discussing the momentous happenings of the day, of which I discovered they knew little if any more than I did. But it was exhilarating, and just the type of stimulation I had been hungering for. So in November, 1921, I joined the Socialist Party of America and got my red membership card. Even though the meetings were quite dull, I attended them regularly. I kept up with Party doings through the daily *Call* and tried to read all of the tracts and books. I even got up on

113

speaking ladders and addressed the indifferent populace in the downtown area.

The techniques of street meetings were interesting. The ladder having been erected at what was presumed to be a strategic point, the speaker would mount and the party members would gather in closely to make it appear to the unwitting that there was some interest in what was being said. This would attract a straggling of passersby who would listen idly for a time. To keep them from sauntering off, one of the comrades would interrupt the harangue to ask a pertinent question or sometimes an impertinent one. An argument would then ensue between the speaker and questioner. Another comrade would then loudly protest that in the interest of free speech the speaker should be permitted to proceed. More people would gather around to see what the shouting was about, and another comrade would circle around the little gathering trying to sell "literature" to any suckers who would buy.

If the street meeting attracted thirty or forty people it was considered a success, and all of the comrades went home happy in the thought that socialism had been advanced. Each one of us took turns speaking at the street meetings, and on the whole we were very unconvincing if one judged by the number of new members we got. If there were ten members at the monthly meeting, we thought things were looking up.

Very shortly I was elected educational director and I launched an ambitious program designed to bring about socialism fast in Syracuse. One of my first ventures was to organize The Negro Community Forum held in the assembly hall of St. Philip's Episcopal Church, in the hope of creating some intellectual ferment. The party paid for the advertising leaflet which promised that there would be discussions of science, history, politics, literature and drama. For the first meeting there would be two instrumental solos and lectures by George S. Schuyler on "An Intelligent Program for Intelligent Negro Workers" and Frederick Sander would discuss "The Evolution of Industry" in a forum heralded as "nonsectarian and non-political." The leaflet failed to mention that Mr. Sander was head of the local Syracuse

114

Socialist Party and that I was the educational director. It did not matter much because I doubt that there were more than ten people present.

I also wrote a couple of four-page pamphlets expounding the principles of socialism. Our biggest meeting those days was when August Claessens, an effective organizer from New York City, came to us and drew a record audience of about fifty. August and his wife traveled the country while he lectured the faithful and whatever prospective members who could be persuaded to come out. He was a balding fellow with a gift of gab and a sense of humor, which was a rare commodity among Socialist speakers, writers and thinkers. Of all the Socialist books I read, only one, Paul LaFargue's *The Right To Be Lazy*, had any laughs in it. The rest were gloomy to the point of sheer boredom. The nearest counterpart among American Socialists was James Oneal who wrote what is still a Socialist classic, *The Workers in American History*. I recall that about that time he wrote in *The Call* a highly amusing piece on "The War of the Marxians" which dealt with the current conflict between the numerous factions of Communists then battling for supremacy on the American scene.

I developed a close friendship with a union painter, Rollen Bolton, a droll fellow, somewhat on the cynical side, who had also read most of the standard works authored by the prolific Socialist hacks. We got together often over beer either at his house or in my flat. These talks were rewarding to me because I had at last found somebody who had begun to doubt the Socialist claims, arguments and predictions. We questioned that every occurrence could be explained on the basis of the class struggle; that the poor were getting worse off all the time; that capitalism would destroy civilization; that a swarm of bureaucrats in Washington could run the country better than the decentralized free enterprise power structure. We noted that the results of socialism in the Soviet Union had been chaos and famine, compelling a return to capitalism under the name of the New Economic Policy. Worse, we both began to question Marxist Holy Writ in party meetings, thus quickly isolating ourselves. This was treason but we both enjoyed it and had fun twitting the orthodox.

I tired of the handy man role and its hazards and uncertainties. So, there being a new construction job just starting on Warren Street, I chucked the whole self-employed business and went to work as a hod carrier and building laborer. It was hard, outdoor work, and more difficult than inexperienced people would imagine. It takes considerable skill to do so-called unskilled work and last at it. We began at the foundation, filling trucks with dirt, which is a tough job if you do it all day and are inexperienced. Then with sixteen-pound hammers and long chisels we dug through the fused gravel for the foundation of the piers. Then step by step, week by week, we worked our way to the roof, six flights up. The most exhausting work was the pouring of concrete in the wall forms. At that time the work could not be halted until an entire section was filled, else cracks would remain. The form had to be filled to the top, and it had to be done with wheelbarrows pushed up an incline, turned on a boardwalk and then dumped. It took nice footwork, brute strength, agility and timing. The pouring had to go on regardless of the hour until the form was filled to the top. This often required overtime under floodlights. At the end of the run one could hardly open one's hands and the pain at the small of the back was killing. A hot tub later at home revived one, but there was always tomorrow. I finally became hardened to the work, and I did not regret leaving my former occupation.

The superintendent of the job was a big, hale Scotsman with white hair and a bull voice. He was disdainful of the young novice workmen with cigarettes dangling from their mouths. He called them "cigarette men" and jeered at their failure to measure up to the demands of the hard tasks. "This ain't no sanitarium," he would roar as a shovel man would lean wearily on his tool. "Come on, man, and sink that pick," he would holler, as the tool jumped back from the gravel. Cement runs weeded these fellows out very fast, and as they fell out and signified they could not continue, he would yell: "All right, go to the shed and get your time."

However, he appreciated a fellow really trying, and I tried hard, although at times I could scarcely carry on. I never gave him occasion to yell at me, and as the weeks extended into months, we became quite friendly. It was a union job and after a week or so a newcomer had better join. I still have my card No. 1082 in the International Hod Carriers Building and Common Laborers Union, Local 40, Syracuse, New York, dated August 24, 1922. I attended several meetings at the union office but nothing happened there beyond the routine. Everything was pretty cut and dried. I later learned that it was one of the biggest rackets in organized labor, which is saying a lot. I was the only Negro member of the local.

The vast majority of the workers were Italians and Irish, many of them grown gray and even white-haired in the business. They worked with ease and knew exactly what to do to save themselves from strain. They were good humored and cooperative, ready to share their wine or a sandwich with you. One old Italian who usually mixed the mortar (a tough job) never seemed to tire as his whole body went with the motion. A florid Irishman in his fifties could negotiate a ladder with a hod full of brick as easily as men of half his years. These men had worked on construction business all over the country, and the bosses knew and asked for them whenever a new job started.

I was the sole Negro laborer on the job until some cement finishers came. There were two or three Negroes among this aristocracy of labor. They earned at that time fourteen dollars a day. They worked a few days on floors and roofs, and then moved on to some other job, just like the structural steelworkers, the bricklayers, electricians, and plumbers. Those latter unions had no Negro members then and rarely have them now. Negro exclusion from skilled unions has invariably been the rule in the United States. It is a vicious circle: without job mobility there can be little economic and social mobility, and civil rights become more or less academic to those destined to remain common laborers. The situation has been little changed since 1922, except that exclusionism and discrimination is constitutionally outlived and now less open than it was.

I occasionally met some old friends from school days, but my way of life precluded socializing, because after work I was either reading, at a Socialist meeting, or at a theater. Though I was a bachelor, I was too tired after the arduous work day to have much inclination to play. I was reading and learning much in books and magazines, and closely followed the news of the day.

There were some women in the Socialist local but only one was intellectually alert, a tall, graceful, young woman who was recording secretary and well grounded in the Marxist theology. It was a pleasure to talk with her. I early detected that there was an affair going on between her and the middle-aged, married secretary of the local. This suspicion was confirmed about a year later when I learned that they had decamped for Philadelphia, where they married after he had secured a divorce.

With the building completed and scaffolding cleared away, the job was at an end. In one of those sudden decisions I have always been prone to make, I decided to return to New York. I was tired of the scene, tired of the Socialist Party, and tired of the provincialism of Syracuse. So to the surprise of Lila and Mary Louise, I announced that I was leaving, and in a few days I left.

CHAPTER 9

IT WAS early December, I had a few dollars, and the clickety-clack of the car wheels on the rails was music to my ears. It was not quite as exhilarating as was the first trip ten years before because in the interim I had seen much of the world that I had dreamed about at seventeen. Now I was bent on renewing my acquaintance with the Big Town about which there was still a lot I did not know. I intended to enjoy New York more than I had before.

Not only that, but I wanted to also meet a different type of colored person than I had during my initial stay. I rented a room on West 136th Street in the Phyllis Wheatley Hotel, owned or operated by the Universal Negro Improvement Association headed by the flamboyant Marcus Garvey. The place was spick and span. In the entrance hall there was a large and striking painting of the famed Negro poetess of Revolutionary days gazing down benignly from the wall. This hotel was in startling contrast to the dingy headquarters of the UNIA around the corner on West 135th Street and to the squat, ramshackle Garvey auditorium on West 138th Street ambitiously called Liberty Hall.

The movement was riding high in December 1922. There were uniformed guards, Black Cross nurses, various business enterprises, the weekly *Negro World,* and a nobility. There were Knights Commander of the Nile, Dukes of Uganda and other honored ladies and gentlemen. The UNIA had its own flag.

The meetings at Liberty Hall were usually packed, and as the ceiling was not over fifteen feet high, there was a ventilation problem when the sprawling place was crowded. I attended a couple of these meetings which were well conducted. There was, of course, a UNIA band and choir. In many ways Garvey anticipated Hitler, who was then unknown save by a handful of followers. Garvey was a short, smooth, black, pig-eyed, corpulent West Indian from Jamaica who had come to the United States a few years before, panting like so many Negroes before him to solve the color problem. A charismatic character, he drew followers by the sheer weight of his personality and convictions, and hypnotized them with his bull voice and his cry of Africa for the Africans at a time when the independence of the Dark Continent was the sheerest wishful thinking of a few racist zealots.

He brought with him from Jamaica the hatred of white people and mulattoes which is probably the most intense in the world, certainly far exceeding anything in the United States. His screams for the supremacy of everything black won readiest response from the considerable colony of West Indians in Boston, New York, and Philadelphia who felt kindred animosity toward British and French imperialism. It had been a Haitian *aide-de-camp* to the Emperor Menelik of Abyssinia, Benito Sylvain, who organized the first Pan-African Conference in Paris in 1899, to which delegates were sent from the United States and various parts of the Caribbean. In London a Negro West Indian doctor made a similar effort some years later. However, the first pan-African sentiment arose in the United States among Negro freedmen more than a century earlier when there were spirited debates between those who favored emigration to Africa and those who did not. Even as a small boy I had read of the journey of Dr. Martin R. Delaney of Pittsburgh on the eve of the Civil War to what is now Nigeria to negotiate with local chiefs for leases of land on which to settle American freedmen. Just prior to Garvey's arrival in the United States, an Oklahoma Negro who was called Chief Sam had led an ill-fated group of Negroes to Liberia.

At any rate, the Garvey Back-to-Africa movement caught on somewhat among the submerged Negro nine-tenths and there were UNIA chapters in many parts of the country somewhat after the manner of the present-day Black Muslims, with hatred of whites as the motive power. But the bulk of American blacks were completely indifferent or derisive, and the Talented Tenth were even more so. It was from the latter that the vocal opposition, invective and ridicule came. Another factor that had strengthened the Garvey propaganda was the several race riots over the country in 1919 and 1920 when worse racial clashes occurred than did anywhere during the 1960's. There recurred the feeling on the part of some Negroes that there was no future in the United States for them.

My feeling was then, and it is stronger now, that Negroes have the best chance here in the United States if they will avail themselves of the numerous opportunities they have. To be sure it is not easy being a black man in the United States but it is easier than anywhere else I know for him to get the best schooling, the best living conditions, the best economic advantages, the best security, the greatest mobility and the best health. Only by travel and reading can this be found out, but the vocal leaders have never concentrated on telling their audiences that fact and explaining how despite handicaps their living can be made better. What they do by their agitations is to stir up desires and demands which cannot be realized for some time to come. Meanwhile the people have to live and strive, and to do that they must have feelings of hope. In short, they need more optimism and less pessimism. Frederick Douglass saw that and so did Booker T. Washington. Once we accept the fact that there is, and will always be, a color caste system in the United States, and stop crying about it, we can concentrate on how best to survive and prosper within that system. This is not defeatism but realism. It is tragic and pointless to wage war against the more numerous and more powerful white majority, and so jeopardize what advantages we possess.

These were some of my thoughts as I went around to the various meetings in Harlem and listened to the speakers. There were several groups opposing Garvey's grandiose schemes, especially his Back-to-Africa views. The masses of Negroes were indifferent because they were American-born and reared, and while they had come from Africa originally, they had only the slightest sentiment about it, knew nobody in Africa except some of the missionaries their churches had helped to send there, and had no desire to go. White Americans were not going back to Europe except to see distant relatives after they had become well-to-do; so it was nonsense to talk of Negroes going back to Africa. When the Negroes talked about the "Old Country," they meant Virginia, the Carolinas and the Deep South.

In playing upon the color differences among the Negroes, Garvey performed another disservice to the group. It was natural that he should raise that issue because it was a powerful one throughout the Caribbean and Latin America where blacks were generally at the bottom of the social scale, although in the majority. It was particularly marked in Jamaica from whence he had come. Those of light complexion were hated more than the handful of whites, and in turn the octoroons, quadroons and mulattoes despised the blacks, and neither mixed socially with them nor married them.

In the United States, on the other hand, while mixture between whites, Indians and Africans had produced a population with as many different colors as Joseph's coat, socio-economic conditions were totally dissimilar to those in the American tropics. The population of mixed ancestry was proportionately much larger and completely unmixed Negroes were in the minority. Moreover, the one-drop racial theory prevalent throughout the United States (whereby any person with one drop of

"Negro blood" was legally regarded as Negro) worked against the growth of color classes within the Negro group, whereas the opposite was true in the Caribbean and Latin America. Many of the light-skinned in those parts were accepted socially as white, the colored Brazilian even referring to the process as "improving the race," which almost no American Negro would say publicly. In Brazil, too, such near-whites and almost-whites from much-mixed Bahia are derisively dubbed *Bahia brancos* or Bahia whites, meaning that they were only so regarded in that state.

This is not to say that color distinctions were not made and did not have significance within the Negro group. They were and are. There were, and to some extent still are, "blue-vein" societies and church congregations in many cities of the Southern states, and cruel distinctions are still made. Very light women rarely married black men, and then chiefly because the latter were successful. When a very light-skinned man married a much darker woman it was regarded as incongruous; but light-skinned women are preferred alike in India and Africa, for that matter. No matter how inoffensively the skin-whitening advertisements in Negro newspapers are worded to spare the embarrassment of the more sensitive readers, they are there and in profusion. One of the ironies of the time was the huge skin-whitening advertisements in *The Negro World* opposite flaming editorials extolling pride of blackness. But as the black Negroes emerged from the cotton patches to prosperity, success, education, and refinement, social distinctions became blurred and more and more of them were accepted. In short, American Negroes were moving away from an anachronism still prevalent in tropical regions. So the Garvey gambit did not become popular, especially when he jeered at respected mulatto leaders like James Weldon Johnson and W. E. B. DuBois as "white men" and damned the NAACP as the National Association for the Advancement of *Certain* People. It did not help matters when Dr. DuBois wrote of Garvey as "a little black man."

In addition to the NAACP, there was in the Garvey opposition the African Blood Brotherhood, headed by an octoroon named Cyril Briggs. Its mouthpiece was *The Crusader*. There was not an

African in its following but all were mixed bloods and the whole group was Communist-inspired.

There was also a colored Socialist group called the Friends of Negro Freedom of which A. Philip Randolph and Chandler Owen were the heads. They were co-editors of *The Messenger,* a monthly magazine devoted to "scientific socialism" and containing monthly denunciations of Garvey and Garveyism, along with sharp criticism of the NAACP. In addition, the Friends of Negro Freedom ran a forum every Sunday afternoon in a vacant store in the Lafayette Theater building on West 131st Street. Its principal target was Garvey and the UNIA, but it had many outstanding speakers on subjects of contemporary interest and importance.

There were also meetings and forums at the Harlem Branch YMCA and the West 137th Street branch of the YWCA. A popular meeting place was the YWCA cafeteria where many people went for lunch and chatting.

There was, I soon discovered, considerable intellectual ferment in the community, and this was encouraged by the dedicated white librarian of the neighborhood public library, Miss Ernestine Rose, who had literary evenings for the community.

Colored New York at that time had a merited reputation for being well dressed, and a conscious effort was made to appear on the streets and avenues looking one's best. Canes and spats were common, and a colored woman would not be seen on the street in a house dress. The colored community still occupied a small section of Harlem surrounded by Finns, Russians, Italians, Germans, Latin Americans and Jews.

Thanks to the enterprise of Lester Walton, a newspaperman who became manager of the Lafayette Theater, the community was offered Shakespearean and other classic dramas at both the Lincoln and Lafayette theaters (both now converted into churches) with parts played by prominent Negro actors. This was a boon to the Negro public which was not available elsewhere in colored America. These Lafayette Players were tops and I spent many pleasant evenings watching them play to packed houses.

Of course the principal fare offered was vaudeville, and the best Negro variety artists were billed. It was there that I first heard Mamie Smith singing the blues, and many of the best musicians of the day. Fats Waller played the organ at the Lincoln, and on Seventh Avenue near West 135th Street, Pace and Handy had an office for their Black Swan Records, which are now collectors' items much sought after by jazz fans.

I attended meetings downtown at the People's Institute in Cooper Union, the Labor Temple on 14th Street and the Rand School of Social Science (or Socialist Science!), where I heard some of the most distinguished thinkers of the day, such as Norman Angell, Will Durant, Everett Dean Martin, John B. Watson and Alfred Adler. At the time there was a great struggle between the various Communist factions jockeying for power in this country as in Russia and elsewhere, and there was much discussion and debate. There was no basic difference between them. They reflected the various party factions in Moscow. Personally I was indifferent as to whether socialism should come in one country first or in all of them simultaneously. In either event I felt that it would be an ill day for the people, as it had been in Russia and Hungary.

More important to me at the time was the fact that my money was running out and I needed a job fast. For nearly a month everything was going out and nothing was coming in. Having discovered that I could eat more cheaply on the Bowery than I could in Harlem or anywhere else, I found that I could spend a nickel for subway fare and still save money.

During one of my strolls along the Bowery I passed an employment office advertising for workers on the Erie Railroad. The pay offered seemed attractive for the period and for my need. I applied and was accepted. The gang was scheduled to leave the next morning, so I went back uptown and spent my last night in the Phyllis Wheatley Hotel. Having been hardened by the building construction work in Syracuse, I did not doubt that I could easily do the toughest tasks on the railroad.

We went across on the ferry next morning to New Jersey and there took a work train to Spring Valley, about thirty miles from New York on the west side of the Hudson. We were assigned to bunks in a remodeled freight car which was clean, tidy and warm. I worked with the gang in charge of the section between Spring Valley and Suffern. Our job was to replace rails and ties, change frogs and switches, and do anything else directed by the section boss. To the positions of work we rode back and forth on handcars which had to be lifted off the track whenever a train was scheduled to pass. This was not difficult for a half dozen brawny men, and the section boss knew when each train was expected. However, by the amount of work there was to do on the section (a mile long) I surmised that our work was temporary.

Ill fortune struck within a few days in the form of a sudden blizzard which heaped snow waist high on the tracks, making it difficult for trains to get through. It was imperative that switches under three or four feet of snow be dug down to and freed of snow so they could operate. We battled all day in the bitter cold to attain this end, and far into the night, with promise of extra pay. When the job was done, we were all very much exhausted—and then during the early morning hours it snowed again!

The snow was not as heavy as before, but we worked all day keeping the yards and the switches in moveable condition. This was just the beginning of the winter, and we were told that these heavy snowstorms were common and we could understand why there was a heavy turnover on the job. There was nothing to do but work, sleep and eat. So when we got paid, most of us made it back to New York and the Bowery.

I did not return to Harlem but shacked up in a flophouse until the next morning, carefully putting my meager currency in the bottom of my socks and leaving the socks on while I slept on the hard cot. I think the lodging cost a quarter or maybe less. A fair meal could be secured nearby for an equal amount, and nobody was overly concerned about sanitation and nutrition.

Next morning I went to another employment office and in a short while shipped out to work in a railroad yard or repair shop near Bethlehem, Pennsylvania. It was dark when we arrived but I sensed that there was something wrong about the place. There seemed to be a lot of extra bunks in the barracks, there were armed guards around the periphery of the place, and at mess that night I learned from others that it was a strikebreaking job. Some of the Negroes were quite cynical about it, saying that was the only way they could get work.

Well, I was not that badly off. I went immediately to my bunk, grabbed my little suitcase, put on my overcoat and went right up an incline to the gate in the barbed wire fence. An armed guard halted me.

"Where do you think you're going?" he asked.

"I'm going out," I answered. "Why?"

"You can't leave now," he said. "Besides, you're liable to get hurt going through town. Those people are on strike and they don't like you fellows."

"They won't bother me," I said rather cockily. "I'll tell them why I left."

Reluctantly he let me through, and somewhat skirting the town, I made for the road back to New York. This was not easy. In the first place it was black dark and there was little traffic on the road back there in late December 1922. So I spent the night in an unoccupied shed on the outskirts of town until sunrise.

I walked for many miles, lugging my suitcase and trying to hitch a ride. I finally succeeded in getting one which helped me along for many miles, then I got another, and by means of trucks, private cars, and local trains, I got to the ferry and across to New York. I had not fared badly but I determined never to take any strikebreaking jobs. It was not that I had any loyalty to organized labor with its rather general policy of Negro exclusion, but because I had no desire to be a strikebreaker in industrial warfare.

Back to the Bowery, the cheap meals, the curbstone camaraderie, and the dingy employment offices. I could have gone to Harlem but it was less expensive among the bums, and the chances of getting work were better. Sure enough, the very next day I got a job on the dock at the foot of Joralemon Street in Brooklyn. Completely unfamiliar with stevedore work, I had a tough time trucking the huge loads over the cobblestones from ship to warehouse. The money was really hard-earned and I was frankly glad when we were let go. I never tried longshoring any more, figuring that there must be easier ways of making a living. The docks were so well organized that it was impossible for a non-union man to get work on any of them except in case of great emergency. On the main docks a Negro, even if a member of the union, could not work. Most of the colored fellows belonged to a Jim-Crow union in Brooklyn which was restricted in the docks it could work.

There came a heavy snow the next evening and the only Bowery denizens on the street were "smoke" bums prostrate in doorways. My money was rather low and I was speculating on how I should spend it, or avoid spending it, as I stood in a sheltered door next to a brightly lit cheap restaurant, when a 'bo came shambling down the street, smoking a big cigar, hands buried in his shabby overcoat pockets and leaning against the wind. He paused and eyed me, probably figuring I was worse off than I was.

"Friend," he said, "I know where you can get a feed and a flop until you get on your feet. Wanna go?" It was a foolish question.

We trudged up the Bowery, past Cooper Union, and turned right on Tenth Street, battling the blinding snow all of the way. Finally we came to a big, darkened church on the corner of Avenue A, went around to the side and stumbled down a dozen snow-caked steps to a basement door. Yellow light shone through cracks in the window shades and we could hear the sound of loud talk and raucous laughter.

My newly found friend knocked, the talk ceased, a chair was pushed back, the heavy door was thrown open, and light, heat, and tobacco smoke rushed out to greet us. We entered and I was introduced to Stumpy, a fat, tanned, bald-headed old fellow with a big brown mustache, mischievous eyes and a wooden leg.

A motley crew, perhaps ten in all, sat around a big dining table in the center of a twenty-four-foot room with a high ceiling. They were the type to be found in any Bowery gathering on a winter's night. They were young and old, punks and weather-beaten veterans of highways, jails, almshouses, and hobo jungles. Some were looking through dog-eared old magazines, others sipping coffee from big agate cups, still others just smoking and talking. They greeted us in the casual manner of Hobohemia.

My friend Old Bill Wilson threw off his overcoat and I followed suit. He was a gray-haired, slightly stooped bum with shaggy gray eyebrows, intelligent blue eyes and an aquiline nose somewhat red on the tip. We drew up chairs and Stumpy hobbled around getting us coffee, bread, and stew. A fire was blazing merrily in a big fireplace, much heat was coming from a big kitchen range in the corner, and the radiator in another corner was popping. Heat, shelter, and food!

I borrowed a pipeful of tobacco from Jerry, a gray, morose fellow of indefinite age, who kept his mouth shut and played solitaire most of the time. Then I began to inquire about this idyllic club of the dispossessed.

Our haven was the large basement of the church, an area which was seldom used by the people who owned it. Three young unmarried clergymen lived in quarters upstairs and an upper room was used as a school of some kind. The commodious basement was the domain of Frank Elliott, the middle-aged janitor, a former hobo and gangster who refused to forget the dispossessed of the world. One room was used for general assembly, another provided sleeping quarters with several cots, with mattresses and blankets, and there was additionally a small auditorium with chairs, platform, and piano, which was not used at all except when our ranks were swelled beyond the ordinary. The building was in the parish of Saint Marks-on-the-Bouwerie.

Frank Elliott explained the rules to me, as he did to each newcomer. A tall, greasy brunette, perpetually clad in brown overalls and an olive drab Army shirt, his straggling brown hair kept falling over his searching brown eyes. He had a belligerent jaw and his loose, full lips were caught to one side when he spoke, but opened very wide when he laughed. He knew the Bowery like a book, had fought and got drunk in all of its notorious joints, and his picture was in Rogue's Gallery.

"You take a day's work when you can get it, see?" he explained, standing with legs wide apart and scratching his ear. "When you get a coupla bucks, put one in the kitty" (pointing to the tall coffee can on the mantel over the fireplace). "That's how we're able to buy chow. When you ain't got nuthin', don't worry; some o' th' boys will have somethin'. Play fair with us and we'll give you an even break. Get me?"

For a couple of days the snowstorm afforded us all work. Twelve hours a day out in the biting air, and we each got ten dollars. The kitty was overflowing and the gang feasted off steak, potatoes, onions, bread, and coffee, with occasional bits of pastry. Then the sun came out strong and the snow shoveling jobs melted away. We had nothing to do but sit around, smoke, play cards, read, debate, and swap anecdotes. There were lively arguments about the worst experiences, the toughest towns in which to be stranded, and the worst prisons in which to serve time.

"What th' hell do you know about stir?" challenged Sweeney, a big, hard-faced, profane Irishman with wicked little eyes who had once studied for the priesthood. Almost every word he uttered was obscene.

Sweeney would then launch into a discourse on domestic and foreign prisons in which he had done time. Once he got started he talked on and on, and no one could interrupt him except Frank or Old Bill. He would glare murderously at an interrupter and then outshout him with his bull voice; but he interrupted others whenever he chose. He boasted of being a white man, he hated priests and Englishmen, and he declared with finality that there were no good women.

The butt of all his jests and the recipient of much of his abuse was Stumpy, the old cook whom he taunted with, "Why in th' hell don't you go jump in th' river? What good are you? You're all shot. You'll never be able to make a livin' with that peg leg."

Stumpy took it all with seeming good humor, perhaps because it was all so true. Sometimes his old eyes would glisten dangerously but would quickly resume their expression of calm, philosophical resignation. He was too ancient and battered to defend himself. He had to take the abuse of younger, stronger men and pretend to like it.

Robert, a young, slender, lazy, no-account dreamer with strag-gling brown hair, pasty face, and red-rimmed eyes was almost as garrulous as Sweeney. He would sit for hours and talk about socialism and the rights of man when he was not poring over some radical pamphlet. He seemed weak and uncertain of him-self, claiming to be too ill to seek even an easy job. Snow shovel-ing, he said, hurt his back. He never put anything in the kitty until Frank demanded that he do so. He held that "We're the proletariat an' th' world owes us a livin'."

Sam, the resourceful, bullet-headed little Negro, characterized Robert as "positively th' laziest joker I evah seed. Ah doan blame your folks for kickin' you out!"

Sam considerably livened things up in the basement, and his droll comments pacified occasional belligerents. He got more odd jobs than anybody else and was always putting something in the kitty.

Sam voiced the thought of the rest of the gang about Robert. No one was expected to work steadily but every man was in duty bound to add something to the common treasury. Even old rheumatic Jerry with his slightly trembling hands managed to get a few chores now and then.

Jerry and Slim, a tow-headed West Virginia mountaineer with vacant blue eyes, were close friends. Together they had been on the road for years and claimed familiarity with hobo jungles from one end of the country to the other. Slim could scarcely read a cigarette advertisement, but he loved to philosophize about life and comment on the ills of society, especially when he and Jerry got full of "smoke," that atrocious though popular Bowery con-coction of wood alcohol and water. An ex-drunkard, Frank was dead against drinking, but when Jerry and Slim turned up on the fag end of a tremendous drunk, looking as if they had been dragged for miles behind an automobile, he always forgave them.

"Now whut th' hell are we here fer?" Slim would ask nobody in particular. "We're here jest tuh eat, drink and be merry. I ain't got nuthin', you ain't got nuthin', an' ain't none of us gonna have nuthin'. Whut's in this studyin' books 'n' things? Doan do you no good. Lookit Old Bill: he knows everything an' he ain't gotta quarter. Here I am dumb as hell 'n' I gotta dollar'n a half."

"An' you ain't gonna have that long," Sam would comment, to the accompaniment of uproarious laughter around the table.

Two of the inhabitants never sought odd jobs although their occupations were odd, and they contributed regularly to the kitty. They were inseparable pals, Mabel and Cleopatra, good looking and in their early twenties, dissatisfied with the Creator for assigning them to the wrong sex. Mabel was a tall, slender Scandinavian type with blonde, pomaded hair; Cleopatra was a short, plump Italian with curly black hair, a front tooth missing, and a lisp. They addressed each other by their feminine nicknames, walked mincingly and rolled their eyes coquettishly, and used such expressions as "Well, for Gawd's sake!" "Now *Ma-a-zie!*" and "I'm a decent, respectable woman!"

Mabel worked Bryant Park, Madison Square and Union Square; Cleopatra patrolled the Bowery from Cooper Union to Chatham Square, frequenting the dingy moving picture theaters and the lobbies of cheap hotels, and sometimes ventured into the financial district.

It was pleasant sitting around the big table on snowy evenings talking about everything under the sun, boasting of amorous exploits, planning for the spring trek to far-off places, playing card games. It was a special treat when Old Bill, the hobo intellectual, lectured. He spoke correctly and distinctly, carefully choosing his words, and with sarcastic, humorous asides. It was easy to close one's eyes and imagine some professor lecturing a university class. He knew all of the things Robert pretended to know. He had once edited an Industrial Workers of the World weekly and contributed to the *Hobo News.*

He went regularly to the free lectures at the People's Institute in the Great Hall at nearby Cooper Union and sometimes I accompanied him. Under his cot he had a beaten old suitcase half-filled with radical pamphlets and pencilled manuscripts. Even Sweeney listened respectfully when Bill held forth on Marx's theory of surplus value, on proletarian art, Walt Whitman and crowd behavior. Whenever he got a day's work, he would make his contribution to the kitty and then disappear for a day or two, returning with bloodshot eyes and reeking of cheap liquor. I liked and respected Bill even if I did not agree with him on the evils of capitalism and the supposed glories of socialism.

There was consensus on the uselessness of Robert. Frank reluctantly broke the bad news to him, pointing out almost apologetically that the worst of the winter was ended and gave him a dollar out of the kitty. While everybody felt relieved at his going, they were somehow shamed into silence. Even Sweeney had nothing to say.

Had they done right? What would become of one so helpless in this civilization of steel and stone; reluctant to panhandle and too dumb to steal? He might get a job dishwashing (the mecca of down-and-outers) or find succor at one of the Bowery missions or the municipal lodging house.

These men were accustomed to tough luck and tragedies. They were cynical and realistic, yet withal compassionate, kindly, and generous, but in their hard world Robert was just too much.

One source of income I soon discovered after moving to the basement was lighting fires for orthodox Jews on Saturday mornings, their Sabbath, when they were willing to pay somebody to perform their normal household chores. The change came in handy.

It was a leisurely life, if an inpecunious one, I scanned all the latest periodicals and the daily press. I spent fruitful hours in the reference rooms at the 42nd Street library and roamed through the Museum of Natural History. I went regularly to the forum of the Friends of Negro Freedom where some of the sharpest minds in Harlem assembled to make irreverent comments on subjects sacred and profane, and sometimes to affairs at the 135th Street library and the YMCA on the same block. I was impressed by the fact that there are so many cultural advantages entirely free in New York every day of the year. One needed only carfare, and sometimes not even that.

Going to the forum on Sundays, I became acquainted with A. Philip Randolph and Chandler Owen, co-editors of *The Messenger* and operators of the Friends of Negro Freedom, which was largely a paper organization. When Owen left to go on the road to get advertising from affluent Negro business concerns to bolster the flagging finances of the journal of "Scientific Socialism," Randolph suggested that I might like to help him out in the office. The idea of being associated with an important publication fascinated me, but I could not see how I could possibly live on the ten dollars weekly which I was told was the limit the magazine could afford. I would have to pay half that much for a small room, and there would be little left for food and laundry.

I was still staying in the basement but the demise of this haven was approaching. Spring was close and trees were budding in the parks. Jobs were now more plentiful and everybody was busily acquiring stakes essential for hitting the road.

There were a few dollars in my pockets. I had a fairly good suit, and if things got tight, I could always pawn my overcoat until fall. So I found a small, neat hall room in a private house on West 130th Street between Lenox and Fifth Avenues for five dollars a week. During the weeks I spent in the basement I had learned a lot about a seamy side of the world which I was not to see first-hand again.

The block onto which I moved was then the southernmost limit of black Harlem. It was clean, tree-lined and trim; one of the most attractive in the community where most of the well-kept homes were owner occupied. My tiny room was at the front end of the hall on the third floor. The landlord was Bob Harris, a rotund, overweight, cheerful black fellow with a smooth fat face and pop-eyes. He had once been butler for a famous theatrical impresario and had traveled widely with his boss, meeting most of the important people of the theater, and learning how the good life was lived. A man of no schooling, he was highly intelligent and had good taste in furnishings and food. From basement to roof his house was immaculate and he spent many hours daily keeping it so. He had acquired tapestries, a grand piano, oil paintings, Chinese porcelains and expensive rugs. He roamed the antique shops on Third Avenue in his leisure time acquiring rare additions to his treasures. He daily patronized Weisbecker's, then the most exclusive food shop in Harlem, returning with big steaks, mushrooms, and other delicacies. The man ate prodigiously and was always inviting anyone who was present to join him. His cooking was as great as his generosity.

His roomers were a headwaiter in an exclusive night club, a gambler, a numbers runner, and I, the poorest of the lot. His two best rooms he reserved for transients; men and women of wealth and position who found this hideaway safe and convenient; who could not afford to be seen in downtown haunts; who would like to spend an evening or a weekend in romantic seclusion. He was a teetotaler but his connections were such that he always had a supply of fine wines, liquors, and brandies throughout the prohibition period.

By contrast the office of *The Messenger* was a disappointment. It consisted of two tiny rooms on the third floor of a converted brownstone house at 2305 Seventh Avenue. The furnishings were nondescript, the files were disorganized, back copies of the magazine were scattered about indiscriminately, and finding anything was a chore. There was but one typewriter, a battered old Underwood. With my long clerical experience in the Army and at the disciplinary barracks on Governor's Island, this disorder was distressing to me, and I began straightening things up the first day.

A. (for Asa) Philip Randolph was about six years my elder, and one of the finest, most engaging men I had ever met. Slender, brown-skinned, handsome, erect and always immaculately dressed, he was undemanding and easy to get along with. He was leisurely and undisturbed, remaining affable under all circumstances, whether the rent was due and he did not have it, or whether an expected donation failed to materialize, or whether the long-suffering printer in Brooklyn was demanding money. He had a keen sense of humor and laughed easily, even in adversity. I have never fancied people who beefed and bewailed their lot when things went wrong.

I soon discovered that the magazine's revenue came largely from meager advertising and from subscriptions and newsstand sales which then totaled about 5,000 monthly. There might have been occasional donations from Socialists downtown, but I never inquired. However *The Messenger* might feel the fell clutch of circumstance, Randolph showed no dismay and his aplomb seemed impenetrable. With the sonorous voice and the delivery of a Shakespearean actor, he calmed all tension, anger, and insistent creditors.

The Messenger was a good place for a tireless, versatile young fellow to get plenty of activity and exercise. I swept and mopped the office when necessary, was first to arrive and last to leave, opened the mail and answered much of it, read manuscripts and proofs, corrected copy, went to the *Brooklyn Eagle* job press, handled the subscriptions and distributed the magazines to newsstands in Negro areas. In between these chores I would take Randolph's dictation directly on the typewriter.

Many a time we would stop and laugh over some Socialist cliché or dubious generalization, and at such times I realized Randolph was wiser than I had imagined. Still, there was a strain of idealism in the man that has persisted through the years from his arrival in New York in 1915 when he began organizing hotel workers. His first publication effort, together with Owen, was *The Hotel Messenger,* which later became *The Messenger,* a journal of "Scientific Socialism" with a definite Marxist orientation. This was an innovation in Negro journalism. Both Owen and Randolph were conscientious objectors during World War I and were, I believe, briefly confined on Governor's Island. During the time of the post-war race riots, an article on the Washington, D.C. shootings, carrying accompanying cartoons showing the Negroes making the world safe for democracy with guns abroad and in Washington, incurred the wrath of the Department of Justice. The article aroused the ire of Representative James M. Byrnes of South Carolina (later senator, Supreme Court justice and Secretary of State) who brandished it on the floor of the House and called for its suppression.

Previously, when twelve black soldiers were hanged in Houston for shooting up the town, *The Messenger* carried Alexander Grimké's scathing poem on the Twelve Black Martyrs of Houston. *The Crisis,* the NAACP magazine edited by Dr. W. E. B. DuBois, had previously rejected it because it was too incendiary and might get *The Crisis* into trouble. DuBois, a Socialist like the other founders of the NAACP, was currently trying to get a commission in the Army. At that time he also carried an editorial "Close Ranks. Let Us Forget Our Grievances," which Negroes generally denounced as appeasement when military discrimination and segregation were rife.

Alexander and Francis Grimké were distinguished colored South Carolinians, pastors of churches in Washington, D.C., and flaming militants of the day on racial questions. About the same time Dean Kelly Miller of Howard University wrote his open letter to President Wilson, "A Disgrace To Democracy," which had a very large sale in a Negro America whose fathers, husbands and sons were going "over the top."

Chandler Owen, a plump, light-brown-skinned man, shorter than Randolph, a North Carolinian and graduate of Virginia Union University, was a facile and acidulous writer, a man of ready wit and agile tongue endowed with the saving grace of cynicism. He had already seen through and rejected the Socialist bilge, and was jeering at the Bolshevist twaddle at a time when most intellectuals were speaking of the "Soviet experiment" with reverence. Incongruously his conversation contradicted or disputed everything for which *The Messenger* professed to stand. He dubbed the Socialists as frauds who actually cared little more for Negroes than did the then-flourishing Ku Klux Klan. Owen was gifted in hyperbole and his sarcasm was corroding.

Much of Owen's bitterness probably stemmed from the experience of his brother, a highly skilled tailor, who had been unceremoniously brushed off by one of the Marxist clothing unions he had sought to join in order to become a cutter, the highest paid work in the shops. Being co-editor of a Socialist magazine was no help when Chandler tried to exert pressure to get his brother accepted. Of course at that time no craft unions accepted Negro members except in separate Negro locals. To be sure, Negroes could join the clothing unions, which swore by Marx and Engels, but only as lower-paid cart-pushers and pressers. They were Jewish and Italian unions rather than labor unions.

So Owen and I were quite in agreement about this labor union hypocrisy. These people paid lip service to the brotherhood of man and the universality of the labor interest, but they were not really talking about the Negro. Randolph's pious pronouncements of Socialist cant and clichés in the face of the stark realities was, to say the least, disquieting, although he often had a twinkle in his eye. To be sure, the slogan "Black and White, Unite and Fight" was a good one, except that practically it meant nothing.

In addition to our discussions in the little office, Randolph had interesting guests for breakfast every Sunday morning in his spacious apartment on West 142nd Street just east of Seventh Avenue. There I first met his vivacious gray-haired wife, Lucille, a light-brown matron who operated a beauty shop on West 135th Street opposite the public library from which she derived considerable income, as she was popular, efficient, and modestly-priced. She would giggle ironically over the fact that she had several Jewish customers who came to her shop to get their hair straightened, just like her Negro customers. It reminded me of how Karl Marx (who was himself nicknamed The Moor) jeered over the fact that Ferdinand Lassalle, the German Socialist leader, used bear's grease to conceal the African curl in his hair.

One of Lucille's close friends was A'Lelia Walker, a regal dark millionairess who boasted a limousine, a uniformed chauffeur, a town house on Edgecombe Avenue and a stately mansion at Irvington-on-Hudson, which distressed her white neighbors. Later she bought a palatial town house on West 136th Street where the Countee Cullen branch library is now. It was called *The Dark Tower* and was the center of social life in Harlem and the meeting place for members of both races who wanted to practice social integration as well as preach it.

Always present, too, was Randolph's scholarly brother, James, who was taking a science program at the College of the City of New York on the heights above us. In addition there would be two or three others. The conversation sparkled and nothing escaped the group's probing minds and witty shafts. The Negro

Question was seldom the number one topic. It was often bypassed in favor of other subjects currently popular. Around that table I encountered some of the community's best minds and it added much to my education.

Often after breakfast, which would end around noon, Randolph and I would join the promenaders on Seventh Avenue. There was much to intrigue the artist and sociologist on such a stroll. New York Negroes of the day prided themselves on being well-dressed, preferably in the latest style; the gentlemen wearing gaiters and boutonnieres, and swinging canes; the ladies in the knee-length dresses of the period and often fur coats. Pince-nez were more affected then than horn rimmed spectacles, and it was not surprising to see a monocle or lorgnette on occasion. These people seemed to be proud to be what they were, with no evidence of the inferiority complex and racial self-hate that the current crop of psychologists think they ought to have. They dressed as well as white New Yorkers farther downtown.

The homes and apartments I visited were tastefully furnished. Contrary to legend they were no more overcrowded than those of the whites, and not nearly as much as many I had seen on the Lower East Side while lighting Saturday morning fires. This myth of Harlemites packed together like sardines is a durable one. A comparison of the census for 1910, 1920, 1930 and up to 1960 will show conclusively that the population of the Harlem area has steadily declined despite the Puerto Rican and Southern Negro influx. Harlem has always suffered from a bad press.

The well-being of the community was remarkable in view of the Negroes' exclusion from large areas of employment, a pattern that set in with the increase of European immigration and continued until World War II, a period of more than a century. They were in the main restricted to the low-paid jobs, excluded from the skilled crafts, and subjected to color discrimination in a number of irritating and annoying ways. That they looked and deported themselves so well was a tribute to their resourcefulness, adaptability and ingenuity.

Aside from the Lincoln and Lafayette theaters, none of the considerable number of theaters welcomed Negro patrons in their

orchestra sections. Randolph and I would stroll south on Seventh
Avenue to catch the vaudeville show at the Alhambra theater at
West 126th Street. Entering the lobby, he would flatten himself
against the wall near the ticket window, toss in the money and
ask for two orchestra seats. Sometimes the deception worked, but
when it didn't, we would be sold tickets for the back balcony. It
was much the same at the other theaters on and around 125th
Street, and was worse downtown. Negroes were readily served
only in the cafeterias and restaurants catering to the masses.

CHAPTER 10

SOON AFTER going to work at *The Messenger*, I submitted a first-person piece, entitled "From Job to Job," recounting my work experiences in and around New York City, to Miss Anna Rochester of *The World Tomorrow*, the magazine of the Fellowship of Reconciliation, a Christian Socialist movement. John Nevin Sayre was editor, Miss Rochester was his associate, Devere Allen was managing editor, Alice Parsons was business manager, and there were such contributors as Sarah N. Cleghorn, Walter G. Fuller, Zona Gale, John Haynes Holmes, Grace Hutchins, Rufus M. Jones, Kirby Page, Richard Roberts, Norman Thomas, Ridgely Torrence and Harry F. Ward. All of them rendered conspicuous service to the collectivist front. Associated with it was the Fellowship Press: George A. Beaver, president, Ray Newton, secretary and Hollingsworth Wood of the National Urban League, treasurer. Miss Rochester's acceptance came on March 24, 1923 and it appeared in an April issue. It was the first time I had been in print since the old days in

Hawaii. *The World Tomorrow* was a respected periodical, and since the writings of Negroes were only rarely to be found in contemporary magazines, I was elated over the achievement. Now I knew I could write with the best and it gave some assurance that I was on my way. It was ironical that the first opportunity should be provided by a Christian Socialist periodical.

My experiences with the fringe proletariat during the years after leaving Governor's Island formed the basis for another article soon afterward in *The Messenger* entitled "Hobohemia." I was now also doing a monthly page there called "SHAFTS AND DARTS: A PAGE OF CALUMNY AND SATIRE," which lampooned many of the fads and foibles of the day and was quite iconoclastic. Most Negro publications, then as now, were solemn and serious, containing little wit and humor except in comics. To me nothing was above a snicker, a chuckle, a smile or guffaw.

I enjoyed immensely what I was doing but it was done at a hardship. The original ten dollars weekly was finally increased to fifteen dollars, and even then the going was tough. However, I was not a recluse. I made many acquaintances and some friends, including the brilliant Elise McDougald (now Mrs. Vernon Ayer), a school teacher who later became the first Negro woman school principal in New York City; J. A. Rogers, then on the *Amsterdam News;* Theophilus Lewis, postal clerk, theatrical writer (who years later became drama critic of the Jesuit weekly, *America*); Robert W. Bagnall and William Pickens of the National Association for the Advancement of Colored People; Wilfred A. Domingo, Jamaican importer of tropical products and member of the minuscule African Blood Brotherhood; Edward W. Perry, a journalist who was interested in the little theater movement among Negroes; Gwendolyn Bennett, an artist; and several others. Later on when Theophilus Lewis and his wife took an apartment on Seventh Avenue, I boarded there, along with Bruce Nugent, a young artist with a style reminiscent of Aubrey Beardsley, and Wallace Thurman, author of a novel, *The Blacker the Berry.* Lewis was an avid reader of *The Smart Set,* edited by Henry L. Mencken and George Jean

Nathan. He later became a protégé of Father John LaFarge, and converted to Catholicism.

Bagnall, an NAACP field secretary, had led the "invasion" of West 127th Street which became the southernmost boundary of Harlem. He and his wife were *bons vivants* and always had interesting guests from various strata of society, among them the singer and fashion plate "Broadway" Jones, and the baritone Jules Bledsoe who first starred in *Show Boat*.

On West 139th Street, just below City College, there was a row of private houses, brown on one side of the street and yellow on the other side. It was one of the most beautiful blocks in New York City, having been designed by Stanford White. William Pickens lived in one of the yellow houses, and I was welcome there.

Almost daily I lunched at the YWCA cafeteria with J. A. Rogers, a Jamaica-born journalist whose first book, *As Nature Leads*, had added to his reputation. He was a former Pullman porter who had studied art in Chicago and had a tremendous knowledge of the historical background of the Negro and especially of miscegenation around the world. He was usually present at our Sunday forums and the gab sessions we often had on Saturday afternoons in *The Messenger* office after we moved from 2305 Seventh Avenue to 2311, a more spacious location where we had the entire first floor. Other participants in those sessions were Henry F. Downing, an Indian-looking man with a bush of snow-white hair, who had once been U.S. consul at Luanda, Angola, and before that a paymaster in the U.S. Navy stationed in New York. He had written *An American Cavalryman*, a novel based on the career of U.S. Major Charles Young, a Negro West Pointer, along with several plays in England. He was the son of the distinguished restaurateur, George A. Downing, who had once operated one of the finest restaurants in downtown New York and whose large supply of vinegar had been used to thaw out water pipes enabling the fire department to save the city from being gutted during the big fire in the 1840's. Downing was a walking compendium of Negro history and lore, and I learned much from him, especially about the early Pan-African efforts starting with the first conference held in Paris in 1899 to which Dr. W. E. B. DuBois never referred, although he was an American delegate to the gathering sponsored by the Emperor Menelik of Abyssinia and arranged by Benito Sylvain, his Haitian *aide-de-camp.*

Another habitué of our Saturday round-tables and Sunday forums was T. Thomas Fortune, venerable journalist and one-time editor of the *New York Age,* closely associated with Booker T. Washington's public relations work. Another man, equally distinguished, was the Garveyite, Sir William H. Ferris, graduate of both Harvard and Yale theological schools, author of *The African Abroad,* a monumental work published in 1912. There later joined us a young intellectual from Danville, Virginia, James W. Ivy, linguist and authority on literature and the Negro in Latin lands. He later became editor of *The Crisis,* succeeding Roy Wilkins in that post.

Presiding over these Athenian conclaves would be, of course, the dapper, amiable A. Philip Randolph, with Owen when he was in town. His deep drawl poured oil over the stormy waters of dispute that inevitably arose among these intellectual *prima donnas.* William H. Ferris, a shabby little brown man with pockets ever bulging with newspapers and magazines, had acquired his knighthood from Marcus Garvey, and made the best philosophical defense of the charismatic Jamaican that I had heard. Strangely, this black scholar reminded me of Old Bill, the IWW philosopher of the basement.

In 1923 the Communists were no more concerned with the Negro than were the Socialists who had always taken the position that with the coming of collectivism the race problem would be automatically solved because capitalism would be destroyed (even though there had been a color problem thousands of years before capitalism). To be sure, the Communists were pregnant with theories and had some elaborate plans, as revealed by the documents captured at the Bridgman, Michigan conference in August, 1922, presided over by Joseph Pogany, the young Communist associate of Bela Kun, the Red butcher of Hungary. The

Communists were currently divided into a dozen warring sects on the bases of European nationalism and Marxian differences, all primarily concerned with the progress of Red subversion and sabotage in their own countries. Each wanted to be recognized by the Kremlin as Lenin's Chosen People.

In the United States, the minuscule African Blood Brotherhood, chiefly a West Indian anti-Garvey organization, plugged the Communist line. Its leader was Cyril V. Briggs, who could "pass" for a white man, a fact that Marcus Garvey would never let him forget. None of the members were unmixed African. Prominent among them were a Dutch Guiana mulatto, Otto Huiswoud, who had recently returned from the Bolshevik Promised Land (where they promised everything and delivered nothing) along with the Jamaican novelist and poet, Claude McKay, the only two "American" Negroes to attend the Kremlin conference to conquer the world. McKay stayed behind in Europe, but Huiswoud came home to infect "his" people with Communism. Like the others, Richard Moore and W. A. Domingo, he knew nothing whatever about America, and less about Aframerica.

The only other Red outfit concerned at all with "saving" the Negro from capitalism was William Z. Foster's Trade Union Educational League, a "transmission belt" to bore from within the labor unions and to attempt to integrate Negroes into them. It had started that year and never got off the launching pad in its effort to kill free enterprise. In the first place, most of organized labor had a vested interest in free enterprise, the only system under which free unions could survive. In the second place, they wanted no integration of Negroes in their ranks, and interpreted Foster's labors as a bid for miscegenation, on which subject they were as one with the Ku Klux Klan.

There was a forum being started at the 135th Street public library, and it was arranged in June, 1923 for me to debate Otto Huiswoud on the subject of the Negro and Communism. There was no other person around willing or able to debate him, all the others being intellectual Socialists. We had quite a turnout and the debate was stirring. It was probably the first debate staged in the United States on this momentous subject that has created more heat than light during the forty years since. I took the position that the Negro had difficulties enough being black without becoming Red; that an attempt was being made by Communists to make a dupe out of the Negro which could only end in race war and his extermination; that this could benefit only the Kremlin cabal, not the white laboring classes who would be as enslaved as the Russian people. This was all pertinent since we had just experienced a spate of race riots all over the country, the Ku Klux Klan was mobilizing and marching everywhere, and the government had just recently scraped together a shipload of the most obnoxious extremists and shipped them to Russia on the U.S. transport *Buford.* With Communism bringing only misery to white people, what could it offer non-whites?

Otto Huiswoud was an avid agent of the Communist International who in the mid-Thirties succeeded George Padmore as executive secretary of the International Trade Union Committee of Negro Workers and editor of its appropriately red-covered propaganda organ, *The Black Worker,* established under direction of the Red International of Labor organized in Hamburg in 1930.

Son of a wealthy Trinidad physician named Cream ("Padmore" was George's party name), and a graduate of Howard University, Padmore was for long the leading Negro Communist in the British Empire. He later authored several anti-colonialist books. He fell from Kremlin grace when in 1935 he opposed Red policy in Africa during the opportunistic Soviet swing in which the Bolsheviks made a deal with the French and British to suspend the war on "imperialism" in exchange for recognition by the Western Powers. Essentially a black nationalist rather than a Communist (although he was both), Padmore could not rise to the Moscow opportunism. He criticized the deal by which Stalin supplied Mussolini with oil in Greek tankers for Il Duce's conquest of Abyssinia. While the old League of Nations applied "sanctions" against Italy, its outstanding founder-member, Great Britain, let the oil ships go through the Suez Canal. However, it demonstrated its friendliness to Haile Selassie by giving him asylum in England when he was chased from his homeland by the Italian dictator.

The rise of Hitler to power (made inevitable by Stalin's orders to the German Communist Party) compelled a hasty transfer of the International Trade Union Committee of Negro Workers from Hamburg to Copenhagen. The Kremlin decided to fire Padmore and sent Otto Huiswoud to Copenhagen with a letter of peremptory dismissal. Huiswoud then took over the job of subverting Africans, albeit this Surinamer had never been to Africa.

Padmore hastened to Paris where he eluded several attempts to assassinate him during the height of Stalin's purge of Old Bolsheviks who failed to follow the party line or were suspected of defection or potential opposition. He escaped to London, the heart of his hated British Empire, where he remained, subverting African students, until the 1950's when he went to Ghana as the right-hand man of his protégé and loyal follower, Kwame Nkrumah. While my debate with Huiswoud was in June, 1923, this digression shows that thereafter he remained a Red Uncle Tom always ready to do the Kremlin master's bidding.

For the next year I kept abreast of the ramifications of the Communist conspiracy, attended meetings and forums downtown, and kept up *The Messenger's* correspondence with European Socialists and alert Negroes in Africa and the West Indies. We had numerous exchange newspapers and I was able to keep up with the Negro press and even a few Ku Klux Klan papers. I was doing all of the detail work on circulation and advertising; corresponding with contributors; reading manuscripts; and generally putting the magazine to bed and waking it up. The financial state of *The Messenger* was perpetually parlous. Stuart Chase came occasionally to do our books and was puzzled over how we kept going. So was I. We often laughed over the miracle.

At this time Ira F. Lewis, general manager of *The Pittsburgh Courier,* then second largest in circulation of the Negro weeklies, asked me to do a column, but the amount offered was only three dollars a week. I was not insulted; I was delighted. I knew I

147

would soon get more and I did. Even *The Messenger* gave a few more weekly dollars. So early in 1925 I was earning as much from journalism as I had from building construction three years before!

There were very few American Communists then and even the most extravagant claim did not put the total over 14,000. Of these about 150 were Negroes who tiresomely baited the "reactionary" Negro church, press, and civil rights organizations to no effective end.

The colored and white Communists of the time were bottom drawer people without education or stature, and most ineffective in selling their Red wares. Many of the white Communists were aliens unfamiliar with the English language. It was not until the early New Deal years when the party dropped the "no collaboration with the bourgeoisie" line and began to woo the middle class, colored and white, that its membership and influence grew rapidly. It was the Socialists (who had long had the so-called intellectuals through the tireless efforts of the Fabians of the Intercollegiate Socialist Society) who by then had infiltrated all of the Ivy League colleges. They were led by such pioneers as Gaylord Wilshire, Walter Rauschenbusch, George D. Herron, Leonard Abbott, J. G. Phelps-Stokes (founder of the fund bearing his name which has become a pasture for retired Negro college presidents), his Russian Socialist wife, Rose Pastor Stokes, Clarence Darrow, Lincoln Steffens, Professor Richard T. Ely, Franklin Giddings, John R. Connors and Thorstein Veblen. Others were Charlotte Perkins Gilman, Upton Sinclair, Harry W. Laidler, Jack London, William English Walling (who founded the NAACP along with five other white socialists and one black one, Dr. W. E. B. DuBois) and such eminent socialist leaders as Morris Hillquit, Norman Thomas and Algernon Lee. I learned of this Socialist influence quite early in my studies of Marxist propaganda and infiltration.

Harry W. Laidler had been the pioneer propagandist in selling Marxism to the college students through the ISS. The Harvard chapter was headed by Walter Lippmann, associated with Heywood Broun (who organized the American Newspaper Guild), Kenneth MacGowan, and Lee Simonson.

Shortly there were fifteen chapters and 300 members clamoring for Socialist curriculums. Leading the pack at Columbia University were Charles A. Beard, John Dewey, and Franz Boas. Other ISS executives were Evans Clark, Dr. Frank Bohn, Orway Tead, Henry Bruere, Frederick C. Howe and Algernon Lee. The latter doubled as head of the Rand School of Social Science, a Marxist school modeled after the London School of Economics, put over on the British by the English Fabians (Bernard Shaw, Sidney and Beatrice Webb, H. M. Hyndman, Ramsay MacDonald, Sidney Olivier, Annie Besant and so forth) dedicated to bringing socialism to England by not calling it socialism.

After the word Socialist acquired a very bad odor from the Russian Revolution with its butcheries, and the five Socialist assemblymen elected in New York's 1920 elections had been promptly ousted following the investigations of the Lusk Committee, the ISS decided to change its name. Thus the Intercollegiate Socialist Society became the League for Industrial Democracy (which meant the same thing but was more broadly based) and had the same executives. Other leaders of this Jekyll-Hyde Marxist endeavor were Dr. Robert Morss Lovett, Charles P. Steinmetz, Paul Blanshard, Norman Thomas, Paul Porter, Leroy Bowman, George Soule, and the peripatetic and potent Harry W. Laidler.

A hurricane of pro-Socialist pamphlets deluged the market and soon the *LID News Bulletin* could boast of having hornswoggled 35,000 students. It supported every strike and labor upheaval, and was soon getting substantial subsidies from radical labor unions, especially the needle trades. They popularized such Socialist euphemisms as "social justice," "progressivism," "social reform," "social planning," "welfare state," and "industrial democracy."

As soon as I discovered that the real differences between these "respectable" reformers and the younger brash Communists were tactical and strategic, rather than fundamental (since both sought the same collectivist goal), I was profoundly enlightened. So far as a free society's survival was concerned, these Socialist wolves in the sheep's clothing of Fabianism were probably as dangerous as the Communists, if not more so.

This did not come to me suddenly like a bolt out of the blue. I had read the work of these men and women, attended meetings and lectures where they expounded their views, and noted the respectability which they generally enjoyed. It took some time to sense the proportions of what seemed to me to be a conspiracy to plant collectivism in America and nourish it to the final harvest. Many of these people might charitably be said to have been caught up in this movement without realizing its profound import. In their suspicion and hatred of free enterprise capitalism, they were working toward the same kind of ant-heap slavery inherent in collectivism. They talked hopefully of the "Socialist experiment" in Russia which would eventually wash off the blood of its accouchement and become pure, healthy, and progressive, not realizing that you cannot "experiment" with full-fledged collectivism; that it is the end of human freedom.

There was no one with whom I talked and no one I read who seemed to understand this trend in world affairs which has increasingly become a stampede, except Albert Jay Nock and Suzanne LaFollete of *The Freeman*. Certainly, the Negro intelligentsia were unaware of it. In their discussions they almost seemed like a colony of ants, on the end of a log floating down the Mississippi River to the sea, talking about destiny.

In March, 1924, Dean Kelly Miller sent out a call for a Negro Sanhedrin and I went to the planning conference on West 134th Street as a delegate from the minuscule Friends of Negro Freedom. There were others representing the African Blood Brotherhood, the International Uplift League, the NAACP, the National Race Congress, and the National Equal Rights League. The call for the Negro Sanhedrin was signed by James Weldon Johnson, Kelly Miller, William Monroe Trotter, D. N. E. Campbell, W. A. Domingo, Richard B. Moore, Otto E. Huiswoud, Robert W. Bagnall, Richetta Randolph, James M. Neill, Matthew A. N. Shaw, and myself.

These people with such disparate interests and views, and a pompous pretension of representing significant memberships which they did not have (save for the 100,000 or so in the

NAACP), made me dubious about the outcome of these deliberations. The wrangling between the leonine Trotter from Boston and the sarcastic Kelly Miller from Washington, and the quarrels of the liberals and radicals did not make me hopeful.

It remained for a German to solve the problem of luring the middle class and some of the upper class into the Communist fold. The great weakness of the party was its rough, gorilla base that was sufficient for the tasks of murder, subversion, and sabotage, but did not attract the sort of people who composed the Fabian Socialist movement for collectivism by indirection.

This man was Willi Muenzenberg, an early protégé of Lenin when the latter was hibernating in Switzerland. Later Muenzenberg transferred his activities to Berlin and founded the Communist Youth International which staged its first World Congress in May, 1920, in Moscow. He became its first president. Rapidly this became a juvenile Communist Third International (Comintern), paralleling the parent in all respects. Indeed, it grew so fast that the Comintern took over its direction and delegated Muenzenberg to organize the International Workers Aid, a labor insurance business which, along with the contacts made by the Communist Youth International, touched a lot of middle class people. In America it was termed the International Workers Order, or IWO, a notorious Red transmission belt. The IWO was among the first non-party Communist organizations to penetrate the non-Communist groups of the middle class, an example for all future organizations serving the Red solar system. Moreover, it was financed by the dupes themselves.

A gifted organizer and publishing genius, Muenzenberg became the Hearst of the Comintern, publishing two Berlin dailies which exceeded the sales of the combined German Communist press, and an illustrated rotogravure weekly with the largest circulation in the country. His secret was publishing material the workers could and would read instead of the almost unintelligible Communist party language which nobody could understand.

Muenzenberg's claim to enduring fame was his discovery of the fellow traveler, the individual who works for and often profits from Communism without avowing it. Knowing that practically everybody believes he can write, Willi's proliferation of newspapers and magazines catered to this half-educated element by inviting manuscripts of narration, fiction, and poems of quality unacceptable elsewhere. This was called proletarian literature, and did not belie the name. To the delight of the newly recognized authors, the editors paid for it, too, and touted them to the skies. Many people who could actually write palmed off manuscripts rejected elsewhere, giving them a working class slant. Thus a large number of non-proletarians were sucked into the Red movement. They helped to make Communism acceptable and respectable by selling their talents. In time, Muenzenberg corrupted not only German writers and poets but also many throughout Western Europe.

Rapidly this trend became worldwide. It was he who inspired the Comintern to push the Popular Front which enveloped disparate Marxian groups all over the world, including the United States, where it won colored and white *petit bourgeoisie* and aspiring intellectuals.

A gambler, cynic, and opportunist extraordinary, his policies, adopted by the Comintern, indirectly wooed the black bourgeoisie into the Red ranks which earlier they had spurned. By the mid-Thirties they were hooked. In the mid-Twenties, however, this was still in the future. There was then nothing the Communists were doing which was the least attractive to Negroes of high or low estate, what with attacks on the Negro churches and established race organizations. Their tactics repelled possible recruits who had always been suspicious and distrustful of poor whites pretending to "save" them. The only radical labor organization which had been able to attract a goodly number of black workers was the Industrial Workers of the World, the IWW, which some cynics nicknamed I Won't Work.

In October 1925, the minuscule TUEL (Trade Union Educational League) being already proved moribund, and which William Z. Foster admitted was "isolated from American life," the same conspirators convened to set up the American Negro Labor

Congress. Lovett Fort Whiteman, a Texas Negro Communist of the African Blood Brotherhood clique, was chosen president. The new organization died aborning.

The Pittsburgh Courier engaged me to go on the road to write my observations on the Negro South and incidentally to solicit agents. This offered me a golden opportunity to learn at first hand about the people I had been largely generalizing about, so I accepted. It was an assignment that was to last from November 1, 1925 to July 4, 1926, and carry me thousands of miles.

In preparation for the assignment, the *Courier* prepared and widely distributed a four-page leaflet which stated that I had been chosen to:

> make a nationwide tour of the urban centers of the country and write about the conditions and progress of the Negro population. . . . He is well-equipped to make an interesting, informative and instructive survey of the various Negro communities in the United States. Mr. Schuyler is not an optimist or a pessimist; he is a realist. He approaches his subject with the objectivity of the reliable observer, leaning more toward science than sentiment. He is primarily interested in presenting a picture of such and such a community; how the people live, what work they do, who are the celebrities, the relation between the races, the school conditions, the fraternal orders, the churches, the cultural movements; in short, every phase of life in that community. What he gives you is an accurate picture of the community not "touched" by the brush of the propagandist. Mr. Schuyler is not interested in proving anything; he is presenting a word photograph. It may or may not please you: you may like or dislike it, but you will be impressed by its judicial poise, its keen penetration, its sophistication and urbanity, and withal, the writer's rich background of experience and information.

It did *not* say that I had never before been below the Mason-Dixon Line.

I sought to live up to that puff, but the money was very short—fifty dollars weekly for pay and all expenses of transportation and upkeep. From Philadelphia I traveled to Harrisburg, Pennsylvania, stopped off for my first visit to the *Courier* office on Fourth Avenue, and then entered the South at Wheeling, West Virginia. I visited every city with as many as 5,000 Negroes in Kentucky, Tennessee, Arkansas, Texas, Oklahoma, Louisiana, Mississippi, Alabama, Florida, North and South Carolina, Georgia, and Virginia.

Transportation and accommodations, always Jim Crow, ranged from good to the worst imaginable. The ordinary facilities a journalist would use were denied to me because everywhere separate-but-equal prevailed, especially the separation. In some places in the Mississippi Delta there were restaurants which served colored and whites on opposite sides of oval counters with food from common kitchens, but that was as far as integration went. The hotels and rooming houses at which I stayed were operated by Negroes, and they ranged from satisfactory to the very worst. I did not mind staying in Negro places, for after all I was writing mainly about Negroes, and have never been fascinated by mingling with white people *per se*. It would have been very helpful in many places if I had been able to check in at a white-operated hotel and eat there.

Sometimes it was an ordeal getting adequate service from the time one stepped off a train or bus (bus travel those days was truly rugged). In many places the dark traveler had to get a taxicab driven by a Negro because white taxicabs would not carry colored people, even though empty. Usually a Negro taxicab was somewhere around the corner, but if not, one had to be called, maybe by an accommodating white cab starter. Perhaps in the next town white taxi drivers would vie for the Negro patronage. I learned very rapidly that almost every town differed in its interracial etiquette. On one interurban streetcar line, I found Negroes seated in the *front* of the car whereas in the two towns it connected, they sat in the rear of the trolley cars.

Almost everywhere the Negro taxi driver was of great assistance to me. He knew every Negro-owned hotel, rooming house, restaurant, barber shop and pool room. I learned that the people who knew every town best were the taxi drivers, policemen and bellhops (far better than the average citizen) and I found all to be helpful, colored or white, when asked. This was a boon because I had a maximum of work, a minimum of time in which to do it, and a paucity of contacts. Usually I knew not a single soul when I arrived except possibly one of the *Courier* agents whom I had never met personally. I would have his name and address from the long list supplied from the circulation department. So to find out the salient facts about the black city within the white city and the relationships between the two in a brief time took a bit of planning.

Before I arrived in a town I already knew its total population figure, the number of colored and white people, transportation facilities, sources of income, schools and colleges for whites and Negroes. I had to clothe this bare skeleton of facts with personal observations and as many interviews as possible within the alloted time, and cross check the answers I received to some thirty questions I usually propounded. Additionally, I sought to hire an agent for the *Courier* if there was none, or visit the one we had.

I kept up this hectic pace for eight months without respite, without missing a town, and without untoward incident. I nowhere concealed my mission and purpose, and everywhere got the cooperation from the colored and white I solicited. One sheriff even offered to let me sleep in the jail if I could find no better accommodation. His offer was not accepted, but he meant well.

From the beginning I realized that my purpose was not to reform the South but to report on it, and to try to improve the *Courier's* reputation and increase its sales. If local Negroes had not been able in decades to improve their lot, what alien could do so in a couple of days, or should even try? I felt then and feel now that it is the responsibility of the people of every community to solve their local problems. So I obeyed the laws, asked pertinent questions, kept my eyes open, and wrote down the facts and my conclusions. I tried to present an accurate picture, not a caricature; to remain an observer, not become a partisan. I have always felt that to be the role of a good reporter.

Naturally I had (and needed) more contact with the colored than with the white people, but what I had with the latter was proper. I was courteous and well-mannered but never obsequious, and any attitude of some whites that was intended to make me feel that I was a member of an inferior caste failed because I ignored it. Many a crude and hostile storekeeper or clerk who had originally greeted me with a gruff and offensive manner became affable and friendly after a few minutes' conversation. When curious and suspicious police officers asked me what I was doing in town, I told them frankly and forthrightly. There was no point in pretending that I was anything but what I was because some local Negro informer would tell them anyway, and probably had already done so, as often happened. So swiftly does news travel.

I soon systematized my routine: learning the town by being driven about, the while interviewing the taxi driver, then talking to the landlady or hotel man, the barber and others, after getting my roll of current *Couriers* from the postoffice for distribution as samples as I went about. In the afternoons I visited the professional people to get their version of what I had earlier picked up. A large city took more time, naturally, than a small one; and where the latter might be done in a day of intensive work, a large town might take two or three days. Some interviewees were more frank than others, but I learned that frankness is no guarantee of truth, and truth does not mean the same thing to everybody. A reporter must avoid being gullible. I found a great deal of local pride.

Going from town to town in this manner, I gathered an immense amount of information, observations and impressions. It added much to my education. This intimate knowledge of the South and its people served me very well in later writings and discussions, and I later applied the methodology perfected in these daily investigations to Europe, Latin America, and Africa. I made a large number of acquaintances who later proved to be valuable and trustworthy sources of information.

Some of these, a number of them white, became my good friends. Many of my most pleasant experiences have been in the Southern states, and I learned that race relations there varied from county to county and from state to state, and I came to quickly detect the varying nuances that make communities distinctive, and these influences on the direction of Negro life. To me the myth of white "hatred" of Negroes was soon dissipated. I learned that it was dangerous to generalize; that while the protocol of race relations was everywhere maintained, it was more loose and variable in some places than in others, and in some people more than in others; that people were humans and individuals before they were racial stereotypes. I have since found that this holds true all over the earth.

Prior to leaving New York on my long journey through the South, I submitted an article, "The Negro Art Hokum," to *The Nation*'s Fred Kirchwey. The venerable weekly, then as now, was Fabian Socialist. The article ridiculed the current gabble about a distinctive Negro art and literature. I argued that such artistic performance by colored American artists would in the very nature of things be indistinguishable from other American art; that the American Negro was just a lampblacked Anglo-Saxon, and could no more escape the imprint of his environment than colored people in other lands had done. He was an American, albeit a lower caste one, and had no more recollection of, connection with, or interest in Africa than any other American. This was treason at a time when there was so much talk about African heritage.

For months I learned nothing about the piece. Finally in the early spring I received a letter from Miss Kirchwey, forwarded from *The Pittsburgh Courier* to Tyler, Texas. She explained that the delay in publishing my article was caused by the necessity of letting a lot of Negro intellectuals around town, like James Weldon Johnson and Charles S. Johnson, read it and getting their opinions of it. Later in the spring *The Nation* finally published "The Negro Art Hokum," and I received a check for fifteen dollars.

Returning to New York, I found that so far as the Communist conspiracy was concerned, I had missed nothing. The Reds were getting nowhere either with blacks or whites, but a few zealots were trying. Things were better in New York, socially and economically. There was very little unemployment and a great deal of gaiety. The Roaring Twenties was quite a reality. Few were concerned with Communism or socialism. Through the intermediary activities of Carl Van Vechten and others, downtown was "discovering" Negro Harlem and vice versa.

Randolph was engrossed in the organization of the Brotherhood of Sleeping Car Porters. I had been one of the speakers at its founding mass meeting in Elks Hall on West 130th Street the previous August. Neither the Pullman Company nor the American Federation of Labor had yet recognized it. Wallace Thurman, the author of *The Blacker the Berry, Infants of the Spring,* and the Broadway play *Harlem,* had my old job at *The Messenger.* My sole income from *The Pittsburgh Courier* was for my column, and it was very small. However, in August, 1926, Ira F. Lewis, the general manager, asked me to try my hand at writing the paper's editorials, offering an addition to my stipend. I began in the middle of August and with the exception of a few intervals when I was out of the country on foreign assignments, I continued writing them until November, 1964, when new ownership and new management suddenly relieved me of that chore, after thirty-eight years of commenting on national and international events for our readership, which sometimes totalled 350,000.

The Communists, then led by the likes of Jack Stachel, Jay Lovestone, William Z. Foster and Benjamin Gitlow, had no viable tactics for corralling Negroes. The good life of the mid-Twenties was so dazzling that Negroes could not be lured to Red meetings to be told how miserable was their lot under capitalism. Nor could many young Negroes be suckered into interracial house parties where greasy, unattractive, white Communist Party girls pawed over them while guzzling bootleg gin and spouting Marxism. Some few Negroes attended these sessions for the physical and alcoholic advantages accruing from such association. A handful were hooked but the others went two or three times and abandoned them for greener fields in the Village.

For a while there was a type of labor school set up in Harlem. Such places, however, could not compete with The Bamboo Inn, The Savoy, The Nest, the YWCA, the YMCA, the numerous church activities designed to hold members, and the numerous basement clubs on side streets between Lenox and Seventh Avenues. What little the Reds sought to sell Negroes, they were not buying.

Personally, I was thinking a lot about what I had seen during my travels in the South by way of Negro progress in farming, business and insurance, and the potential for self-help with which I have always been concerned. I saw no future for radicalism in that equation. It might well retard the Negro's progress.

In December, 1926, Wallace Thurman quit *The Messenger* for bigger things and Randolph appointed me managing editor. As the official organ of the Brotherhood of Sleeping Car Porters, there was more money for salary and expansion. I started using colorful covers drawn by an artist friend in Greenwich Village; introduced a page of satirical cartoons by Wilbert L. Holloway of *The Pittsburgh Courier* (with whom I have collaborated ever since), used some articles from abroad, encouraged J. A. Rogers to do a monthly article on great men and women in Negro history (thus anticipating the rash of such articles and books in the 1960's), got Eugene Gordon of *The Boston Post* to make a monthly appraisal of the best editorials appearing in the Negro press, began a series of "inside" stories on Washington's Negro society, and tried to get a good short story for each issue. Among the first were tales by Zora Neale Hurston and Langston Hughes.

Simultaneously, I was doing a weekly satirical column for *The Interstate Tattler,* which featured Negro show business and night life. *The Nation* carried my sarcastic piece "Blessed Are the Sons of Ham" and *The New Masses* ran my collection of sketches on the seamier side of the South entitled "Southern Snapshots" which appealed to its Communist taste. Significantly, Mike Gold, its fire-eating Red editor, left out those sketches he

159

thought might be offensive to white people, in typical bourgeois journalistic manner. Mike, who had once joined with other Reds in working out a blueprint for taking over New York City when the Revolution came, was sufficiently agile to wangle ten thousand dollars out of the Wall Street banker, Otto Kahn, to establish a proletarian theater in the Village. This was one of the first, after the Provincetown Playhouse, of the rash of side street little theaters infesting the area now. One of Mike's first playwrights was John Howard Lawson, who later was among the notorious Hollywood Ten who defied the House Committee on Un-American Activities. Around that time the new *American Mercury* had carried Eugene O'Neill's phony *All God's Chillun Got Wings,* which was regarded as daring enough in those days for Mayor Hylan to refuse permission for colored and white children to appear in it. The "liberal" *New York World* came out editorially against it, I recall, because it dealt with interracial marriage which some thirty states then banned.

Significantly, *El Sol,* a Communist magazine in Mexico City, promptly reprinted "Southern Snapshots," but the honorable Mike Gold never saw that I got paid for it. Other Red magazines may also have carried it in the general piracy characteristic of the solar system of Communist publications.

After my Southern tour, I concluded that most of the Negro's difficulties and problems could be greatly ameliorated through his own efforts in cooperation with willing whites who recognized that such would be mutually advantageous. I had seen where this had been done on many occasions in real estate, insurance companies and banks. There was no lack of communication between members of the two "races" who had anything to communicate. Agitating for anything other than our present form of government would be futile and dangerous and would retard Negroes rather than advance them. I was convinced that they would be far worse off under any collectivist system, and for that matter, so would the whites, as is amply demonstrated in Soviet Russia.

Now another Negro conference was being planned, this time by the Negro business and educational community of Durham,

North Carolina, for the Christmas holidays, 1927, in cooperation with the white community. Durham was an outstanding example of what Negroes could accomplish for themselves. It was headquarters of the North Carolina Mutual Life Insurance Company, the largest Negro-owned business in the country. There was also a flourishing bank, a fire insurance company, many successful smaller businesses, and the impressive North Carolina College for Negroes. There were numerous Negro-owned tobacco farms in the vicinity. The stress at this upcoming conference would be on self-help, and there would be speakers from many parts of the country. Randolph and I were both going.

At the invitation of Henry L. Mencken, who was always favorably disposed toward Negro writers who had anything to say, I did an article called "Our White Folks" for the December, 1927 issue of *The American Mercury*. It was an irreverent, slashing appraisal which so delighted Mencken that he made it the lead article, a great distinction. The piece was extensively advertised in newspapers, magazines and on all street newsstands and those in the subways and "els." It received vast comment in the press here and in England, and I received literally hundreds of letters.

This was followed by my satirical piece, "The Negro's Greatest Gift to America," in the collectanea, *Ebony and Topaz*, edited by Charles S. Johnson, investigator of the Chicago race riot, editor of the National Urban League's magazine, *Opportunity*, and later the first Negro president of Fisk University. It was a distinguished gathering of colored and white talent—poets, artists, and essayists. Today it is a collectors' item. My piece later appeared in a Modern Library collection. The gift I referred to was simply that of being present here, which made white people assume a superiority unknown in Europe.

CHAPTER 11

THAT SUMMER my whole life had been changed by the arrival in New York of one of our contributors from San Francisco, Josephine Cogdell. She had written poems and essays for us but had not informed us that she was coming to the metropolis. Then one day, unannounced, she walked into my office. Beautiful, charming, vivacious, fashionably dressed, sharp, witty, and well-read, she was something very special. It was one of my busy days, but we talked all afternoon about reading and writing, about literature and politics, about art and travel, and I think we had dinner at Tabb's, a fine restaurant at 140th Street and Lenox Avenue across from the Savoy, where often thereafter we went to dance. She was blonde and shapely.

Daughter of a Texas rancher and banker in the Fort Worth area, she was liberal on the race question without being mawkish and mushy. She saw Negroes as I saw whites, as individuals. She had been a Mack Sennett girl in Hollywood, and a model and ballet dancer in San Francisco. She had a surprising grasp

of international politics, and she had seen through both socialism and Communism, and their inevitable connection. This
was rare in the intellectual milieu of the time when almost
everyone was agog over the Soviet "experiment." Perhaps that
was due to the fact that, like myself, she had actually read the
grist of collectivist "classics" rather than skimmed through a
few Red pamphlets. On the Pacific Coast she had met such
Communist stalwarts as Mike Gold and Jim Dolsen, the numerous hibernating Indian revolutionists, the food faddists and
many members of the queer sects proliferating in California.

We got on famously that summer and fall, making the rounds
of theaters, movies, dance halls, lectures, and exhibitions from
Greenwich Village to Harlem. She was the first girl I had ever
met who embodied all the things I most desired in a woman.
It was inevitable that we should fall in love and marry. The
place was New York's marriage bureau and the date was January 6, 1928. We are happily married to this day.

The colored community was so impressed by my *American
Mercury* article that a testimonial dinner was arranged for me
by Mrs. Geraldine Dismond (now Gerry Major of *Jet*), a leading Harlem socialite and columnist on *The Interstate Tattler*.
It was held in the heart of Harlem in the Venetian Tea Room,
and the diners were a cross-section of the professional and business community. It was an auspicious occasion, and I could
not help reflecting that just five years before I had been vege-
tating in the basement at Tenth Street and Avenue A!

Another by-product of *The American Mercury* article was
being invited to speak in many parts of the country. Miss Emma
Lou Sayers, a Los Angeles journalist, arranged for speeches
there and in Oakland, Seattle, Pasadena, and San Diego. I
appeared at Carnegie Lecture Hall in Pittsburgh, the Berean
School in Philadelphia, and several other places. This became
an annual thing until near the end of World War II. Topics
in the early days were "Psychoanalyzing the Negro," "Feminism
and the Race Problem," "Negro Art and Other Illusions," "The
Negro's Next Step" and "Consumers' Cooperation." In later
years as I went around the college and forum circuit, I talked

164

mostly on the need for self-help, organizing for economic advancement, and youngsters preparing for new fields of employment rather than concentrating on teaching and preaching.

I had been much influenced by Albert Jay Nock and his weekly individualist magazine, *The Freeman,* where Suzanne LaFollette was managing editor. It more nearly expressed my conservative views than any publication of the time. I was delighted when it devoted an entire page to a piece I had written in *The Messenger* dealing with economic self-help through consumers' cooperation. At the same time I was closely following the writings of Dr. Henry P. Warbasse of the Cooperative League of the United States. It seemed to me then that a combination of consumers cooperation and an investment trust offered most to the Negro.

When *The Messenger* died in July, 1928, it was the editor of *The Pittsburgh Courier,* the late Robert L. Vann, who came to the rescue. During a talk in New York, he asked if I would be interested in going to Chicago to edit a weekly magazine insert for a large number of the bigger Negro newspapers. It was to be published by the W. B. Ziff Company, the foreign advertising agency for almost all of the Negro newspapers. The magazine was to be printed three weeks in advance and freighted to the various newspapers involved in the enterprise. The combined circulation would be more than a quarter million copies, and this would bring in considerable advertising revenue for the members to share. William B. Ziff was an enterprising live-wire salesman who had got his start selling advertising space for *The Chicago Defender,* then the largest circulating Negro newspaper, which copied closely the format and flamboyance of the *Chicago Tribune.* William B. Ziff was a Jew, and he had prospered, for when he started, Negro advertising solicitors were not welcome in the big advertising offices. Indeed, some of the more enterprising had to go up in freight elevators. This is further evidence of how far America has come in race relations.

I accepted the position enthusiastically. Along with my *Courier* pay, the new salary would make my income greater than it ever had been. So leaving to Josephine to send the new furnishings we had in our three room apartment on St. Nicholas Avenue, I departed for Chicago and a new adventure.

By Labor Day I was in a spacious office in the Transportation Building on the corner of Harrison and Dearborn Streets in the Loop. After looking around on the South Side for a couple of weeks, I rented a very nice four room apartment in the 5100 block on South Parkway opposite South Park which was just opening to colored occupancy. It was a lovely nest and when Josephine came she was delighted with it, and with furnishing and decorating it.

The magazine insert was printed by *The Drovers' Journal* press in the stockyards. It had a rigid deadline for all copy. Strictly at eleven o'clock Saturday mornings I had to be there with the complete dummy, taking the elevated to the plant. Everybody observed this deadline except the advertising solicitors, and this became the weekly headache. I had set a deadline of five o'clock Friday evening for advertising copy. Coming in early on Saturday morning I would put the final touches on the dummy and take the elevated in time to get to the press at eleven. At least that was my plan, but just as I would prepare to leave the office for the press, here would come a salesman with a 500-, 1000- or 2,500-line advertisement or two. This necessitated tearing down the dummy to find room for the new advertising, since we could not go beyond a prescribed number of pages. This made me late at the press and we had to pay for overtime, against which Bill Ziff vociferously complained. He would not back me up on the advertising deadline because he said he could not afford to refuse any revenue.

This situation became intolerable, so in February, 1929, I gave notice to Bill that I was quitting. Of course he begged me to stay but I could take it no longer. I did relent to the extent that I would stay on for another month to train a successor.

There was a young man among Ziff's salesman who had just graduated from an Ivy League college and was learning advertising. He was Benjamin J. Davis, Jr., son of the wealthy Benjamin J. Davis, editor of *The Atlanta Independent,* powerful fraternalist and Republican National Committeeman from

Georgia. I had met the elder Davis when I visited Atlanta during my Southern tour. Young Ben was as amiable as his father, and we had a good time during the month we were together. He dined at our apartment several times and listened to our latest records.

Ben was not a Communist then, was not even thinking about it, but even after he became one we always got on well together. He was one of the few Communists I knew who had a sense of humor. I think his treatment as a young lawyer in the Atlanta courts was a contributing factor in leading him astray. Then, too, Ben had a considerable streak of opportunism and cynicism. The following year the office of the Illustrated Feature Section was moved from Ziff's office in Chicago to that of the *Afro-American* in Baltimore. He bought several of my feature stories. One in particular was ridiculed as far-fetched sensationalism because I predicted that Negroes would some day rule Manhattan Island. In 1952, a Negro, Hulan Jack, became borough president, and twelve years later another Negro, J. Raymond Jones, became chairman of the Democratic county committee, or leader of Tammany Hall.

Leaving Josephine behind to pack up in Chicago, I returned to New York City and rented a three room apartment in a brand new house on Edgecombe Avenue on what was facetiously called Sugar Hill because so many high-income Negroes lived up there. My income was not nearly as high as it had been recently, but with speaking engagements and free-lance writing, and writing fiction for the *Courier* under various *noms de plume,* I was making the grade.

Communist efforts to subvert and corral the Negroes were in the doldrums. There was a lot of theorizing but no practical plans. This probably reflected the uncertainties in the world Communist movement, Stalin not yet having consolidated his power. So-called white chauvinism of the mainly foreign-born American party membership, who understood little about the Negro and cared less, was a barrier to attracting Negro members. With the coming of the resolutions of the Sixth World Congress in 1928, which stressed equal rights and the determination to enter into and direct the Negro struggle, things began to pick up. Several Negroes were recruited to go to Russia as technicians, which was a greater opportunity than they had at home. This got quite a play in the Negro press. Then, in 1930, the Comintern invented the concept and slogan of Self-Determination for the Black Belt (a Negro "Republic" in the South). This puzzled and revolted the black comrades. I wrote at the time that this was merely a revival of the old slave plantation under Communist direction, and that the Negroes would have none of it.

To woo the black bourgeoisie, the League of Struggle for Negro Rights was formed with the poet Langston Hughes as president. This gave the Reds their first inroad into the Negro middle- and upper-class element. The LSNR was simply another Communist front with a telephone-booth size membership, but the effectiveness of such cells cannot be gauged by size. Hughes had won the acclaim of the white literary world during the misnamed Negro Renaissance, so he was honored and respected among the Negro Talented Tenth from whence the fellow travelers of the future were to come.

Other than commenting saltily on these developments, there was little for a Negro anti-Communist to do in that period. However, I was busily engaged in other and more important endeavors. I had several speaking engagements, I was doing free lance writing for the Illustrated Feature Section which I had edited in Chicago, columns, editorials and short stories for the *Pittsburgh Courier,* and additional contributions to the *American Mercury.* These included "Keeping The Negro in His Place," in August, 1929; "A Negro Looks Ahead," in February, 1930; "Traveling Jim Crow," in August, 1930, and "Black Warriors," in November, 1930. I was in good company in those pages with such fellow contributors as James Branch Cabell, Lloyd Lewis, Benjamin DeCasseres, Howard W. Odum, George Jean Nathan, Chester T. Crowell, J. Frank Dobie, Sherwood Anderson, Herbert Asbury, Henry F. Pringle, Edward Sapir, C. Hartley Grattan, and Hoffman Nickerson. Altogether my association with the *American Mercury* under its various owners and editors extended from 1927 to 1961, during which time I had a score of my articles printed.

My literary association with E. Haldeman-Julius of Girard, Kansas, began in the fall of 1928 when I had a piece published in his short lived quarterly, the *American Parade*. The article was "Racial Intermarriage in the United States" which he later republished as *Little Blue Book No. 1387*. Later I did another piece for him, "The Stronghold of Prohibition," on the workings of Volsteadism in Mississippi, which appeared in a magazine he published irregularly.

Haldeman-Julius, an East Side New York Jew, a Marxist who married a wealthy Kansas girl and went out there to live, was a publishing genius who in many ways reminded me of Willi Muenzenberg, except that he took no active part in politics. He published for the masses, bringing out hundreds of titles in the familiar blue paperbacks that sold for only a nickel. He specialized in publishing boiled-down versions of classics. At the same time he, like Muenzenberg, was able to attract many writers of standing. For instance, in the issue of *The American Parade* in which my piece on intermarriage appeared, there were such contributors as Remy de Gourmont, T. Swann Harding, Bertrand Russell, Clarence Darrow, and Walter White.

One of my best literary portraits was "Woof" which appeared in November, 1928, in the one issue magazine *Harlem* which appeared while I was in Chicago. Woof was the nickname of First Sergeant William Glass of Company H, Twenty-Fifth U.S. Infantry. The editor of *Harlem* was Wallace Thurman, and the first (and last!) issue had as contributors such figures of the "Renaissance" as Alain Locke, Walter White, Georgia Douglas Johnson, Richard Bruce, Langston Hughes, Allison Davis, Aaron Douglas, and Roy de Coverly. It also included one of the finest short story writers colored America produced, Dr. George W. Little of Homestead, Pennsylvania, the capable chronicler of a steel mill town. His story "Two Dollars" in *Harlem* was sent in to Thurman, who was crying for first class stuff, because it was a little too strong for the Illustrated Feature Section. I subsequently bought several of Dr. Little's stories when I was handling features for the *Courier*. Ironically, this man never appeared in any of the collections of "best stories."

One of the *avant garde* publications of the time was *The Modern Quarterly,* edited in Baltimore, Maryland, by V. F. Calverton (George Goetz) and Samuel D. Schmalhausen. Calverton asked me to do a piece for them and "Emancipated Woman and the Negro" appeared in the Fall 1929 issue. Among the contributors were Eugene Jolas, Pierre Loving, Edwin Seaver, Herbert Gorman, and T. Swann Harding. In the following issue I reviewed for the *Quarterly* a book of black folktales by Samuel Gaillard Stoney and Gertrude Mathews Shelby, entitled *Black Genesis*. More interesting were the other reviewers, including Floyd Dell, Gamaliel Bradford, Charles Yale Harrison, and John Chamberlain.

By February, 1934, when the *Modern Quarterly* had become *The Modern Monthly,* I did a piece entitled "When Black Weds White." This was reprinted as the lead article in the June, 1934, issue of the German magazine, *Die Auslese,* which reprinted each month the twenty-five most important articles which appeared in the leading magazines of the United States, England, Germany, Holland, Italy, Spain, Japan and China. In August, 1930, the young *Reader's Digest* bought the rights to my "Traveling Jim Crow" and carried a truncated version.

Calverton used my "Negro's Greatest Gift to America" in his *Anthology of American Negro Literature*. More important, he encouraged me to write by first book, *Black No More,* a satire on the American race question, which was the first, I believe, to treat the subject with levity. He was instrumental in getting The Macaulay Company to publish it, and it came out in January, 1931, with very good reviews.

Aside from writing, lecturing, and my weekly editorial task, I developed an interest in Harlem politics, as a student rather than a participant. Despite the growing Negro population and voting registration, all of the Democratic district leaders were white, the most prominent at that time being James J. (Jimmy) Hines, mentor of the gangster Dutch Schultz and owner of several bars. Although there were more Negro Republicans than

Democrats, sentiment was changing. To speed it along, Ferdinand Q. Morton, the Harvard-educated Mississippian who was the first Negro member of the Civil Service Commission of New York City, got together with a group of like-minded Democratic Negro jobholders and established The United Colored Democracy, a large clubhouse located in the center of Harlem on Seventh Avenue. Young bloods of the community assembled there nightly to talk, make acquaintance, and play poker. It was there that I made friends with Ferd Morton, Dr. Louis T. Wright (later surgical director of Harlem Hospital), Chauncey Hooper (later retired as brigadier general in the New York National Guard) and Charles E. Toney and James Watson (who each later served twenty years as municipal judges). There also I met Lonnie Hicks, retired piano player, gambler, and operator of the Symphony Club in the basement of the Lafayette Theater building who introduced me to many of the old timers in music and show business. Lonnie contributed heavily to the United Colored Democracy and was a close associate of Morton and Dr. Wright. Their objective was to win control of the area from the whites and, accordingly, the fat political patronage.

I never joined the Democratic Party but I wrote a couple of campaign pamphlets for it. I have usually voted Republican although I have often wondered why I should, especially with the increasing me-tooism of the party spokesmen and bosses.

Later, when there was need for a mouthpiece for the group, Lonnie subsidized a small newspaper, the *National News,* which I edited in the spring and summer of 1932.

However, my principal interest in 1930 was trying to organize the Young Negroes' Cooperative League for the purpose of having groups in each city to study the principles and practices of consumers' cooperation, form buying clubs and eventually open stores. I had given a great deal of thought to this, written about it, and discussed it with Cedric Long of the Cooperative League as well as Dr. Warbasse. Since the urban Negroes lived in sharply defined neighborhoods, then as now, the idea was to organize the Negroes on a neighborhood basis for retail selling and then cooperate with the whites in the district and area wholesale cooperatives. This would avoid the obstacles that have tripped so many interracial efforts while at the same time enabling the two groups of consumers to function to mutual advantage. So far as I know, nobody has come up with a better plan for general advancement and the increase of interracial amity and understanding to the profit of all.

I zealously proselyted the colored community through my column which was widely read, and in a few months there were several score adherents in a few dozen cities. I put out a pamphlet which was widely distributed across the country. Before long there were a dozen buying clubs in operation. I do not have the capacity for group organization, and the group needed an administrator, somebody with a clear understanding of the principles of Rochdale consumers' cooperation, and there had not been sufficient time to develop such people. I had no money, income from dues was of necessity slight, and I had to devote most of my time to the sheer mechanics of making a living. Nevertheless by the end of the year the prospects were hopeful.

The summer saw me attending the annual conference of the NAACP in Springfield, Massachusetts. Afterward, in August, I was asked to teach newswriting and reporting to about 150 farm and home demonstration agents at an agricultural extension course held at South Carolina State College at Orangeburg. The course was for two weeks and the summer was one of the hottest on record. The Department of Agriculture under whose auspices the school was held later informed me that my contribution had been very important. It was the first time I had taught a class since the post school at Fort Lawton, Washington, eighteen years before.

During that late spring, at the behest of Wallace A. Battle, field secretary of the American Church Institute for Negroes of the Protestant Episcopal Church, I visited the largest four of the eight schools operated in the South for Negroes. These were St. Augustine's, St. Paul's, Vorhees, and Fort Valley. I had first met Mr. Battle five years before when I visited Okolona Institute, Mississippi, where he was principal. He was later stationed in New York and we were good friends. The article I subsequently wrote about the schools was published in *The Spirit of Mission* for February, 1931. Incidentally, the first time I saw a copy of the magazine was in the library of the Episcopal mission in Cape Mount, Liberia, as I had left the United States before it was published.

Toward the end of 1930, I got a call one day from George Palmer Putnam, the publisher, who was then heading a newly organized firm, Brewer, Warren, and Putnam. He was much disturbed about conditions in Liberia where a League of Nations mission (whose secretary was Charles S. Johnson) had rendered its frightening report on the selling of "boys" to the Spanish plantations on the island of Fernando Po off the coast of Nigeria and on the deep involvement of the President and highest officials of Liberia. They were getting fifty dollars for each "boy" recruited and this was being split three ways; one-third for the district commissioner who "recruited" the laborers with his armed forces, one-third to the President, and one-third to the Spanish consul, also a Liberian.

The usual method, it seemed, was to surround a village before dawn, fire a volley from the old Krag rifles, and then pick out the "boys" wanted as they rushed out of their huts, and march them tethered to a coast warehouse to await the Spanish vessel which would transport them to the malarious island a thousand miles to the southeast.

Mr. Putnam thought there was a book in it and he was looking for someone to write it. He asked Arthur Spingarn, the lawyer, bibliophile, and later president of the NAACP, to recommend someone, and Spingarn referred Putnam to me. After some initial conversation, Putnam asked me if I would come to his apartment on West 58th Street near the Plaza Hotel, and bring down some of my published work. I took my *American Mercury, The Messenger, Nation,* and pieces published by Haldeman-Julius, along with some columns and editorials from *The Pittsburgh Courier.* This made quite a little package, and apparently the doorman mistook me for a messenger. At any rate he directed me to the next door, a few feet west on 58th Street, which turned out to be the delivery entrance. Rather irritated by this, I returned to the lobby and asked that George Putnam be called on the telephone. He told me to wait there, and in a few minutes he was down in a raging fury, bawling everybody out for insulting his guest.

I merely mention this incident because it was typical of the times, and shows how far New York has come since then. A couple of years later when I went to visit Harvey Firestone, Jr., in his suite at the Ritz-Carlton, the elevator operator hesitated about carrying me up until the frightened desk clerk gesticulated and yelled across the lobby, "It's all right! It's all right! For Mr. Firestone!" When I related the incident to Mr. Firestone, he was angry because he had previously advised the management that I was to be brought up without ado. He called the manager and admonished him.

A couple of hours later when I came downstairs, I noticed that there was a uniformed flunkey standing at the revolving door pushing it as each guest departed so the latter would not have to do so. As I approached the door, his white-gloved hand froze to his side, and I pushed the door open myself, finding the whole thing vastly amusing. The holier-than-thou attitude of "liberal" New York toward its Southern sister cities is one acquired only in the past thirty-odd years with regard to the accommodation of Negroes.

George Putnam and Amelia Earhart, the aviatrix, were then engaged, and she was there in the suite, looking exotic and relaxed in lovely Oriental pajamas. They were very hospitable and in an hour's chat the project was agreed upon. I was to go to Liberia, cover the country getting evidence to substantiate the charges of slavery and oppression, write a series of articles for an as yet undetermined number of daily newspapers, and gather material for the book.

Two things, speed and secrecy, were essential, so aside from the publisher, Josephine, Julian Mason, editor of the *New York Evening Post,* who was arranging the sale of the newspaper series, and Arthur Springarn, nobody knew where I was going or why.

There was a hectic month of preparation, getting necessary credentials, boning up on Liberia and telling Ira F. Lewis of the *Courier* enough to assure that my weekly paycheck would keep coming to Josephine during the months I was gone. I promised to keep writing my column *Views and Reviews* but the editorials would have to be written in Pittsburgh. I did not tell either Vann or Lewis exactly why I was going abroad—only that I was taking a trip. I took these precautions because I knew the reputation of the Liberian government, and that it was especially touchy after the international exposure of its sins. Then, too, I had read the report of Poston, the special emissary of Marcus Garvey to Liberia, and the very unflattering opinions he expressed. More important than anything else, I had seen the eyewitness statements of Henry F. Downing, author of *An American Cavalryman* and one-time U.S. consul in Luanda, Angola, who knew Africa's West Coast like a book.

Communications except by costly cable or wireless were difficult. There was no air mail, and even if there had been, Liberia had no airport, and did not have one until World War II when the United States built both an airport and a dock. Only about one ship a week touched at Monrovia. There were not a hundred miles of road in the country, and that mostly on the Firestone rubber plantation, so all travel would be on foot or in a hammock. I had to buy hobnailed leather boots and a tall thermos bottle with a leather case from Macy's, hunting shorts, shirts, and a white pith helmet from Abercrombie & Fitch, a .45 automatic pistol and ammunition. Added to all that, I knew nobody in the country and could trust no one, save possibly the Virginia-born Negro businessman, Thomas Faulkner, who had been a long-time thorn in the hide of the government because he was progressive. Even getting a passport was a chore because birth records were rarely kept when I was born, and I had to gather affidavits to support my nationality. My military descriptive list was helpful. At least ten days were required to get a passport after application, and then came the matter of a British visa, as I would have to remain in the United Kingdom for ten or twelve days to make connections. There I planned to get my Liberian visa. Just to play safe I got both French and Spanish visas.

In addition to all this, Josephine had few friends or acquaintances in Harlem, so there would be long months alone. There was Mrs. Elise Ayer, the school assistant principal, and Miss Ella J. Baker who was associated with me in the Young Negroes Cooperative League; and such friends as A. Philip Randolph, Theophilus Lewis, L. F. Coles and my *Courier* colleague, Floyd Calvin. Otherwise she was, no matter how resourceful, alone. Nor could one telephone in an emergency. In Monrovia I heard there were telephones but the system was so bad that it was simpler to use messengers. Outside Monrovia one used drums. So traveling to Liberia then was like journeying into outer space today; except that nowadays everybody knows where your space vehicle is, all of the time, and there is ready intercommunication. All news in Liberia would be history. This was something to ponder.

Finally, on Saturday, January 24, 1931, I was off, first class, on *R. M. S. Scythia* under Captain G. Gibbons, from New York to Cobh and Liverpool. Josephine saw me off on that pleasant afternoon. When the crack Cunard Line vessel stopped in Boston the following day, I surprised Josephine by telephoning her from the ship for a final goodbye.

The *Scythia* was all that the discriminating passenger could reasonably expect. It was quite luxurious, with spacious salons, large library, store, and majestic dining room reached by a grand staircase; an elaborate cuisine, with menu and wine list of equal size. There was a five-piece string orchestra for dinner and for dancing. Everyone dressed for dinner and the general atmosphere of affluence was demonstrated by the huge bowls of caviar wheeled from table to table along with other hors d'oeuvres. Cheese was served not in individual portions but with the entire cheese on a wooden platter. Waiters were inconspicuous, attentive but not unpleasantly obsequious. The

176

wine steward with his broad chain and keys strode majestically among the tables. This was a far cry from the hog maw, chitterling, and barbecue rib joints in which I had eaten usually during my eight-month journey through Dixie.

Being alone, as well as colored, I was assigned to a two-seat table. On some occasions, however, other passengers invited me to their tables. Colored first class passengers, stewards informed me, were rather unusual; but before the voyage was even half-finished there was no evidence of racial aloofness. Indeed, I got some valuable tips from businessmen who had visited Liberia.

Knowing I was visiting England, I had written ahead to the Cooperative Wholesale Society of Great Britain at One Balloon St., Manchester, telling them that I was en route and the probable time of my arrival. Aware of the difficulty Negroes were having with hotel accommodations in England, from reading of the embarrassing experiences of the four Mills Brothers, Marcus Garvey, and others, I wired from the *Scythia* to the swank Midland Hotel in Liverpool for a reservation for room with bath. I hoped thereby to circumvent the obvious anti-colored conspiracy. However, when I arrived at the Midland, the woman desk clerk quickly announced that the hostelry was "full up," which was astounding at that season, months before the tourist rush. Unabashed by my incredulity, she said she could get me a room at the Northwestern, their second-class hotel, which turned out to be satisfactory.

This was one of the chain of hotels owned by the London, Midland and Scottish Railway, and when you stayed in one, they would make a reservation for the next one in your itinerary. This worked for the Midland in Manchester (and the Cooperative Wholesale Society may have had something to do with it) but it did not work in London. Upon my arrival at the LMS hotel there, the desk clerk admitted she had my reservation but that they were "full up" because the boat train had just arrived from Holland. She recommended several other hotels in the vicinity, but after trying a dozen the cab driver took pity on me and told me of a theatrical hotel on Shaftesbury Avenue hard by Piccadilly Circus, where I was accepted.

In Liverpool I bought about fifty dollars worth of trinkets and useful items from Woolworth's three-and-six-pence store as "dash" or presents to town chiefs in Liberia and also made a very fruitful visit to a mission serving colored people there. Most of them were sailors and almost all were married to English women. These white wives fought to get a square deal and equal rights for their husbands and children, but it was tough going. There was absolutely no work for colored people, not even sweeping streets or the lowest domestic work. There was nothing ahead for colored girls except marriage or prostitution. I subsequently discovered that a similar condition existed in Manchester, Birmingham, London, and Cardiff. This was scarcely calculated to enhance my esteem for the British Empire, especially when I learned that there had been race riots during and after World War I between black imported labor and domestic workers.

In Manchester the CWS people rolled out the red carpet. I was given a special luncheon and Harry Massey of the publicity department was assigned to take me on a tour of some of the 110 factories of this concern, the largest of its kind in the world. It was most instructive and inspiring. On another day I accompanied Massey and his cameraman many miles upcountry to Skelsmeredale, a coal town, reminiscent of parts of West Virginia, except that the working people wore wooden shoes which clattered on the cobblestones as they walked. We dined at the home of the cooperative's president, and later I had the experience of speaking a few minutes to the assembled members.

Massey and his associate had been so painstaking and diligent in showing me everything available that I asked them to join me in champagne and hors d'oeuvres at the Midland in its large supper room with trellised ceiling five stories high. They enjoyed it immensely but then seriously asked me not to mention it to the people at the CWS headquarters! Apparently the class system was still strong in England. People still spoke with almost comical respect of members of the nobility. And one evening after the public houses had closed I asked a fellow I was interviewing to come up to my place, continue the talk and have a couple of drinks. He recoiled with consternation and said, "Oh, no sir. That's too good for me!" It was hard to imagine the average American saying that.

Removed from the American scene I knew nothing of the great interest and even furor raised by *Black No More,* and under the circumstances there was no way for me to find out until I returned from Africa. I did get one letter from J. A. Rogers who was in Paris, fresh from Abyssinia where as correspondent of the *New York Amsterdam News* he had covered the coronation of Ras Tafari as the Emperor Haile Selassie. I had sent him the book sometime before my departure, with my Manchester address in care of the CWS. He was vastly delighted by it.

Also while I was away, Farrar & Rinehart published on March 19, 1931, a symposium, *Behold America!,* edited by Samuel D. Schmalhausen, in which there were thirty-three essays covering many intriguing and provocative subjects. My contribution was "Some Unsweet Truths About Race Prejudice." Some other contributors were Harry Elmer Barnes, Robert Morss Lovett, Robert Herrick, John Haynes Holmes, T. Swann Harding, C. Hartley Grattan, Jerome Davis, John T. Flynn, A. J. Muste, James Oneal, Louis B. Boudin, McAlister Coleman, Henry Seidel Canby, Ernest Gruening, Pierre Loving, Gorham B. Munson, Edwin Seaver, Roger Baldwin, and V. F. Calverton. It was a 755-page tome, slightly on the Left, but several of the essays still live.

By this time I was deep in Liberia. I had left Liverpool on the M.V. *Adda* of the Elder Dempster Lines (Commander J. G. Shooter) on February 11, 1931, on the 3186-mile journey to Monrovia. There were 144 passengers in the "First Saloon," 33 in Second Class, while in the Third Class was one passenger noted by name and then "fifteen Natives" for Freetown. The color system was evident in that all of the colored first class passengers were conveniently assigned to the same table. These were Charles E. Mitchell, the new U.S. Minister to Liberia, and Mrs. Mitchell; Bishop Monroe H. Davis of the African Methodist Episcopal Church, Rev. T. J. Hughes and myself.

After the first rough two days across the Irish Sea and the Bay of Biscay during which few passengers used the dining room, it was clear sailing across a glassy sea. It was the most pleasant voyage in my recollection. The conversation at our table was scintillating, and with deck chairs abreast, the bishop, the diplomat, and I had a merry time.

Minister Mitchell was president of a small bank in Charleston, West Virginia, and had been business manager of West Virginia State College at Institute for a quarter century. He was a lifelong Republican and a power in West Virginia politics, whom I had first met when I visited the vicinity in November, 1925. Until he was appointed, ministers to Liberia received 5,000 dollars yearly while all other ministers (white) received twice as much. Mr. Mitchell would accept the job only with the stipulation that he was to receive the same pay as the others. He was also the first U.S. minister to bring a limousine to Liberia, although there was little occasion to use it, owing to the paucity of roads. Mrs. Mitchell, an inveterate traveler, had visited Europe a dozen times but had never been to Africa.

Bishop Davis, a big, hearty, jovial man who smoked cigars made from tobacco raised on his own plantation in South Carolina with his name stamped on the cellophane cover, had been in Africa before and his first foreign jurisdiction had been Liberia. He wanted no more of it. He denounced the Liberians as corrupt and as crooks of the worst kind. His knowledge of the country and his estimate of its ruling class were very valuable to me in understanding the people with whom I had to deal for the next several weeks.

Traveling with the Mitchells was most fortunate. It helped me in my dealing with the Liberian government. I stayed at the American Legation as their guest, ate at their table, and motored with them to the Firestone Plantation and the Booker T. Washington Industrial School at Kakata. Mr. Mitchell had brought his own cook-chauffeur, A. Wicks, with him to "keep these rascals from poisoning me." This was no mere persiflage. The last State Department man, a Mr. Reber, who served in the interim after the last Minister, Mr. Francis (who died in office), narrowly escaped poisoning through ground glass in his stew at a farewell dinner given for him. The thick forest areas of West Africa are virtual pharmacies from which hundreds of poisons can be extracted from berries, barks of trees, and the phantasmagoria of reptiles, animals, and insects. The natives are adept in the use of the homemade potions which can whisk one to the cemetery in jig time.

Although I had read and heard much of Monrovia, the capital since the "republic" was founded in 1847, I was quite unprepared for the squalor, filth, and degradation I encountered. Compared to it such all-Negro American towns as Boley, Oklahoma and Mound Bayou, Mississippi, were palatial. Monrovia with its unpaved, rock covered streets, unpainted ramshackle houses, and general slatternly appearance was repugnant and depressing. The swarms of goats helped keep down the weeds but nothing could keep down the odors and the mosquitoes. I described all of this in my newspaper series, in an article in *The American Mercury* ("Uncle Sam's Black Stepchild") and a piece in *Globe* magazine ("Monrovia Mooches On").

I had, of course, all of the necessary credentials. There was one from Julian Mason, editor-in-chief of the *New York Evening Post* (January 21, 1931) reading: "This letter will introduce Mr. George Schuyler who is serving as special correspondent of the *New York Evening Post* in looking into present conditions in Liberia."

Another, dated January 16, 1931, was from Edward K. Warren of Brewer, Warren, and Putnam reading: "This will introduce Mr. George S. Schuyler, distinguished American author and journalist. Mr. Schuyler is going to Liberia at our request, gathering material for a book which we shall publish. We bespeak for Mr. Schuyler friendly consideration and assistance."

On February 23rd I got my permit of residence in Liberia and four days later I had an interview with President Edwin Barclay in the Executive Mansion. On March 9th I was given permission by the Secretary of the Interior to carry my pistol with cartridges into the hinterland, its number having been registered with the War Department on March 3rd. All of these formalities were necessary to avoid difficulties outside Monrovia. Finally I used my powers of persuasion to get U.S. Minister Mitchell to permit young Vice Consul William George to accompany me on the long trek, which would be added protection en route besides affording me friendly companionship.

With the assistance of Mr. Hines, superintendent of the Firestone plantation (which had three or four thousand laborers), I was able to get a number of "boys" as carriers and, most important, a guide named Blackie (because he always wore a black shirt) who knew the country and the different tribal dialects.

The "boys" were to stay with me throughout the trek, being paid at the rate of one shilling (24-cents) a day upon their return. This was the prevailing rate, and any violation of it would bring the accusation of having flouted the wage standard of the country. Firestone had run into trouble with the Government by paying some of the more apt employees as much as fifty cents and one dollar daily. I intended not to make that mistake. However, I made up for this by making a side agreement that I would myself pay six pence a day for their food. This was an enormous concession because other bosses made them feed themselves out of their shilling pay. I did pay Blackie fifty cents daily because he was the guide and foreman.

The full crew that accompanied me for the entire 600 miles consisted of Zinna, Blackie, Zo, Lefto, Johnny, Davie, Bobo, Dinah, Todie, Georgie, Yama, Newboy, Mose and Bobo Number Two. Zinna was my steward. He prepared all of my meals, and I had him taste them before I ate. This was just playing safe in case some witch doctor got ideas!

With 150 pounds of salt, a case of Scotch and two cases of trade gin, 100 pounds of leaf tobacco, a water filter, pots and pans, cheap cutlery for George and me (the carriers ate with their hands), folding chairs, cots, medical supplies, folding bathtub and other paraphernalia, including a locked tin box full of British coins, we shoved off on the morning of March 10th in a Kru boat for Roysville. One can estimate the size of it from the fact that there were in addition to our group, ten oarsmen and a helmsman. We paddled for several miles at sea and then a mast was put up and we had smooth sailing for several hours to Roysville where we camped on the farm of a Liberian senator.

Next morning we marched to Teh, where the chief staged a dance for us and we "killed" one of the fifths of Scotch. George had a portable phonograph and some hot records. Our first night of the trek was a success. The Kru boatmen returned to Monrovia next morning and we hiked to the shore of Lake Pissu, hired a giant war canoe for ten dollars to have ourselves paddled to Robertsport (Cape Mount) by ten paddlers and a helmsman. We arrived tired out after dark, and George and I put up at the Episcopal mission where I first saw the issue of *The Spirit of Mission* containing the article I had written on the four largest Negro schools operated by the Episcopal Church. This did not hurt us with the missionary in charge.

Next day we bought additional supplies at a store in Cape Mount and on March 15th took off for the hinterland. Cape Mount was our last glimpse of civilization before more than a month of steady marching, going from town to town, except when we camped one night in the open in crossing a sixty-mile wilderness where there was no habitation at all and the trail was obviously little used. Usually the jungle was so thick that one had to stick to the trail which was from six to eight feet wide, and was so matted on the sides that only an elephant or perhaps a bush buffalo could break through it. A man with a sharp bush knife would require almost all day to cut a swath. One was impressed with the power of the elephant when one saw an opening as wide as a barn door where one of the pachyderms had bulled its way through. We passed one herd of five elephants one day at a distance of about ten feet. Two were lying down and the others were feeding. They just eyed us and we discreetly tiptoed by. Even without seeing a bull elephant, it is frightening to come upon his spoor. I had nothing but my .45 Colt automatic—and I had not come there to hunt anyhow. It was mighty eery to sleep in the open in the jungle and hear things moving about, cracking twigs and brushing trees and bushes. We had a fire to discourage leopards and such, but I slept with my pistol by my side. George did the same with his .38 Smith & Wesson. It was great to see dawn come up out of the steamy jungle and to hear the sunrise greeted simultaneously by every living thing: reptile, bird and mammal, from the bottom to the top of the forest. But with trees 200 feet high, matted to each other by giant vines, with roots taller than a man, one saw the sun only occasionally.

Villages ranging from fifty to five hundred huts were from fifteen to twenty miles apart. The chiefs were hospitable and always provided a neat guest house for us and "dashed" George and me whatever food, rice, palm oil, and palm wine we needed. We paid for what was supplied to the carriers, but they ate separately according to tribe and did not look upon each other as brothers. They also slept separately with their respective tribesmen. They were all black but there any similarity ended. They spoke only rudimentary English and when I had to address them it was through Blackie. Talk about uniting the black brothers was grimly laughable.

At each town I interviewed the chief, "dashed" him salt, tobacco, safety razor and blades, mirrors and a bottle of gin, and pumped him for information relative to the recently "suppressed" slave trade. I got a lot of information, too, some of it accompanied by tears, as they related how they had been treated for failing to "recruit" enough of their young men for Fernando Po. A typical punishment was to spread-eagle the chief on the ground with wrists and ankles tied down, and then have one of the soldiers vigorously flog him as his people were forced to look on. Some towns had been visited by tax gatherers as often as four times a year. In one town the people grew so tired of these visitors that they just abandoned their home and went far into the bush where they erected a new town. I was taken there by a circuitous route along an almost indistinguishable trail.

So it went for well over a month. I was worn thin and my notebooks got fat. Fortunately I had my portable typewriter along and as in my tour of the Southern states five years before, I did some typing of notes daily. Early in April I contracted malaria at the mountain town of Sublima, as I noted when I climbed a steep hill in that mountainous country. I fell exhausted at the summit and noticed that my arms and torso were quite dry instead of pouring perspiration. There was still a long way to go and making it was an ordeal. When I returned to Monrovia, I had thinned down from 160 pounds to 125.

Mrs. Mitchell was kind enough to provide me with some of the best food. (People ate well only when a steamer came from England or America.) The malaria did not become acute while I was in the great heat of the Liberian coast, in Freetown, Sierra Leone, or even in Dakar, Senegal, where the Barber Line freight-passenger boat stopped en route to New York; but once we turned north, it became pretty terrible. What with alternate burning and freezing I could do little writing during the three-week trip.

My friend L. F. Coles met me at the dock in Brooklyn, and after passing through customs I got a taxicab for the long trip to Harlem. Coles filled me in on what had happened since my departure. My homecoming was both happy and sad: happy to be back with Josephine and sad because I was so ill that at times I could scarcely lift my head, while at other times she had to pile blankets on me although it was mid-May and quite warm.

Nevertheless, I had to prepare the newspaper series and then the book. This necessitated going downtown to confer with Julian Mason and the *Post* managing editor, and with George Palmer Putnam. Then when the articles were finished I had to take them down to the libel lawyer's office on Park Row. As my malarial attacks grew worse every day at about four o'clock when the temperature changed, I tried to get home before that hour; but one day while waiting for George Putnam, a terrific attack of fever assailed me. The girls were all fluttering around but there was nothing they or anyone else could do about it.

Since malaria is basically due to malnutrition, I treated it accordingly, with fresh chopped steak, strawberries and cream, raw milk, raw clams, and green salads. I weathered the storm and before long the fever left never to return. I give thanks to the man from the Rockefeller Institute of Tropical Disease with whom I dined one evening at the Firestone Plantation. He prescribed the treatment which I used, and scoffed at the use of quinine.

The six articles I prepared appeared during the last days of June and the first days in July, 1931, in the *New York Evening Post*, the *Buffalo Express*, the *Philadelphia Public Ledger*, the *Washington Post* and one or two other papers. Additionally the *Evening Post* in its weekend rotogravure section carried two pages of my pictures of Liberian native life. It was the first time anything like this had happened to a Negro newspaperman. T. Thomas Fortune had once been an editorial writer for the the *New York Sun*. Lester Walton had been a feature writer for the *New York World* and Eugene Gordon had served as feature writer of the *Boston Post*, as had Noah D. Thompson on the *Los Angeles Express*. But so far as I know a colored writer had never before served as a foreign correspondent for an important metropolitan newspaper.

The series was well advertised through newsstand placards and space in other media. It was the talk of the town, especially among the Garveyites and the "black nationalists" who expect a Negro newspaperman to lie to satisfy their egos. I have always refused to do this, regarding it as unworthy. I believe in calling the shots as I see them. I did just that two years later when I wrote "Uncle Sam's Black Stepchild" for Mencken's *American Mercury*. This unchauvinistic approach may make many enemies but it engenders much respect for a writer. Later, in 1937, I painted a full-scale portrait of the capital of Liberia in *Globe* entitled "Monrovia Mooches On."

After I had turned over the manuscript of my second book, *Slaves Today!*, to the publishers, I devoted my attention to the Communist conspiracy and consumers' cooperation.

CHAPTER 12

WHEN THE Scottsboro case broke, I was out of the country and out of touch with what was going on, but upon my return I saw clearly the Communist design.

On March 31, 1931, nine Negro boys were indicted at Scottsboro, Alabama, on charges of having raped two white girls on a coal car of a freight train passing through northern Alabama. After long sessions and legal maneuvers and two reversals by the U.S. Supreme Court, most of the defendants were freed. The Scottsboro case was the *cause célèbre* of the time. The Communists stole it from the NAACP by legal trickery and exploited it for years through the International Labor Defense.

When the NAACP lost control of the case through the machinations of Benjamin J. Davis, Jr., who had scurried around the South and secured the signatures of the parents to turn the defense over to the International Labor Defense, I recognized all the earmarks of a Communist plot. It was an integral part of the Communist strategy laid down in the papers captured at the

Bridgman, Michigan, raid in August, 1922. It was in conformity with the Moscow ukase of October 26, 1928, that: "The main Communist slogan must be: The right of self-determination of the Negro in the black belt."

From its founding in 1919, the Comintern saw the need for utilizing racial and nationalistic prejudices and antagonisms to split populations and stir civil war, and in consequence the value to them of the Scottsboro case was clearly seen. They operated similarly in other parts of the world, not just in the United States. As there was just one country within the confines of the United States, it was necessary to create another, so there would be a black country and a white country warring against each other, and thus undermine the American system. Therefore, the Negro problem would be solved by liquidation of the Negroes.

The 1930 resolutions of the Comintern had pointed out that an essential part of the black-belt program called for confiscation of the property of the white landowners and capitalists for the "benefit" of the Negro farmers. Parroting the Comintern, Clarence Hathaway, then editor of the *Daily Worker*, demanded that:

> The land of the Southern white landlords for years tenanted by the Negro tenant farmers be confiscated and turned over to Negroes . . . secondly, we propose to break up the present artificial boundaries established for the convenience of the white master class, and to establish the state unity of the territory known as "the black belt" where the Negroes constitute the overwhelming majority of the population; thirdly, in this territory we demand that the Negroes be given the complete right of self-determination; the right to set up their own government in this territory and the right to separate, if they wish, from the United States.

The general Negro consensus at the time was that this was the sheerest lunacy. According to the U.S. Bureau of the Census

188

figures, there were at the time in the South 535,433 Negro home-owners, 177,604 Negro farm owners, 18,064 Negro owners of retail stores, 16 Negro banks, 30 Negro insurance companies, 35,000 churches and fraternal halls owned by the colored people, over 250,000 motor vehicles, to say nothing of fisheries, cattle ranches and other enterprises owned by Negroes. Obviously all of this wealth would be confiscated along with that of the whites.

This seemed incredible to most Americans but not to those who had studied the propaganda victories of the Communists elsewhere. The most fantastic programs appeal to some elements of any population, and the inroads into Negro society by the Communists utilizing the Scottsboro case became very great in a short time. Volunteers to aid the International Labor Defense arose on every side. At least twice the number of Scottsboro mothers as there actually existed were sent about the country to appear in Negro churches. Collections were taken up to fatten the Communist income. William Z. Foster boomed that "It is impossible for the Negro people to achieve their full economic, political and social equality as Americans unless they organize as a nation." All of the Communist leaders, colored and white, parroted this defeatist philosophy that only by dividing the country into black belts and white belts could the Negro possibly become free.

Ordinary Negroes were won over because they did not see that the speakers sent to their churches were Communists bent on destroying a way of life of which they approved, but saw them simply as advocates of justice for nine black boys caught in the toils of Southern justice. They did not know that other speakers of this same type were lecturing similar audiences all over the world on the evils of the capitalist system and its "lynch terror."

I knew that the Communist Party had sent six Negroes, along with twenty-four whites, to Russia on September 2, 1930, armed with fake names and phony passports. These Negroes were carefully selected in the hope that they would unquestioningly carry out orders. Delegated to spy upon them and keep them in line was Mrs. Raissa Berkman Browder, wife of Earl Browder, U.S.

Communist Party head. Even these handpicked Red Uncle Toms rebelled against the black-belt line.

Soon after I returned from Africa, specifically, in August, 1931, another big delegation, including fifteen Red Negro "students" were sent to the Lenin School, a vast swamp of intrigue attended by from 1,500 to 2,000 students from fifteen countries, one half spying on the other half. They came back to the United States and plunged into the promotion of the campaign to raise money for the Scottsboro Defense, although the ILD lawyers were allegedly serving without fee.

Enormous sums were being collected and Negroes were coming to regard the Communists as their greatest friends. The Negro press generally swallowed the Communist propaganda hook, line, and sinker just because the Reds were speaking out for justice for the Scottsboro boys. Preachers whom Reds had previously denounced as enemies of their flocks, now welcomed Communist speakers to their pulpits to take up collections ostensibly for the Scottsboro boys. This money, which was never properly accounted for, ran into hundreds of thousands of dollars. Attorney Samuel Liebowitz, the volunteer ILD defense counsel, who later broke with the Reds because they double-crossed him, said the total was $250,000. The Communists conceded that it amounted to $125,000. Out of this each of the boys' mothers was given $10.00 monthly for maintenance and the boys themselves were sent $2.00 weekly for tobacco in prison. According to Liebowitz the two appeals cost $12,000.

As Manning Johnson, high Negro Communist Party official, testified years later on the Red insincerity in the Scottsboro case:

> We were constantly told by James W. Ford and others that we were not interested in saving the lives of the "damn" Scottsboro boys; that we were interested in using the Scottsboro case to penetrate the Negro churches and civic organizations which we could not reach except for a cause of that kind, and in the course of the development of this campaign to raise the slogans of the Communist Party, and during our contacts with these large masses of

Negroes to seek out the best elements among them and recruit them into the party.

Johnson also later testified that:

In the Negro commission of the national committee we were definitely told by James W. Ford and other leaders of the party: "We don't give a darn about the Scottsboro boys. If they burn it doesn't make any difference. We are only interested in one thing, how we can use the Scottsboro case to bring the Communist movement to the people and win them over to Communism."

As an ominous augury of coming events, the Camp Hill massacre of the same period occurred when a white Communist organizer went into that eastern Alabama town determined to set up a Sharecroppers' Union. This resulted in five Negroes being lynched, twenty wounded, thirty-four imprisoned, and the burning of Negro churches. Similar orgies occurred elsewhere in the area and in Mississippi.

It was abundantly clear to me that I must devote all of my energies to fighting this conspiracy to destroy the Negro population to ensure a Communist victory. I had one potent weapon —my typewriter. Since 1927 I had become nationally and internationally known through my writings in magazines and newspapers. Knowing what I did about the Communist world conspiracy against civilization, it would be criminal not to expose to the world, and especially to the Negroes, what was behind the machinations of this Kremlin criminal cabal. With all the dedication and energy at my command I plunged into the controversy, and I have been in it ever since. Because so many of the so-called intellectuals of the group (thanks to the wooing of the middle class by the League of Struggle for Negro Rights plus the Scottsboro case), had been won over to the Communist ideology, I had first to turn my guns on them.

Since I wrote both the editorials and a column in the *Pittsburgh Courier,* I possessed a double-barreled shotgun. One of my first targets was the Communist-front member and managing editor of the *Afro-American,* William N. Jones. The *Afro-American* of Baltimore, Maryland, had the second largest circulation of Negro weeklies, after the *Pittsburgh Courier,* and was very influential among Negroes along the Atlantic Coast. Stung by a column in which I had taken him and his ilk to task, Jones excoriated me in turn.

On August 15, 1931, in the very heart of the Scottsboro case and the uproar over the Camp Hill massacres, I wrote:

> My good friend, William N. Jones of the *Afro-American,* affects not to understand my position on the Scottsboro case and the Communist racketeers, although I really strove to make myself very clear. . . .
>
> I disagree with the tactics of the so-called Reds in dealing with the Negro and also with the advice they give him. I claim that they make the Negro problem worse instead of better by their insane tactics. They give the murderous Southern Neanderthals the very opportunity and excuse they are looking for to commit additional homicide. Mr. Jones says: "I believe the Communist policy of driving a wedge between the white worker and the slave-driving white ruling class which is fostering race prejudice for its economic advantage, is the most vital weapon any group has ever tried to use."
>
> This is all well and good if and when it drives said wedge, but it seems to me that in Alabama, for instance, it is merely resulting in white worker and capitalist uniting in posses and hunting down unfortunate Negroes. I am sure it will be healthier for Negroes in the South if the Communists (who must show Moscow a "good" record) would concentrate on the white proletariat and leave the Negroes alone for a spell or until the white masses are sufficiently emancipated to not be misled by the Negrophobic propaganda of the Southern plutocracy. I am quite in agreement with A. J. Muste of the Brookwood Labor College, who said recently: "The Communist Party in

the United States today suffers from a mechanical dictation from the outside which severely handicaps it in dealing with the American situation. It does not have its roots
primarily in the American soil. It has pursued a divisive
and sectarian policy in the trade unions. It has abandoned
an honest effort to build a mass labor policy. It talks a
fantastic and doctrinaire language which American
workers do not understand.

"It does not make the occupants of an insane asylum
any more rational by bringing in more lunatics nor does
it improve conditions in the Dixie madhouse by an invasion of crazy Communists who think they can save eight
young Negroes from the electric chair by calling for social
equality, and denouncing the governor and the judge."

This was a typical column of the time. I was relentlessly harry-
ing the Red brethren and the increasing number of black mouth-
pieces they were corralling. I became the target of the Red
smearbund, and because there were so many Fabians and out-
and-out Socialists infiltrating or dominating high places in the
intellectual world, I was increasingly handicapped in many snide
ways; but I have always liked a good, no-holds-barred fight, and
in this one I knew I was on the side of the angels. I followed
every twist and turn of the party line, and tried to explain what
it meant.

There was the column I wrote on January 30, 1932, in which
I said, in part:

My chief criticism of the Communists in this country has
been that too often they are guilty of doing the very
things of which they accuse capitalists: that is, prevarica-
tion, misrepresentation, libel, and violence. . . . I can see
no sense in booting double-dealing, chicanery, lying and
racketeering from the seats of power under capitalism only
to bring them back under Communism. Recently a reporter and photographer had to argue for over an hour
down at the Pennsylvania Station in New York City with

a group of these alleged Communists before two of them could be gotten to pose for a photograph with the mother of one of the Scottsboro boys. And yet the governor of North Carolina readily posed a while back for a photograph flanked on one side by a Negro girl and on the other side by a white boy.

Such incidents, however, are insignificant compared with the campaign of vilification carried on by the Communists against the NAACP. No Ku Kluxer ever denounced the latter organization more vigorously and unfairly. The Communists know they are lying when they assert time and again that the NAACP wants to see the boys convicted and is betraying the race.

For years we have had an efficient civil rights organization in this country known as the American Civil Liberties Union, which has won many notable battles for free speech and free assembly thus permitting radicals to put over their message. Now come the Communists and form an American Civil Rights Union for ostensibly the same reason, but actually to undermine the older organization whose "crime" is that it is largely composed of the hated liberals. This founding of organizations with names similar to those existing is an old trick with our American Communists and is done chiefly for the purpose of confusion by which these fellows hope to profit. Having forged a twin organization, they immediately proceed to denounce the other as counter-revolutionary, bourgeois and traitorous to the workers.

It is impossible to differ with our American Communists or take them to task for obvious tactical errors without being immediately labeled as an agent of J. P. Morgan and the National City Bank. They have quite the same sort of grooved mentalities as Ku Kluxers, Garveyites and other race fanatics, black and white. The course they tentatively pursue is held the only true one and whoever takes exception is denounced as an enemy of humanity, even though they may have to change that course in a few months.

Like the Garveyites, and professional Anglo-Saxons, these quaint folk are devoid of a sense of humor. Their claptrap is unbelievably wearisome to anybody with adult mentality, and in their effort to appear revolutionary they often succeed merely in becoming ridiculous. No wonder they have driven the most intelligent comrades from their party.

In the early spring of 1932, I agreed to edit the *National News*, a local New York weekly which was to voice the views and interests of the Negro Democratic element seeking larger powers in the community as represented by Ferdinand Q. Morton, Dr. Louis T. Wright, and Lonnie Hicks of the United Colored Democracy. While it created a stir in the community, it was an unwise step because there was insufficient money behind it to compete with the two existing weeklies in the community, and inevitably it folded. I was the one most harmed by the demise of the newspaper, since now I had no steady source of income and had to rely on free-lance writing and lecture engagements for which it was the wrong season of the year.

On June 27, 1932, I received a very friendly letter from Amelia Earhart who was living in Rye, New York, telling me that she had worn on her transatlantic flight the elephant-toe bracelet I had brought her from Liberia the year before. "Indeed," she wrote, "I have become so attached to the bracelet that I wear it almost constantly." To be sure, all of her subsequent photographs showed her wearing it, but whether she wore it on her ill-fated flight around the world, I do not know. Elephant-toe bracelets were a rarity then as now. Sliced from the toe, hollowed out, polished, and then studded with silver, they were among the most valued examples of African art that I brought back from Liberia, Sierra Leone, and Senegal.

During this period I had published in *The Crisis* for January, 1932, an article on the Young Negroes Co-operative League and what it had accomplished to date in encouraging colored folk to take economic steps to help themselves. I had hoped that the NAACP would show some interest and activity along this line since it had hundreds of branches. I spoke on the subject at the annual NAACP conference, but nothing came of it.

In April, 1932, *The American Mercury* published my provocative piece, "Black America Begins to Doubt," which was a critique of the Negro churches. In this issue I had such company as Hoffman Nickerson, Jack Conroy, John Nicholas Beffel, George Milburn and Albert Halper.

In June, I contributed "Quality versus Quantity" to a special Negro issue of *The Birth Control Review,* along with Dr. W. E. B. DuBois, Charles S. Johnson, Dr. M. O. Bousfield, Elmer A. Carter, S. J. Holmes, and Dr. W. G. Alexander.

The August issue of *Opportunity* carried my long review of *Race, Class and Party* by Paul Lewinson (Oxford University Press, New York) which remains one of the outstanding works on Reconstruction.

The American Mercury ran in November, 1932, my "Black Art," a portrait of my grandmother. Contributing also to that issue were John Fante, Benjamin DeCasseres, H. E. Buchholz, and Hoffman Nickerson.

In December I reviewed for *Opportunity* John L. Spivak's *Georgia Nigger* (Brewer, Warren and Putnam, New York) and did an article on "The Economic Outlook for the Negro" for *The Forum,* a quarterly review published in Bridgetown, Barbados.

The University Scholarship Foundation ran a National Negro Forum program over Radio Station WEVD on November 17, 1932, which stirred considerable comment judging by the large number of letters and telephone calls received. I had talked on some contradictions of race prejudice.

In September, 1932, when things were not looking well for me after the *National News* expired, Ira F. Lewis telegraphed me an invitation to resume working for the *Pittsburgh Courier* and I did so forthwith, writing a column and all of the editorials. My connection with the paper has continued to the present.

I aroused the ire of the Communists in general and one of their parrots in particular, managing editor William N. Jones of the *Afro-American,* when I wrote unfavorably about one of those periodical hunger marches on Washington which the Red brethren stage to capitalize on misery. I wrote:

> To be perfectly frank, I cannot work up any sympathy for the hunger marchers wending their way toward Washington. I seriously doubt that anything can be accomplished by this latest stunt except to furnish food for the tabloids and to supply the more militant of the marchers with a nice assortment of black eyes and bumps.

I doubt that anybody in the United States who makes his or her needs known this winter or at any other time during the depression will starve. Whatever can be said against the Americans (and a whole lot can be said), they are generous at such times as these. Hence, I am of the opinion that about as much can be obtained by staying at home as by going to Washington. These hunger marchers, few of whom appear to be hungry, are either ill-advised or are just Communists, afflicted with the martyr complex and a vague notion that the revolution is right around the corner; and imagine they are doing a service for humanity by sniffing tear gas and stopping policemen's clubs and boots.

Because the Communists were exceedingly lucky in Russia, they imagine that they will have the same luck elsewhere. They confuse the American capitalists with the decadent Russian nobility. Capitalism here is sick, but it is far from being dead. If it were supported only by those who squeeze great profits from it there might be a chance for a revolution in the near future, but capitalism in the United States is supported by the vast majority of the American people who will fight and die for it to the last ditch because they believe in it.

What the obtuse Communists fail to realize is that the Americans are much more inclined to the Anarchist theory

197

of great individualism and mutual aid with a minimum of government that they are to an all-embracing collectivism enforced at the point of the bayonet by a small minority of revolutionists who have substituted Marx for Jesus.

That was in December, 1932, and it did not go down well with the comrades. What was disturbing to me was that the managing editor of the second largest Negro newspaper should come out so boldly on this issue in championing the Communist viewpoint. Apparently the Reds had been doing a lot of spadework (with no pun intended!).

More momentous things were in the cards for later that month. The NAACP had been receiving dire reports from the Mississippi Delta about exploitation bordering on peonage of workers on the Mississippi Flood Control Project. Miss Helen Boardman, a former Red Cross relief worker, had made an initial investigation in the summer of 1932 for the Association. A bill by Senator Robert F. Wagner had been introduced to investigate the charges of peonage. It languished in the Committee on Commerce, and would have to pass the Committee on Audits and Expenditures before reaching the floor of the Senate. The NAACP wanted the great number of Negro workers to share in the $325 million being spent through private contractors.

The NAACP decided to make a full-scale investigation on the ground in secret, and I was chosen to be one of the investigators, along with Roy Wilkins, the assistant secretary of the Association. We went immediately to Memphis, Tennessee, where we closeted ourselves with the shrewd, gracious Robert R. Church, the Negro millionaire boss of Republicanism in that area, in his lovely home. Church briefed us on the area we were to invade. It was quite familiar to me, since I had covered that country in 1926, and had been there a few times since; but it was all new to Roy. We needed someone with whom we could make contact fast in case of trouble. We could use Bob Church only indirectly and through another name.

This turned out to be a wise provision. The name chosen was that of one of Church's henchmen. We dined with him and his lovely daughter, Roberta; and the next day we went to a store specializing in workers' clothing. We bought overalls, sheepskin lined coats to put over our street clothing, little sacks to hold extra underwear, and toilet articles. Presto! We were incognito.

We took a morning Yazoo and Mississippi Valley Jim-Crow day coach and were on our way. Roy got off at Greenville and I went on to Vicksburg. He was to cover the Mississippi side while I worked over in Arkansas. Both of us were to seek work in the levee camps or on the quarter boats thus getting firsthand information. I avoided contact with any of the people I knew in Vicksburg and went to a cheap rooming house.

Next morning I took a bus to Lake Providence, Louisiana, where there was a large levee camp. In one or two days I learned from the workers themselves that they often worked from twelve to sixteen hours a day, depending upon the foremen's demands, for which they were paid one dollar a day, and then had to pay exorbitant sums for commissary, ice water, and cook's charges. They lived in floorless tents and filthy quarters with no garbage disposal or screening in malaria-infested country. It was not uncommon for slow or recalcitrant workers to be buffeted and beaten.

While I understood quite well the intentions of the NAACP, I found that the investigation was ill-timed, being too near Christmas when it was not only very cold but when there was practically no work in progress. Thus, while I sought work, there was no hiring being done because of the season; but I gathered valuable information. I had to be extremely careful, make no entries in my notebook until I got to my room, and tell nothing about myself. I knew this was tough country, and any Negro who seemed suspicious could easily get put on the chain gang for loitering. The countryside was full of such loiterers and the police were watchful.

It was icy cold throughout the Delta region that winter. Many Negroes were on Red Cross relief, working a day for every dollar's worth of goods they received. Women were often wearing trousers or overalls, sometimes with high-heeled shoes. Everything was frozen solid. The wooden houses were draughty. When it did not snow, it rained. All in all I visited camps outside Tallulah, Mounds, Delta Point, Lake Providence, and Steinberg's Camp. At the latter workers got $1.50 daily and fed themselves. Beds cost $2.00 monthly. Some mechanic's helpers got $2.50 daily. Some of the quarter-boat boys from the camp at Waterproof, Louisiana, worked on the quarter-boat and laid mattresses, getting $2.20 daily with board. These were rough people. They worked ten hours a day, sleeping and eating on the boat.

Down near Natchez, on the Arkansas side, were camps I visited at Eyebrow and Deer Park. There the men's pay varied from $1.25 and $1.50 daily, tops being $1.75 for a ten-hour day, with pay every two weeks. Men working on the dragline at Locust Ridge got $1.50 a day when paid. There was neither camp nor commissary there, the men having to stay at home or room in town. The pay was a trifle better at Duckport and Waterproof. If a worker got $2.00 a day, $1.00 was taken for board. Practically everybody appeared to be broke. I was careful never to display anything but silver money and normally kept very little in my overall pocket. My chief treasury was my shoes.

When in the Natchez vicinity, I came across from Vidalia, Louisiana, and chanced visiting my old friend Dr. Dumas, former president of the National Medical Association. He was a distinguished, courtly, and wealthy mulatto who owned a large white mansion atop a double terrace, six blocks of downtown real estate and a big plantation. He was one of a considerable number of Negroes in the vicinity who were planters and slaveholders before the Civil War over on the Louisiana side. But when he wanted to send his children to college at Howard University, he had to route them through New Orleans to get Pullman accommodations.

Of course I did not go to Dr. Dumas's mansion in my hobo outfit, I went to his office and waited with the patients, then revealed myself to him when I got inside his examining room. He was astonished to see me and much concerned about my roaming over the countryside gathering information for the NAACP. He knew the risks involved, not just with the whites but with the blacks. When I visited Natchez three years later and was stationed in Jackson covering the whole state for the *Pittsburgh Courier,* he insisted that I share the luxury of his home. But on this occasion I stayed in an alleged Negro hotel which was so ramshackle that it had no knob on the bedroom door. I had to move the end of the bed across the door so that any effort to open it would awaken me. As a precautionary measure I left my shoes on, with the money inside them!

Each day I wrote to Josephine, but I was so much on the move over the frozen countryside that I was unable to get any reply. I finally took the Missouri Pacific bug-a-bug (or gasoline coach) to Vicksburg. After securing a room at the house where I had previously stayed, I sent Josephine a telegram, asking her to reply at that address. Then I went off to a movie at the Saenger Theater, ate something, and returned to my room to await the telegram. I even bought extra coal from the landlady for my fireplace so that I could wait in comfort. I had bought the current *American Mercury* and was propped up reading that.

Suddenly there came a loud pounding at the door. I thought it was the messenger from Western Union. I grumbled something about it not being necessary to knock down the house. But when I threw the door open there stood a detective and a uniformed policeman, both with revolvers drawn. Naturally I reached for the ceiling as they shouted, "Throw up your hands, nigger!"

"What's this all about?" I asked.

"Get your things," the detective ordered, and when I did they hustled me into the police car outside and rushed me handcuffed to the police station which was also the city hall. The mayor, J. C. Hamilton, and the chief of police interviewed me. Since they had my notebooks there was no point in not being completely frank about what I was doing. I talked with them for some time and convinced them that I was what I represented myself to be.

Indeed, I surprised them by pointing out that what I had been doing was to their advantage. City employees had not been paid for weeks as the city was broke because of the depression. I pointed out that businesses could not pay their taxes because

Negroes working on the Flood Control Project had not been paid by the contractors who had millons in federal money for their work.

This was an effective approach and they were convinced that I was not one of the two Negro holdup men the police had been seeking. In a subsequent exchange of letters between Walter White and the Vicksburg mayor, the latter explained that a description of the culprits had gone out over the radio, and that in response to this appeal for information, the landlady of my rooming house had telephoned the police. She reported that a suspicious looking Negro was stopping at her place and might be one of the men implicated in the crime.

When the police searched me in the station, they took in addition to my notebooks some thirty dollars I had in my overall pocket and a Schaeffer lifetime fountain pen. They did not know and I did not tell them that I had twenty-five dollars in my shoe.

I was locked in a cell with another man, and as soon as the turnkey had gone I got in touch with the trusty and gave him a dollar to send a telegram to Mr. W. White, 409 Edgecombe Avenue, New York City.

It was a brief notice that I was in jail in Vicksburg. I knew that would bring swift action, so I laid down on my hard cot and took it easy. My cell companion turned out to be a burglar and road agent, a disarmingly good-looking fellow who frankly confessed to a life of crime: robbery, murder, and rape. He had been in numerous prisons, and related that the cause of his present arrest was his holdup of a white couple on the road, and his taking all their money, along with their car. It seemed that he had made a mistake and taken the wrong getaway route which ran him into a police roadblock.

This man's major apprehension was not the sentence he knew he would inevitably get but the terrible kangaroo court of prisoners at the state prison farm at Parchman. Every newcomer was tried by this court and then sentenced to an unmerciful beating at the hands of the execution squad. The authorities condoned, perhaps encouraged, this as a disciplinary measure to straighten out the newcomers immediately. This fellow had escaped from several country jails but Parchman was a tough stir to crack and few convicts escaped from it. For this reason, he said, when he got through with the kangaroo court, he intended to be a model prisoner, make himself useful, and eventually become a trusty, preferably on the prison farm. From there he could escape easily and go on his merry way, as he had in the past.

This man and many of his type could not be reformed as many sociologists and penologists erroneously think. He was beyond redemption, and, as a matter of fact, did not want to change his mode of living. He attributed his several arrests to "mistakes" and "unlucky breaks"; "bad" was getting caught and "good" was escaping detection and punishment. Practically all the other criminals I have encountered think the same way.

Next morning a detective came for me and we went down to the property clerk, a different man from the one who had taken my thirty dollars and my valuable fountain pen. My notebooks were returned but there was no sign of the money and the pen, which the clerk pretended to know nothing about. With the jail door open, I was not disposed to argue with him about it.

On the jail steps the detective assured me that I could go but to get out of town immediately. I told him that I was on my way to the railroad station to take the first train out. He shook his head negatively.

"Don't go to the station," he warned. "You'll be picked up as soon as you get there." Then he pointed up the road and said, "You see that? That's Highway 61 to Memphis. Get on it and don't ever come back to Mississippi!"

Losing no time I headed immediately for the Negro YMCA with whose secretary I was acquainted from my previous visits to the city. I went into his office, and somewhat surprised, he greeted me. I got down to business immediately.

"Take these clothes," I said, "and either give them away or burn them in your furnace. Then see if you can get somebody to drive me to Jackson so I can catch the Illinois Central express to Memphis."

He was very accommodating and after a bit of telephoning found a man who was willing to take me the forty-nine miles to the Mississippi capital city. Once there I stayed right in the Negro waiting room until the train arrived. While waiting I was grimly amused by the fact that a little black woman in a big raincoat was surreptitiously selling copies of the *Chicago Defender* which she kept concealed under it. When I asked her why she was not selling it openly, she just chuckled and asked, "Mistuh, is you kiddin'?"

Roy Wilkins met me at the Memphis station. We went immediately to the Negro hotel and exchanged notes and reminiscences. Walter White had had the wires burning that morning preparatory to making my arrest a *cause célèbre*. It made good propaganda and was milked to the utmost. For that purpose my incarceration had been of too brief duration, but not in my book. I have never had a martyr complex.

Despite the warning of the Vicksburg detective, I was soon back in Mississippi, this time along with Roy, and we visited levee camps in Coahoma county and adjacent areas, seeking work and getting much information valuable for our report. We then took the last bus one night for Memphis, and the following day were in a drawing room en route to New York. We related our experiences to the big annual meeting of the NAACP at the Abyssinian Baptist Church which was packed with people. We subsequently spoke in several eastern cities.

I never pretended that I had been mistreated in Vicksburg except for being arrested and jailed under suspicion of being a criminal. By being careful, I had no other encounters with the police in either Mississippi or Louisiana, and it was lucky that I did not, particularly during my hikes across the country from the main highways to the various levee camps. Many Negroes then were being arrested for vagrancy and on suspicion of criminal plans. Theft, highway robbery, and burglary were the order of the day and night. The depression was on full blast, and nobody had any intention of starving.

Because so much is being made nowadays of the supposed lack of knowledge of their historic background by Negroes and the ignorance of white people on the same subject, it might be apposite to mention that if such ignorance prevails, it is due neither to lack of availability of such knowledge nor lack of efforts to spread it. By this time I had published articles on the subject in *The Messenger,* the *Illustrated Feature Section* and the *Pittsburgh Courier,* and had spoken on it in many parts of the United States, as had other speakers. There were more forums in colored America then than there are now. I had spoken both on the radio and in a lecture course at the Latin Quarter on 8th Street in Greenwich Village, as well as at the Harlem Interracial Forum.

I had been having a lot of fun with the Russian film fiasco which began in 1932. A contingent of two dozen American Negroes had been recruited by the Communists to make a film, *Black and White,* which was intended to show up the horrors of the slave trade and so-called lynch terror in the capitalist world in general and the United States in particular. None of the capitalist states of the West then had given diplomatic recognition to the Soviet Union. Such a film would be a thorn in the side of the free world. The Negroes recruited to act in this film knew nothing about acting, nor did their leader, Langston Hughes. But the whole project was widely publicized, and at a time when the American stage was virtually barred to Negroes except in vaudeville and Negro musical comedies. However, when Langston Hughes had labored over the film script, and all was ready for the shooting, the Reds postponed production and the film never was made. Henry Lee Moon and Theodore Poston returned and explained that the film postponement was due to the desire of Stalin to curry favor with the United States, with an eye to eventual diplomatic recognition, the great desideratum.

On September 15, 1932, I wrote:

Our Communist friends are hard put to it to explain why the Soviet film, *Black and White,* is not being produced after the signing of 22 American Negroes and their transportation to the Bolshevist paradise.

Mr. James Ford, who will be the first Negro Vice President of this glorious republic, if he can get elected this year on the Communist ticket, is quite worked up about the revelations of Messrs. Moon and Poston, two reputable and trustworthy Negro newspapermen who, returning from Russia, have let the cat out of the bag.

Moon and Poston, who went over to act in the picture, sent a long report from Berlin charging that the film had been abandoned because the Soviets are more anxious to get American machinery, money and recognition than they are to show how America grinds down the black folk.

Ford and the other Communist leaders declare (a) that the film project has been postponed until the spring because of technical difficulties and necessary changes in the scenario; (b) that only four of the Aframericans who went across to make the picture are disgruntled, the other eighteen being perfectly satisfied to travel around the Soviet Union on government expense, and (c) that work is being found for the various members of the party until such time as the film producers are ready for their services.

It is boasted that the artists and writers are freer in Soviet Russia than elsewhere, and are given every opportunity to pursue art untrammeled by considerations of a material nature. If this be true, it should be possible to make all necessary manuscript corrections more quickly there than in capitalistic America where all writers (except Communists) are chained to the cross of gold. In America such corrections could be made in a few days or weeks. Why is it necessary to wait eight or nine months in Russia? Is socialism less efficient than capitalism? Are we to believe that the land of Stalin trails the land of Ford?

The Soviet Government, engrossed in settling its internal problems and building socialism in the USSR, has promised many capitalist governments, with which it has diplomatic and commercial dealings, to curb therein its propaganda. Is it unreasonable to suppose that Russia, hoping for U.S. recognition and credits, should refrain from producing such an incendiary film as the proposed *Black and White?* In the spring either a new administration will take charge of America's foreign policy or we shall have four more years of Hoover. Perhaps, the Soviets reason, it were better to postpone the picture until then.

Eight months later there was still no film, so I returned to the subject for the further delectation of the readers of the *Pittsburgh Courier* on June 17, 1933:

It is now summer. An entire year has elapsed since the little group of Negroes left here to make the picture, *Black and White,* which was to show the struggles of the Negroes through slavery to the present day. By the time the Negroes got to Russia, the Communists there had decided to drop the picture project for fear of antagonizing the American capitalists from whom they have long been unable to get official recognition. Instead of telling the Negroes frankly what the situation was, they stalled them off and sent them on a tour of the Soviet Union. Several of the Negroes got wise and boldly charged the Russians with yielding to political expediency. The majority of them just Uncle Tommed and accepted everything with a slavish grin. Worse, they sent long news dispatches back here whitewashing the Bolsheviks and attacking their Negro brethren in the film troupe who had been courageous enough to complain. The picture remains unmade.

Each spring for several years I wrote a column about the *Black and White* film that was never made. The majority of the "actors" became Red henchmen.

There is a decided tendency among sociologists and journalists to assert that Soviet interest in Africa began in the late

1950's when the wave of independence movements started. They infer that prior to that time Red subversion did not operate in the continent. Actually it began as far back as 1930.

I have a letter from George Padmore, the leading Negro Communist in the British Empire, dated December 5, 1932, on the letterhead of the *International Negro Workers' Review*, describing itself as "Organ of the International Trade Union Committee of Negro Workers," Head Office, 8 Rothescodstrasse, Hamburg, Germany. This was before Hitler came to power. This office was an arm of the Communist International and bankrolled by it. I had written to Padmore the preceding April 9th to find out what he was accomplishing with his work among Africans and West Indians. I was then editing the *National News*. I excerpt some of his relevant statements:

> Although our orientation is largely in the direction of the colonies—Africa and the West Indies—since there are twelve million Afro-Americans in that so-called "land of the free and home of the brave," we, as a part of our international duty, try to keep track of the situation in your parts.
>
> Some years ago I was in the states and happened to run into you in Washington. This was some years ago and I presume you will hardly remember me. Since then I have drifted into every port except fascist Italy.
>
> By the way, I was in the West Coast just at the time when you were saying goodbye to the lone star of Liberia. Although we both saw something of that country, our conclusions are different. This, no doubt, is accounted for by our background, ideology and outlook. I am afraid, Schuyler, that you see Liberia as an entity in itself and therefore throw all of the blame of the unfortunate country on a handful of political racketeers in Monrovia. You have not attacked these people more than I have done. But when all is said and done—Liberia and her

little autocrats are merely one of the pawns in the big game of world imperialism. . . .

I wish I could write more, but time is limited this morning. I just got back from a trip to England where I had some very successful mass meetings among the colored seamen in Liverpool, London, Cardiff, on the Scottsboro case. Despite my many years of international working class experience, I was surprised to see the deep interest which these African and West Indian workers take in the Alabama affair. This shows the strong international bonds of solidarity which exist in the working class. . . .

I have previously mentioned that Padmore had been fired by Comintern command. A few years later when the office of this Negro branch had been hastily removed to Copenhagen, he was replaced by Otto Huiswoud, the Surinam Communist whom I had debated on the Negro and Communism back in June, 1923, in New York. Padmore escaped Stalin's gunmen in Paris and made his way to London where he contaminated Africans and West Indians, workingmen and particularly students, until his protégé, Kwame Nkrumah, called him to Ghana as his assistant.

From Padmore's letter it is clear that Communist work in Africa antedated World War II, as it did in the West Indies and in the United States. By the time the African countries began getting their independence there was a second generation of Communists at work throughout the continent. Yet in the mid-fifties when Dr. Max Yergan read a paper at a conference at Johns Hopkins University sponsored, I believe, by the U.S. State Department, he was ridiculed for exaggerating the role of the Soviet Union in Africa.

In January, 1933, Walter White invited me to be a member of a fourteen-member committee of inquiry on conditions at Harlem Hospital "as they effect Negro physicians and surgeons." This was quite a large-scale affair. We went thoroughly into administration and practice at Harlem Hospital. In the background, of course, and responsible for the direction of the investigation, was the astute Dr. Louis T. Wright. At that time this municipal hospital in the heart of the vast Negro community had very few Negroes on its medical staff. Eighty per cent of the personnel was white, while Negroes were virtually excluded as physicians and workers at other city and private hospitals. I learned a lot, not only about hospital administration but also about municipal politics and rivalries within the medical profession. The committee's report was later published in book form.

William N. Jones, managing editor of the *Afro-American*, returned to the attack, charging me with inconsistency and opportunism, and having "leaned forward and backward numerous times in the past ten years." To this, I replied on January 21, 1933:

> But there is nothing sacred about consistency. The Communists here and abroad have proved that. At first the cry in Russia was to give the land to the peasants; now the land has almost all been taken from the peasants. Then it was shouted that capitalism was to be crushed, and the shout had hardly died down before Lenin's New Economic Policy was in vogue, creating a shoal of small capitalists. At one time we were told all the peasants were to be placed on collective farms; then we were informed by Stalin that the rate of collectivization was too swift. We used to hear a great deal about the people exiled to Siberia by the wicked Czar and how that would all end under the Bolshevists. There are now more exiles in Siberia than ever before. There was to be a series of Five Year Plans in sequence without a break. Now that the first Five Year Plan has ended disappointingly, with starvation stalking the USSR, Comrade Stalin and his fellow disciples inform the world that there is to be a Sabbatical year in planning, perhaps to enable the comrades to catch up on their meals.
>
> In the United States our Communist comrades are no less inconsistent. Although they sneer at political action as

a fraud and delusion, they name their candidates for office wherever possible at all elections and fight strenuously for votes which they never get. They contend that the social revolution, which is going on under their eyes all of the time, cannot come save through forcible overthrow of the government, and yet I notice they do not advocate it in public either by tongue or pen. They are the first to yell when the minions of capitalism use force on them.

Three or four years ago they invaded the mill districts of the Carolinas, hailing the restiveness of the factory peons there as the opening of the revolution. After a few encounters with the tough Cracker police, they retired from the field. These comrades denounce the capitalist courts as unjust and biased, and yet they are always collecting money to defend someone in court. They talk of self-determination for the Black Belt, yet I failed to find any of them advocating it in the real Black Belt of the South. Although they frown upon the Theory of Exceptionalism, I note that their speech and tactics differ in Mississippi and Massachusetts.

So if it be true that I am inconsistent and opportunistic, I am following good Communist precedent, which should endear me to Brother Jones, who just recently became enamoured of Communism. Not that I condemn inconsistency. An individual who thinks the same about everything that he did ten years ago is a dunce. Since the Communists themselves change all their plans and tactics whenever defeat looms (and they have changed at least a dozen times as opportunity beckoned), they cannot quarrel with opportunism. Had I always been as logical on this matter of bowing to opportunism as the Communists have, I would be basking in a villa on the Riviera or on the coast of Algiers, instead of dodging creditors in Gotham. . . .

The bulk of Americans still have faith in their democratic machinery, through which they can do (as they have demonstrated) anything they wish when they wish. With the natural conservatism of the masses everywhere, Americans appreciate that change can be both beneficial and disastrous; that progress, so-called, is not necessarily improvement.

Of course the Communists consider anybody an enemy of the people (meaning the Communist politicians) who is unwilling to remain blind to the hard facts of life while unquestionably accepting their untried plans and programs as the law and gospel. It is this fanatical state of mind that causes the good brethren to denounce everybody who sees the world and humanity as it is, and laud everybody who pretends to see the world through red spectacles. I have noted this sad change in many of my friends and erstwhile buddies who have suddenly discovered Karl Marx and devoured the Communist Manifesto (that's about all of Marx they've read). At one time they were genial, affable chaps in touch with life's realities; then suddenly they "joined the party," and lost all sense of proportion and clarity of thought and vision. Where at one time they could hold an intelligent conversation and see around questions and problems of the day, they now are unable to do more than mouth boresome slogans and revel in revolutionary cant fresh from the typewriters of their Moscow masters. They could even swallow and defend the recent motion picture fiasco when the Kremlin knelt to the Klan, with straight and solemn faces. It seems that membership in the Communist party is not conducive to developing a sense of humor, truth, proportion or urbanity.

During this period I was secretary of the Harlem Adult Education Committee fostered by the 135th Street branch of the New York Public Library. Eugene Kinckle Jones, executive secretary of the National Urban League, was chairman, Mrs. Vernon A. (Elise) Ayer was vice-chairman. The members were

Robert W. Bagnall of the NAACP; Harry T. Burleigh, noted singer and composer; Attorney Thomas Dyett; Robert B. Elzy of the Urban League; James H. Hubert, secretary of the New York Urban League; Dr. Lorenzo H. King; Mrs. Peter M. Murray; Franklin H. Nichols; Mrs. William Pickens; Mrs. Albert S. Reed; Ernestine Rose, the 135th Street branch librarian; Cecelia Cabaniss Saunders of the YWCA; Arthur A. Schomburg, the bibliophile whose immensely valuable library on the Negro was purchased by the New York Public Library and formed the basis of the famed Schomburg Collection; Dr. Alonzo De G. Smith and Judge James S. Watson. These were some of the leading people in the Negro community.

There was also the Harlem Interracial Forum which met at the headquarters of the New York Urban League, admission free, on Saturday nights. I spoke in February on slavery in Liberia and V. F. Calverton in March discussed his recently published book, *Anthology of American Negro Literature,* which had included my "The Negro's Greatest Gift to America." I do not recall how long this forum lasted but it was a lively one. There seemed to be more real intellectual stir in the community then than there is now. There was certainly no cultural void. There was interest in many subjects besides that of the Negro here and abroad.

The Native African Union had a forum on West 128th Street where I debated the issue of Liberia with H. G. Mugdal of *The Negro World,* the Garvey newspaper. Frank R. Crosswaith, the labor organizer in the area for the International Ladies' Garment Workers' Union, presided over the Peoples' Educational Forum at 2005 Seventh Avenue, where I spoke that spring on May 8th on "Cooperation, the Road to Negro Freedom."

I came to know the brilliant and peppery Annie Nathan Meyer who wrote the play *Black Souls.* Mrs. Meyer, an elderly Jewish lady, wife of the distinguished Dr. Albert Meyer, was one of the founders of Barnard College. She was a militant feminist, a fine writer and an outspoken Negrophile. She was very wise on Communism and deplored the Red efforts on University Heights to lure Negro undergraduates. This was a period when the young campus Communists sought to look as much like unwashed bums as possible, and she said the only clean ones up there were the Negroes.

Mrs. Meyer, who moved in the highest New York circles, took particular joy in baiting speakers at private gatherings who spoke snidely about Negroes. She caused a big uproar once by castigating Judge Lehman, brother of Herbert H. Lehman, for advising a select dinner party that Jews should not become involved in the Negro struggle. At that time only a few Jews who were not Communists, Socialists, or liberals, were interested in identifying themselves in any way with the Negro cause. In her spacious Park Avenue apartment Josephine and I met some of her converts or would-be converts. She was much impressed by my writings, and asked me to do a program note when her play, *Black Souls*, was produced at the Provincetown Playhouse. My effort was entitled "Redrawing the Color Line." Alongside it was an appreciation by John Haynes Holmes of Mrs. Meyer's work.

The premiere at the little theater on Macdougal Street was an auspicious occasion, not only because the play had a mixed cast but also because it touched forbidden themes such as interracial romances. Negroes who starred in the play were Rose McClendon and Juano Hernandez. *Black Souls* was Mrs. Meyer's eighth play. It was directed by James Light.

It was through her influence that I joined the publicity department of the NAACP where I remained until 1935. During that time I wrote the eighteen-article history of the NAACP entitled "Battering Down the Barriers of Prejudice" which ran in the Negro press. It always fetches a wry smile when I hear people saying that the Negro does not know his past!

During this period I had published "Uncle Sam's Black Stepchild" in *The American Mercury* (June, 1933); "The Negro of American Literature" in *The Forum,* quarterly of Barbados, British West Indies; "Boycott to Get Jobs" (September, 1934) in *The Crisis;* "Scripture for Lynchers" (January, 1935) in *The Crisis;* and "The Separate State Hokum" (May, 1935) in *The Crisis,* in which I debated Oscar C. Brown of the 49th State group and James S. Allen of the Communist Party.

CHAPTER 13

WITH THE deepening of the Depression, the propaganda for Negro boycotting of white merchants became intense, and organizations to promote it grew in Chicago, Washington, Richmond, Baltimore, Toledo, and New York. One of the leaders in Harlem was Vere Johns, a Jamaican journalist on the staff of the *New York Amsterdam News*. Our rival viewpoints were aired in *The Crisis*. I called my view "A Deadly Boomerang," and Johns headed his "We Must Have Jobs."

Even today the boycott is a moot question, and the arguments pro and con still echo in colored America. I held that with only seven per cent of the urban Negro population employable in areas of colored residence, it was necessary for 93 per cent to get employment outside the Negro communities. There colored patronage would be a negligible factor and therefore any boycott attempt would fail in its objective.

"The wisdom of the Negro embarking upon an economic boycott," I stated, "is not proved by the 'argument' that others have resorted to it. In the first place, this Negro boycott is unique in that it is the first ever launched specifically for increasing employment. Practically all others have been instigated for political purposes or to enforce the closed shop principle."

I then gave a resumé of boycotts since the weapon was adopted by the Irish Nationalists in the 1880's under Charles Stewart Parnell and named after Captain Boycott, its first victim. I quoted from Jewish leaders like Rabbi Grayzel of Philadelphia who had recently stated:

> The boycott as an organized and purposeful weapon with which to bring an enemy of the Jews to his knees, is, to say the least, not a reliable weapon. It certainly offers no means for a permanent solution to the problem of recurrent anti-Jewishness. . . . Moreover, *no minority can afford to resort to force.* Even if this boycott against Nazi Germany, aided as it is by a great variety of other economic forces, succeeds, I doubt that we will ever again be in a position to use the boycott as a weapon.

I also quoted from Morris D. Waldman, secretary of the American Jewish Committee, who had recently warned Jews against the

> . . . accentuation of separatist consciousness. . . . We must not permit Hitlerites to throw us back into the moral ghetto of unhealthy Jew-consciousness and an estrangement from non-Jewish neighbors. . . . *We must be wary, too, of translating self-analysis into self-betrayal.* I cannot, for example, warn too strongly against the acceptance of the dogma that occupational guidance is to be based on group quotas. Such a course is not only dangerous to our basic rights but may even be futile.

I urged the Negro boycotters to ponder these pearls of wisdom and to reflect on the history of the use of this weapon in the preceding fifty years. I wrote:

> Unhealthy race consciousness is growing among Aframericans like swine in a fattening pen. Some of our leading spokesmen, to say nothing of the lunatic fringe of professional agitators, are busily feeding the fires of race chauvinism. They not only bay for more segregation but they advocate policies that will assure it. Weak and weaponless, they clamor for economic war, quite willing to sacrifice 887,402 Negro jobs to get 57,144. They would rend the stratosphere with their bellows of protest if white customers insisted upon Negro merchants hiring white help.

I recommended that as an alternative Negroes join in the mutual aid of consumers' cooperation which had proven successful all over the world, saying:

> Everywhere today progressive workers are turning wearily from the trite old racial, national and religious slogans and controversies toward this scientific mutual aid; this enlightened anarchism pointing to a rational society free alike from parliamentary chicanery and the goose-stepping brutalities of dictatorship. Not by embarking upon futile and disastrous economic civil wars but by intelligent mutual aid in cooperation with white workers can Negroes improve their economic status.

Had my advice been accepted and acted upon back in the mid-1930's, the urban Negroes by now would have been immensely better off economically and socially. The Negro preachers almost completely failed to consider the value and promise of consumers' cooperation, and even thirty years later have neglected to do so, with the results which they and the sociologists attribute to racial segregation and cultural deprivation. On

217

the contrary they have recently led their people astray into the fatuities and futilities of the so-called Negro Revolution.

During 1934 I devoted much of my writings to attacks on Communism in general and the conduct of the Scottsboro boys "defense" by the Communists through the International Labor Defense.

In January I twitted them on the failure of their great membership drive extending from December 15th to February 15th as admitted by the *Daily Worker*. The bag of 2,104 new members nationally was reportedly less than average. Not one was snared in New York. "In Chicago where packing house workers are as thick as fleas in a Soviet rooming house, only two were bagged for the Party, both of them unemployed."

I especially noted the disappointing result of the Communist drive among Negroes and quoted the *Daily Worker*'s sad comment: "Why are not more Negroes won for the Party, Comrades?"

In April and continuing through the year, I hammered on the conduct of the Scottsboro case and the faulty (from the non-Communist viewpoint) tactics employed. I paid my disrespects to:

> the proposed march on Washington of several thousand Negroes, a plan emerging from the brains of William Davis, editor of the *Amsterdam News,* and his new-found Communist friends. It is one of the most childish and futile plans ever conceived. There have been many marches on Washington, D.C., for various purposes in the past forty years. Not a single one has succeeded. Even where the Washington authorities could have done something, as in the case of the Bonus Army, nothing was done save to drive the ex-soldiers from the capital with bayonet and bomb. Would thirty or forty thousand Negroes fare better? Of what value was the recent Communist Hunger March on Washington (in which nobody actually marched) except to strengthen the forces of

218

reaction? . . . The Negroes will do well not to have much
to do with these fanatics who call themselves Communists.

A year previously I had made a scathing attack on the entire
Negro press for its:

> gullibility in swallowing the propaganda and boresome
> lies and calumnies of the Communists in the past three
> or four years. With very few exceptions, Negro news-
> papers have thrown discrimination to the winds and
> carried practically all of the lying Communist "news"
> releases that have been sent to them. Although suppos-
> edly edited by intelligent men and women familiar with
> the events of the past ten or fifteen years, they have acted
> as if nothing had ever been done to help Negroes fight
> injustice and color discrimination until the International
> Labor Defense came on the scene to chisel in on the
> race racket.

I rung the changes through the months on the "negligence"
of the ILD lawyers in not filing their bill of exceptions in
ample time for a new trial and suggested that this was inten-
tional; dwelt on the vast sums of money collected with no
details as to how spent; and then on the final Red crime of trying
to bribe the State's chief witness, Victoria Price. I had been
viciously and persistently attacked in the Negro and Communist press "for wanting to see the Scottsboro boys electrocuted,
of being a hireling of the Southern lynchers, of sabotaging the
mass struggle of the Negroes, and of going Fascist." They became
apoplectic when my piece "Liebowitz: Jonah in Modern Dress"
appeared in *The American Spectator,* a publication edited by
George Jean Nathan, Eugene O'Neill, Ernest Boyd, and some
other intellectuals, which cut quite a swath at the time.

But all of this was mild compared to the cries of rage from
the Marxists when I mentioned in a column the conduct of
the Angelo Herndon case, saying that now that the young man

had been granted bail he might probably jump it, as Fred Beal and other Communists had done in North Carolina, rather than go to the chain gang. Herndon had been recruited in Cincinnati and sent down to Atlanta, Georgia, by the Reds to lead marches of hungry and unemployed workers on the city hall and capital. A Greenwich Village Communist woman whom I knew had previously asked me to go down there for that purpose, and I laughed aloud.

So they got Herndon; he carried out his Red assignment, and he was promptly nabbed, jugged, tried and sentenced to the Georgia chain gang; then released on bail. Soon the Communists were parading him around the country at mass meetings that proved very lucrative.

The *Daily Worker* and the *Negro Liberator* screamed hysterically that I was one of "the most vicious pen prostitutes plying his trade in the Negro press." In a letter sent over his signature, Herndon accused, "You have attempted to knife me. . . . This is action worthy of a police agent."

The *Daily Worker* of August 28th came out with a four column headlined story which included a lengthy letter supposedly written by Herndon. From this I gathered that those who wrote it had been more concerned than I thought about my attacks on Communism in general and the Scottsboro "defense" in particular. On September 8th Cyril Briggs of the erstwhile African Blood Brotherhood filled two columns of the *Daily Worker* with a characteristic denunciation of me as "assistant lyncher" for whom "no slander was too cheap." The Communists were horrified at the very suggestion that they might be deprived of this meal ticket.

The *Negro Liberator,* a Communist sheet of the same date, reported how the previous week:

> a group of prominent Negro and white intellectuals and professional people met at 405 Edgecomb Avenue, the home of Aaron Douglas, well-known Negro painter, for the purpose of voicing their protest to the recent vicious

attacks of George S. Schuyler against the defense of
Angelo Herndon and the Scottsboro boys.

The screed carried the text of a letter to the *Pittsburgh
Courier* which shouted that:

> We hold the *Courier* jointly responsible with Schuyler
> for all the disruptive and slanderous attacks which have
> appeared in his column, upon the militant struggles of
> the Negro workers. We demand the immediate dismissal
> of George Schuyler from the staff of the *Courier*. We
> demand an end to the provocations against the Scottsboro-
> Herndon defense and other militant struggles.

Among the twenty-four whose names were appended to this
letter demanding dismissal were Channing Tobias, head of
Negro work in the YMCA; Benjamin J. Davis, Jr.; Langston
Hughes, president of the League of Struggle for Negro Rights,
a Communist front, who had recently returned from a West-
to-East trip around the world at Communist expense after the
Black and White Soviet film fiasco, and who the month before
in *The Crisis* had scored Negro college graduates for their
alleged cowardice; Aaron Douglas, an artist and his school
teacher wife, Alta.

Dr. Channing H. Tobias promptly wrote to Aaron Douglas
saying that his name had been used without authority and that

> I would not even ask the dismissal of Mr. George Schuyler
> because I believe that it is just as necessary to safeguard
> the principle of free speech in the case of Mr. Schuyler
> as in the case of Mr. Herndon. If I understand the case
> of Mr. Herndon, free speech is the principal issue.

The other signers never disavowed the letter. I got a sound
drubbing from Red publications and some of the Negro newspapers, although several of the latter came to my defense.

Most amusing of all was a letter from the American Workers Party's provisional organizing committee of which A. J. Muste was chairman; J. B. S. Hardman of Columbia University, vice-chairman; Louis Francis Budenz, later editor of the *Daily Worker*, executive secretary; and Jack Lever, treasurer. This party had been formally launched on July 4, 1934, and its official organ was *Labor Action*, to which I had once contributed an article on the Agricultural Adjustment Act and its influence. The letter was signed by Ann Shane, secretary of the membership committee, and Larry Cohen, New York organizer. Dated September 28, 1934, it read:

> Dear Comrade: Serious charges have been brought against you by Party comrades because of the nature of certain of your recent contributions to the *Courier* and *American Spectator*. You are requested to appear before the next meeting of the Membership Committee of the New York Branch to answer these charges. The meeting will take place on Tuesday, October second at the Party Headquarters at seven p.m. Should you find it impossible to attend you will please let us know immediately, and the Committee will arrange to hold its next meeting at a time convenient to you.

These people evidently assumed that because I contributed one piece to *Labor Action*, that made me a member of their so-called party. At any rate I wrote them the following letter the next day, September 29, 1934:

> My dear friends: I shall have to disappoint you by refusing to be the guest of honor at your inquisition on Tuesday evening, October 2nd. In the first place I decided some time ago not to be a member of any of the numerous political parties, conservative, liberal or radical, and you are hereby notified that I do not consider myself to be a member of the American Workers Party. Although I have never been sent a copy of your party platform, I

felt at one time that you were going to be a real *American* party. Your present contemplated action convinces me that you have taken over the methods of the Communist Party, and of course I refuse to accept the regimentation of thought which that so-called party imposes.

I have always said and written just what I thought without apologies to anyone, and I intend to continue doing so. Whatever I think is wrong, I shall continue to attack. Whatever I think is right, I shall continue to laud, whether it be left, right or center. In doing so, of course, I incur the enmity of some people from time to time, but I have always been more concerned with being true to myself than to any group or groups. I shall continue to pursue this somewhat lonely and iconoclastic course.

The American Workers Party, which was headquartered at 112 East Nineteenth Street in a building that has long harbored many Marxist organizations, soon went down the drain to join a multitude of militant collectivist outfits that have passed fleetingly across the left-wing stage and disappeared never to reappear.

During this period I was collecting information for a series of articles on the schools in Harlem which appeared in the *Courier* illustrated with my own photographs. This was the first series of its kind dealing with Negro schools.

Meanwhile, I was writing against the idea of a Negro boycott against white businesses. On October 6th, I had this to say by way of critical comment:

As was to be expected, the reprisals against the loudly heralded Negro boycott have started and there is no telling how far they will go. Unthinking Negro groups in two or three cities have run up against ironclad injunctions. A representative of one of the boycott groups confessed to me last week that his group realized it has gone as far as it could in the direction of the boycott. In New

York a group of Jewish business men has protested to Mayor LaGuardia against the anti-Semitic character of the boycott campaign in Harlem, the more lunatic fringe of which is headed by one Abdul Sufi Hamid, whom the Jewish newspapers describe as an Arab but who has been no nearer Arabia than North Carolina. The Jewish Minute Men of America, backed by Jewish newspapers of wide circulation, have banded together to fight what they call a Harlem anti-Semitic campaign. Hysteria on one side has been met by hysteria on the other side. And when two hysterias meet, it is just too bad for one of them.

In New York it is to be feared that the Harlem hysteria will be the loser. Abdul Sufi Hamid's Negro Industrial Clerical Alliance may possibly gain a few members and a handful of jobs for them in the Black Belt but the bulk of Negroes who must perforce find jobs outside Little Africa stand to lose. Thousands and thousands of Negroes in New York are employed by Jews either in homes or businesses. A Negro who operates a large employment office in Harlem told me that he placed the bulk of his applicants in Jewish homes. In New York City there are 1,765,000 Jews and something over 300,000 Negroes. Needless to say, it is the capital of the Jewish world, economically and culturally, as it is also the Negro capital; but the Jews are in a position to buy a great deal of Negro laboring power while Negroes are in a position to buy very little Jewish laboring power. Moreover, the Jews are powerful politically. Congressman Dickstein, head of the committee investigating Hitler propaganda in America, has already turned his attention to the Harlem goings-on which, in reality, are anti-Semitic only insofar as the businessmen against whom the Negro boycott is launched happen to be Jews. But once the sweep of hysteria has started, it is hard to appeal to reason, and so stem the tide.

In addition to Abdul Sufi Hamid's group agitating Harlem,

there were groups led by the Reverend John H. Johnson, young pastor of St. Martin's Protestant Episcopal Church; young assistant pastor Adam Clayton Powell, Jr., of the Abyssinian Baptist Church; and another young fellow named Reid. I am convinced that the agitation stirring the Negro community led directly to the growth of race chauvinism and hence to the first Harlem riot and wave of vandalism that disgraced the community and the Negroes. Great is the power of suggestion, especially in stirring up racial, religious, and nationalistic prejudices, and inciting the mentally retarded to greater flights of envy of the more successful.

The most important intellectual debate, as far as Negroes were concerned in 1935, was that held in *The Crisis* for May 1935, on "Which Way Out for the Negro?" Oscar Brown, a Chicago lawyer who headed the 49th State Movement; the Communist official and writer, James S. Allen, and I were the participants. Brown entitled his piece "What Chance Freedom?". Allen called his "The Communist Way Out," while my position was stated simply "The Separate State Hokum." It is said to be one of my best efforts, and I think it demolished the arguments of my opponents. My introduction set the tone and tempo of the attack:

> Whenever the Aframerican, flailed unduly by poverty, prejudice and proscription, yammers aloud for succor, there is a wild stampede of hungry sociological shamans, loaded down with weird and colorful nostrums, clamoring to assuage his hurts.

> Thus, we have been periodically afflicted with the Back-to-Africa dervishes from the early days of the Republic to the advent of the infantile paralysis of Garveyism; the high pressure Group Economy salesmen who view segregation through rose-tinted spectacles, and the wistful witchmen who see Zion amid the snows of Alaska or the swamps of the Amazon.

> The beleaguered Brother has grabbed at one or the other of these nostrums as the rowels of adversity have bitten deep, but his saving sense of humor and fundamental

cynicism have, after cursory examination, restrained all except the lunatic fringe from swallowing such crackpot proposals. The shamans rattle their shells and toss their gri-gri bags for a season, charm a moron minority with their bombastic amphigories, enjoy a grateful change of diet from neckbones to filet mignon and then, when the disease has run its course and dues grow scarcer than dinosaurs, they hock their wardrobes and hold off their landladies until they glimpse another glorious vision of cash.

Scarce had the wallops of the current depression beaten the Brother to his knees, when these Profiteers of Despair bore down upon him, in response to his fervent yelps, bearing old nostrums in new cellophane. To be sure, the Back-to-Africa blather, sans Garvey, was offered again while learned clerks barked from a hundred platforms the virtues of Black Fascism, but in addition the witch doctors dazzled the Ethiopian imagination with visions of the Separate State.

I then proceeded to an analysis of the positions of the 49th Staters and the Communist advocates of Self-Determination for the Black Belt, and demonstrated the sheer impossibility of realizing either goal.

The impact of my continual attacks on Communism in every sector of its activity here and abroad was not negligible. The *Pittsburgh Courier* at the time enjoyed a circulation of approximately a quarter of a million and reached Negroes from one end of the country to the other. Having supplanted the *Chicago Defender* in influence, it was not only more widely read but, more important, it was widely believed. The Communists regarded me as a serious adversary because they knew that I not only had a hard-hitting column but also composed the *Courier's* editorials. Thus, I got yowls of protest from Reds at home and abroad.

When the new Soviet Constitution was adopted, with all of its paper guarantees of freedom and equality, the ecstatic

American Communists were beside themselves with praise of the document which in reality was meaningless except as propaganda. I pointed out that the same guarantees appeared in our own Constitution and thoroughly deflated the Soviet document. For this I received a long six page typewritten letter directly from Moscow which pasted end to end was about five feet long. It was a terrific diatribe in which I was called everything but a child of God (whom Communists do not recognize, of course). It afforded Josephine and me much amusement. What intrigued us much more than the criticism of my stand on the new Soviet Constitution were the signatures at the end which included every Negro Communist then sojourning in Moscow. The singular thing about those signatures was that they all seemed to be in the same handwriting, that of Eugene Gordon, who had abandoned his wife and child here and gone to the Soviet Valhalla for further indoctrination.

Prior to that, while I was ridiculing the *Black and White* film fiasco, Allan McKenzie, one of the Negro "actors" who had gone to the USSR with a score of others of his ilk, wrote a long dispatch to the *Afro-American* ridiculing my statements that the Russian land had been taken from the peasants, and quoting some Communist report to the contrary. He was probably a better actor than journalist because his dispatch sounded like it had been written by Eugene Gordon. The Communists cannot stand criticism. They prefer a monologue to a dialogue every time. What also greatly annoyed them was that my writings were not confined to the *Pittsburgh Courier* and that I spoke all over the country. Nor could they shut me up by recounting any scandals, as they had done with other opponents.

When Dr. W. E. B. DuBois, editor of *The Crisis,* in a succession of editorials, came out for Negroes completely separating themselves from whites, I wrote and spoke against it as a complete surrender to segregation and therefore acceptable to every Klansman, Fascist, and Nazi. An old Socialist who had increasingly taken positions indistinguishable from those of the Communists, DuBois had even given a Marxist interpretation to the Reconstruction period in his book *Black Reconstruction.* To urge Negroes to cut their communications with whites to an irreducible minimum placed him spiritually alongside the 49th Staters and the Communist Black Belters. As I recall, I was the only writer, Negro or white, who openly took him to task. He had to sever his connection with the NAACP Board, which could not stomach his position. In his nineties, when safely parked on President Kwame Nkrumah's payroll, DuBois at last came out boldly and took membership, not in the Communist Party of Ghana but in that of the United States, doubtless at the behest of his wife, the writer Shirley Graham.

On May 14, 1935, I got a letter from NAACP head Walter White notifying me that after July 1, it would be necessary, by decision of the Board's Budget Committee, to dispense with my services because of the Association's "desperate financial condition." He concluded, "We appreciate more than we can say the splendid work you have done in connection with the Association's publicity."

Fortunately, the *Pittsburgh Courier* had another program for me. With nearly a million Negroes in Mississippi and a circulation there of only 2,000, it was decided that a sustained effort would be made to build it up. By Labor Day I had established headquarters in Jackson, Mississippi, and for the next three months I traveled to all parts of the state by rail and bus, and managed to secure a *Courier* agent in every county where we had none. While lodging ranged from good to bad and the available colored restaurants left much to be desired, I found Mississippi in many ways fascinating, the people kindly and cooperative, and the racial way of life not intolerable. I met most of the prominent Negro businessmen, farmers, educators, fraternalists, lawyers, physicians, and dentists, and was often a guest in their homes. I was welcome because I made a point of being fair. Other Negro newspapers were not. They often carried the must lurid stories with screaming headlines which had no basis in fact. The *Chicago Defender* was the worst and for that reason was not permitted to be sold in some communities, and I really could not blame the people for their rancor. I checked on many of these stories of terror and persecution and found them to be entirely false. Apparently northern Negro newspapers would print anything sent to them.

The *Pittsburgh Courier* had a reputation for being dependable and trustworthy, and I sought to maintain it. I was given two pages for news, feature stories, and pictures of Mississippi Negro life. Everywhere I went I was able to get unusual items such as: a Negro who owned more rental houses than anybody else in Jackson; the colored veterinarian who was famed throughout the state; the doctor in Yazoo City who in the face of considerable difficulty and sacrifice had succeeded in building a private hospital; the farmer who owned a dairy which supplied much of the milk consumed in the capital; the several educators who had built large schools from exactly nothing to several modern buildings; and one principal who was noted and respected among farmers, white and colored, for lending his prize boars and bulls around the county to improve the cattle. The church was an important factor in sustaining the spiritual and social life of the state's Negroes. There were many Negroes with large, well-kept farms with diversified products such as milk and timber. Whatever the quality of schools (and they varied widely), they were all full and there was little talk of drop-outs. Mississippi was and is an agricultural state with all of the usual assets and liabilities, and I felt that there were enough of both to present a balanced picture rather than the bias and distortion which was the usual fare in the Negro and so-called liberal press. Because the *Courier* presented a balanced view, printing the favorable along with the unfavorable news, its circulation rose rapidly from 2,000 to 10,000 by Thanksgiving, 1935, when I returned to New York. Nobody had ever spoken kindly and sympathetically about Mississippi before.

However, all was not sweetness and light. After a month's residence and travel I wrote:

> More and more as I travel through the South, especially in this State of Mississippi, I am impressed by the extent to which the race question colors and warps everything, hampers progress and development, and makes the whole

section a little ridiculous. This is reflected not only in the manners of the people, but even in their facial expressions. The wonder is that the cruelty, oppression and exploitation is not even greater than it is.

In a small Mississippi town of less than 3,000 population where I spent a day conversing with colored folk last week, one very intelligent Negro resentfully expressed the view that: "The white folks have formed a plan against the Negro in Mississippi, and they're always carrying out that plan." He was a man of little education, but with a great deal of experience and knowledge. Others there expressed similar views. The white people would have been greatly surprised, doubtless, to have heard those Negroes angrily hold forth on inadequate relief (or none at all), on discrimination on relief work, on failure to use relief money for the improvement of Negro streets and schools, and for building swimming pools, parks and playgrounds which they so sorely need.

There are many, many white people here, much more than an outsider would suspect, who regret this condition and are doing what they can to change it. Their voice is more powerful and their influence greater than it has ever been before, but unfortunately it is not great enough. Yet, if it were not for them, how much worse it would be!

I note that the white newspapers do not rant and rave against the Negro as used to be their wont. I note also that in the stores the clerks are uniformly courteous, quite as much so as I have found them elsewhere in this Land of the Free. Indeed, if one is all set to expect rudeness, one is often disappointed. This is not only true of the large towns but of the small ones as well.

Despite the great handicaps under which Negroes

have lived and labored here, they have taken such good advantage of the few opportunities they have had that there is today little difference between the city and country Negroes.

Schooling has unquestionably played its part in bringing black and white here closer to the national standard of civilization. Roads, the automobile, telephones, radio, increased newspaper circulation and the sobering effect of the depression have also been contributing factors.

I wrote extensively about Mississippi, almost weekly, as I traveled the state from side to side and end to end. The contrasts fascinated me, and this study in depth added much to my understanding of the Southern region and the changes that had occurred in the ten years since I first traversed it. Then I had only paused a day or two in each place; now I was living in Jackson and roaming the rural places, sleeping under strange roofs, eating strange food and meeting unusual people; learning about local customs. There is a temptation to relate more of what I saw and experienced but this would be a lengthy digression. Suffice to say that my sojourn that fall in Mississippi contributed greatly to my larger education.

So, having increased the state circulation from 2,000 to 10,000, and having found a state representative to take over the job, I returned to New York and the writing and lecturing by which I made my living. In the next ten years I visited the South every lecture season, and in addition to speaking for private groups, I talked in almost every college in the area between the District of Columbia and El Paso, and several high schools. Conversations with college presidents, school principals, and teachers added to my knowledge and understanding.

In my lectures I talked mostly of new careers for Negro youth, Negro history, and consumers' cooperation. None of my talks were incendiary, nor were they intended to be. They were all inspirational and encouraging. It is very cheap and unrewarding to go into a community and stir up suspicion and animosity. One has to have a lot of gall to go into a place and tell audiences what their problems are when they have been doing their utmost for years to solve them. I noticed that there were often white people attending my talks, and in several instances they were Ku Klux Klan officials. I never changed a talk because of that. What I said in New York City, I said in Mobile and Dallas.

One cannot get a complete picture of any Southern section just by talking with Negroes and getting their opinions, and I have been fortunate in making the acquaintance of and corresponding with whites of prominence, and with some of no prominence at all.

One of my best friends was Dr. E. C. L. Adams, the white satirist and humorist of Columbia, South Carolina, who had a plantation on the edge of the Congoree swamp and operated a grist mill, along with his medical practice. His was one of the oldest families in the state, and at one time he sought the nomination for lieutenant-governor. Unhappily for his political ambitions, he wrote a droll book entitled *Congoree Sketches* which satirized interracial relations and held many prominent whites up to ridicule. That did it! Later he wrote a sequel called *Nigger to Nigger* in which the principal characters were Negroes holding conversations among themselves about the white folks. He also wrote a play, *Potee's Gal*.

I spent pleasant evenings at his place bordering the Congoree swamp, sampling his fine oysters, roasts, and impeccable corn liquor. When he visited New York he always looked me up. Dr. Adams was a walking encyclopedia on the history and customs of his state, and he knew well the Gullah dialect of the Negroes between Columbia and Charleston. He was a good friend of the editor of *The State,* Gonzales, who was the great authority on Gullah, a mixture of African, English, and Indian dialects. Dr. Adams was an engrossing raconteur, a witty conversationalist, and had a small coterie of Negro friends.

In Jackson, Mississippi, I became acquainted, through a mutual Negro friend, with Colonel Fred Sullens, editor and columnist of the *Jackson Daily News*. A newspaper veteran, he had covered all sorts of stories, gruesome and hilarious, and knew Mississippi like a book. He was an authority on its customs, history, and politics.

I had a protracted correspondence with Lyle Saxon who wrote the wonderful *Fabulous New Orleans* and was an authority on the lore of that city. There was also a young man who was on the staff of the *New Orleans Times-Picayune*. His name now escapes me but I am indebted to him for giving me much information on that city's Negroes and whites and what actually went on between them.

But closest of all to me was that distinguished Southerner, Henry L. Mencken of Baltimore, Maryland, sometime city editor of the *Sun*, also editor of *The Smart Set* and *The American Mercury*, and for long the dean of American letters. I corresponded with him from the time of my first article in the *Mercury* in December, 1927, until long after he was stricken with paralysis and could only correspond through his secretary. Many of his letters to me appear in *Letters of H. L. Mencken*, selected and annotated by Guy J. Forgue (A. A. Knopf, New York, 1961).

We first met at the office of *The American Mercury*, then located in Knopf's office at 730 Fifth Avenue in New York. Miss Lustgarten, the secretary, was there, but Charles Angoff had not yet come from Harvard to join the staff. When I came in, Mencken, a roly-poly exuberant man of medium height, jumped up grinning and said, "Well, we meet at last!" By that time I had contributed about four articles to the magazine. I stayed for about half an hour and we had a lively chat, a pleasant beginning.

All the other times I saw him were in his home on Hollins Street, and always with his brother, August, present. Mencken boasted of his justly famous cellar, which he did not have to press me hard to sample. As I recall the first time, we discussed his book, *The American Language*, and I remember his view that the language was enriched by just a handful of people rather than the masses. I called his attention first to the late Dan Burley, who was then columnist on the *New York Amsterdam*

News, and a man full of new turns and twists to the language, who had written a small dictionary of jazz and jive terms. He had the same flair as Walter Winchell.

Mencken was affable and hospitable, the perfect host. On the matter of the Negro, he had none of the mawkishness the white professional liberals display. He had no illusions about either colored or whites. He had been surrounded all of his life by Negro neighbors, and knew them as individuals in a way that so many sentimentalists do not. I learned much from him about Negroes in Baltimore and the rest of Maryland. One of the things that struck me in visiting many Southern cities was that one found Negro and white families living side by side in the same block to a greater extent than in numerous Northern cities. I found many such blocks in Jackson, Mississippi. While the children did not attend school together, they played together, which is equally important.

Mencken did an enormous amount of reading and he even subscribed to, and read, the *Pittsburgh Courier.* One night he told me that Julia Bumbry Jones, the woman's editor of the *Courier,* wrote the best column of the kind in American journalism. At a time when very few Negroes were being accepted in the more outstanding magazines, Mencken encouraged them and published more of their output than any others. He often used excerpts from my *Courier* column. In a letter to Harry Elmer Barnes dated December 6, 1945, referring to me, Mencken said: "I am more and more convinced that he is the most competent editorial writer in this great Free Republic." It was a very fine compliment.

During the period of the twenties and thirties, Mencken was the literary dictator of the United States. Anything for which he expressed a dislike had a hard time surviving. He was the hero of all the aspiring literati as well as the smart alecks. He controlled them all and dominated the field to an extent that no one does today. His *Sahara of the Bozart* in reference to the South had a block-buster impact that first put the unreconstructed crackers and the professional moonlight-and-roses Dixie glorification literati on the run. He was a vastly entertaining writer and one cannot help but reflect that there are too few left today who, with something to say, know how to say it.

We were having great fun with our little daughter Philippa. She had learned her alphabet at nineteen months, could write at the age of two, and was interviewed at twenty-six months by Lincoln Barnett (then of the *Herald-Tribune* but now of *Life*). On her fourth birthday she played ten of her own piano compositions over the radio, and at five was studying composition at the Pope Pius X School of Liturgical Music at Manhattanville College of the Sacred Heart. Subsequently she enrolled in the grammar school on the campus and completed the whole course in three and one-half years, graduating with the highest grade. She is a linguist, global performer, composer, orchestrator, author, and journalist. It was wonderful to watch her grow. Born and reared in Harlem, she is an immense credit to it. There are many other outstanding colored youngsters in the community who are never mentioned by the flock of writers who have recently discovered only the area's sores.

CHAPTER 14

IN JULY, August, and September, 1937, I had one of the most important assignments I had yet been given. The *Pittsburgh Courier* had decided on a series of articles on the impact of the industrial labor union drive on Negro labor, and vice versa. The sit-in strikes, imported from France where plants had been invaded during a general strike of the General Confederation, were launched by the newly organized CIO under John L. Lewis, head of the United Mine Workers Union, tying up many auto and steel plants. We wanted to know where Negro labor stood on the fight between capital and labor, whether it was joining hands with one side or the other, what was the current attitude of organized white labor toward the unionizaton of Negro workers, and what effect the new union drive would have on jobs for Negroes.

To this end, I made surveys during those hot summer months in New York City; Philadelphia, Johnstown, and Pittsburgh, Pennsylvania; Youngstown, Warren, Wooster, Columbus, Cincinnati, Akron, Dayton, and Toledo, Ohio; Gary and Indianapolis, Indiana; Flint and Detroit, Michigan; St. Louis and Kansas City, Missouri; Tulsa and Oklahoma City, Oklahoma; Houston and Galveston, Texas; New Orleans and Baton Rouge, Louisiana; Mobile and Birmingham, Alabama; Atlanta and Savannah, Georgia; Charlotte, Raleigh, Durham, and Winston-Salem, North Carolina; Norfolk and Richmond, Virginia; Louisville, Kentucky; Memphis, Tennessee; Jacksonville, Florida; Charleston, South Carolina; Charleston, Fairmont, and Welch, West Virginia.

There was considerable ferment and I tried to get to the bottom of it. In some northern industrial centers there was great interest and involvement; in other places Negro workers were scarcely touched at all. In each place, I visited union headquarters and strike centers, interviewed labor leaders, organizers, and Negro workers. I gathered an immense amount of practical information, and every week I wrote an entire page about what I had learned. It was an important part of my education. I already knew the history and theory behind unionism, but now I saw actual union activity and came to know the men who were heading the unions. It was an arduous job, and in addition to this extra writing and almost daily traveling, I was writing the *Courier*'s editorials, my *Views and Reviews* column, and a one-column front page summary of the general news.

Incidentally I learned a great deal about the infiltration by the Communists. While John L. Lewis was using many organizers, trained and untrained, he was also freely using Communist organizers, especially in the big industrial centers. The new industrial unions were insisting upon constitutional pledges of no discrimination because of color. This was something decidedly new at a time when the craft unions were almost entirely lily-white, as indicated in their by-laws and constitutions. They carried this out in practice nearly everywhere, just as they had since the beginning of American trade unionism in the eighteenth century. The industrial unions were the first to turn the tide.

The Communists in the industrial unions were the boldest and most active in soliciting the cooperation and membership of

238

Negroes, and the freest in giving information about conditions in various centers. This was something I had to accept with caution, knowing them as I did.

In their history of the period, *Black Workers and the New Unions* (Chapel Hill, University of North Carolina Press, 1939), Horace R. Cayton and George S. Mitchell quoted liberally from my writings on this summer survey of national unionization. I think that what I wrote in the widest circulated Negro newspaper had great impact on the colored workers. This series described the organizing efforts and methods, how the Negro workers reacted, the personalities involved on the local level, and the community reactions.

With all of this activity, including lecturing about the country, I was not otherwise idle. A new and beautifully produced, well-illustrated magazine of international scope was launched in St. Paul, Minnesota by J. W. G. Dunn and his brother Montfort Dunn, the art director. It was a most ambitious undertaking begun late in 1936. In addition to articles about various parts of the world, it carried regularly intimate letters from capitals of world interest, a calendar of international events such as fairs, expositions, sporting events, carnivals, and concerts, and a half dozen regular departments, all for twenty-five cents.

I appeared in the first issue, March, 1937, with "Woman Palaver," a description of sex life in the West African jungle. In the same number were such authors as William Saroyan, Vincent Starrett, Louis Golding, Senator Robert R. Reynolds, Paul Morand, Elizabeth Hard, Sisley Huddleston, Adele de Leeuw, Count Byron de Prorok, Ezra Pound, and John Cournos.

In June I did a story, "The Lord's Work," about missionaries in Africa.

In the July, 1937, number my "Monrovia Moches On" appeared, a lively and disrespectful description of Liberia's rag-tag capital.

It was a pity that this magazine had to die so young. There has been nothing quite like it, before or since, for sheer interest, editorial excellence, and graphic presentation.

239

For *The Crisis* I did "Reflections on Negro Leadership" in November, and reviews of Margaret Mitchell's *Gone With the Wind* and Cedric Dover's classic, *Half-Caste.*

By that time I was back with the NAACP as business manager of *The Crisis* which was then edited by Roy Wilkins, the assistant secretary, who was also doubling as publicity director. It was very pleasant there at 69 Fifth Avenue, on the corner of Thirteenth Street. Roy was, as he still is, amiable and engaging. We had adjoining offices and we got on famously lunching together almost daily, until I departed in the spring of 1944, when my work became so demanding what with editing the New York edition of the *Pittsburgh Courier* and other tasks. For several months prior to leaving I had also been editing a monthly NAACP bulletin that went to all of the Association's members.

After I ended my survey of industrial centers during the big labor drive of 1937, I intensified my attacks in both columns and editorials against the rising influence of Communism. On December 3, 1937, I sought to clarify the supposed differences between Communism, Fascism and Nazism:

> What seems to have escaped the generality of writers and commentators is that all three forms of government are identical in having regimented life from top to bottom, in having ruthlessly suppressed freedom of speech, assembly, press and thought, and in being controlled by politicians. . . .

> What is new about these three forms of government is that all are controlled by politicians with a reformer complex; ex-revolutionists who have gained power and have nobody above them to curb their excesses.

> Here, truly, is an unprecedented revolution. From being a mere mouthpiece, the politician has become master. He who was once lobbygow is now Lord Supreme. He has greater power than rulers ever had before him. He uses that power ruthlessly with a tribute to the Higher Good

on his tongue and a genuflection before the statue of Demos.

He definitely ends all guarantees of liberty for which enlightened men long fought and for which millions have died, and introduces a slavery worse than chattel slavery because for this new servitude there is no Underground Railroad pointing the way to freedom. . . . The home which was once a man's castle is now his cell. It is State property, like everything else. Into it any arrogant official may enter at any time for any or no reason. Parents produce children but they have nothing to say about their secular and religious training for that has become the business solely of the State. Under the politician-dictator the church is only a rubber stamp, a propaganda adjunct, or it is destroyed entirely.

One works where, as long, as hard and for as much as one is told by the boss. And the State (the politician) is the boss. It is fatal to strike against the boss. . . . It is just another way of committing suicide. It either means the firing squad for "treason" or "Trotskyism" or it means withdrawal of one's work card (national blacklist) which means eventual death.

Artists and writers wear the politicians' uniform of conformity or they perish. So there is much talk of Red Art, Fascist Art or Nazi Art, much like Aframerican chauvinists woof about Negro art. . . .

The politicians being the only class in society that is charlatan enough to offer a cure for everything, are quick to see their opportunity. They promise the suffering people everything if elected to office, as Lenin promised, as Mussolini promised, as Hitler promised and as our Big Boss promised.

> Order requires regulation, regulation requires regimentation, regimentation is based on a plan, nothing must interfere with the operation of the plan if it is to be successful; criticism of the plan might conceivably hinder operation and must therefore be squelched.
>
> We are rapidly approaching this form of State in this country and practically have it in all but name. It won't be long now.

This was a dire prophecy back in December, 1937, but even allowing for the elasticity of free enterprise to adjust itself to change, I doubted then and do now whether the bureaucracy will ever again permit the economy to be really free.

I recognized that the National Negro Congress organized in 1935 and holding its first conference in Chicago in February, 1936, was a Communist-controlled front designed to envelop and eventually control the NAACP. This suspicion was confirmed when John P. Davis became executive secretary, after splitting with Robert C. Weaver over entering the New Deal government as "Negro advisers" to white executives. James Ford said in *Party Organizer* of March, 1935, "We Communists were never doubtful about the significance of the outcome of the NNC." Nor was there any doubt about the control of the proliferation of youth organizations of the period, which has been properly called the Red Decade. There was the American Youth Congress, the Southern Negro Youth Congress, the All-Harlem Youth Conference, the two latter being Red Jim-Crow versions.

The Communists were learning from their initial errors of attacking religion and the Negro churches, and denouncing the black bourgeoisie. Whereas the League of Struggle for Negro Rights had walloped the Negro clergy hard and was openly dominated by white Communists who constituted 62 of its 86 council members, the National Negro Congress had only 10 white Communists to 65 non-Communists. Although the NNC made little impression on the Southern Negroes, it had considerable influence on young college undergraduates and junior professors.

However, the Party lost many Negro adherents when it was discovered that Russia was selling oil to Mussolini to help Fascism conquer Ethiopia. The big gain was getting A. Philip Randolph to accept the presidency of the National Negro Congress. Randolph had never quite been accepted by the NAACP Brahmins up to that time, and he was panting for leadership.

During this period mine was almost the only dissenting voice. I did not raise my voice only in the *Pittsburgh Courier*. In 1939 I flustered the Red dovecotes with my "Negroes Reject Communims," which Eugene Lyons, then editor of *The American Mercury*, was happy to publish. It summarized the evidence to date that Negroes en masse had been heedless of Communist wooing, but that considerable headway had been made among the so-called intellectuals of the race. It drew a vitriolic retort from Martin D. Richardson in the *Daily Worker* which was compliment enough. The Communists were especially incensed because I exposed how they had taken over the Workers Alliance to the detriment of Negroes and installed Communist functionaries, replacing the colored brethren. Although there were many (normally articulate) prominent conservative Negroes, during this crucial period they were silent.

Almost a year before, the *Pittsburgh Courier* had been threatened with a heavy lawsuit by a Negro labor racketeer in Chicago named J. Livert Kelly. Robert L. Vann, the president of the company, asked me to go to Chicago to find out all I could about the fellow preparatory to preparing a defense if the suit should come to trial.

My report to Mr. Vann, which has never been published because Kelly dropped the suit, was embodied in a letter dated June 8, 1938, and kindly supplied to me from his papers by Mrs. Vann. It reads:

My dear Mr. Vann:
The investigation is moving swiftly to its close. I have a clear picture of the amazing ramifications of the whole crime situation here in which J. Livert Kelly plays such a prominent part. If we had time or inclination to get the

243

whole story it would involve a number of the biggest names in Chicago. Obviously Kelly could not navigate without the nod from the police and politicians. Why, they are actually reluctant to arrest known criminals on the South Side because they are aligned with this boss or that racketeer. The decent people just throw up their hands in hopelessness and terror. And I mean *actual* terror.

In this latter connection, you have no idea of the *danger* in what I have been doing here. It has required lots of ingenuity and contacts to get what I wanted without exposing myself to the guns of Kelly's mob. They know I am in town, and they are suspicious and uneasy.

The other day while I was talking to a tavern proprietor Kelly had shaken down, who should come in the door but Kelly. The tavern man was scared to death and showed it in his sickly smile. However, being a fatalistic chap, I was quite nonchalant. And when the proprietor introduced me to Kelly, we shook hands and Kelly didn't quite catch my name. I said firmly, "George Schuyler."

Kelly was taken aback. I watched him closely for a move for his gun, since his usual tactic is to whip people over the head with his pistol. He said: "You've been opening your mouth pretty wide not to know what you're talking about. I don't like people that open their mouths too wide." To which I replied: "No, neither do I," and looked him in the eye, sternly and unsmilingly. He paused for a minute, then turned on his heel and walked out without another word.

Later he told A. N. Fields, a local *Courier* man, that the *Courier* shouldn't take that suit seriously; that he wasn't going to press it. Fields has obtained some valuable information for me. Of course he doesn't know that I am writing a series of articles. He thinks I am merely looking around as the *Courier* representative. I tell you this to show how careful I have had to be.

Now I have talked with a score of people and have secured almost everything uptown and downtown that is obtainable, including the police record of Kelly (which is as long as your arm) and of his chief bodyguard "Aces Deuces" Dugan. I am now trying to get Kelly's record from St. Louis (which is said to include a prison sentence and also a rogue's gallery picture of him), if possible. I am also trying to get the details about Johnny Wooley, a member of his board of directors, proprietor of the Vienna Bath House and one of the owners of the Big Four Novelties in which Kelly has one-third interest. I also want to make a check back on some statements made by the owners of the Vernon Laundry which is colored-owned and which Kelly has been fighting. . . .

My best Chicago friend, Attorney C. Francis Stradford, legal representative there of the Brotherhood of Sleeping Car Porters, was extremely helpful in establishing Chicago contacts on the highest levels, including the liberal Judge Lyle who knew the racket world intimately but was handicapped by the criminal-ridden Cook County government.

This fellow, "St. Louis" Kelly, was head of a South Side Negro union auxiliary which controlled the waiters, waitresses, and barmaids of the community. A refugee from St. Louis (which was as rough and crude as Chicago), he ingratiated himself with his union superiors by staging Bacchanalian orgies for them at his suite in a hotel on South Parkway, the girls being the pick of the prettier barmaids who belonged to his union. When I visited his offices at 47th Street and South Parkway and heard the shocking manner in which he shouted at these women, calling them everything imaginable, my opinion of organized labor was not enhanced.

"St. Louis" Kelly, a brown-skinned man of medium height with custom-made shoes, hats, and suits which he often changed several times a day, could also be seen at the big prizefights, the labor conventions and banquets, the race tracks, and the larger crap games. He was wont to stage parties at Johnny Wooley's Vienna Bath House where all attendants were female and the surrounding police were apparently blind, since the joint was never raided. He was trying to take over the juke box business, had a considerable piece of the prostitution racket, and was generally loud and wrong. Investigating this fellow did not add to my peace of mind while I was in Chicago.

On May 14, 1939, I joined the Committee for Cultural Freedom, along with a large number of others in the intellectual world, at the invitation of Professor John Dewey of Columbia University. It was an association which was to last for fifteen years. This new organization was in opposition to the Committee for Democracy and Intellectual Freedom and the National Emergency Conference set up by Professor Franz Boas, a veteran Fabian Socialist, and a famed anthropologist of Columbia University. This group was all for denouncing the absence of intellectual freedom in Nazi Germany and Fascist Italy but chose to remain mum on the denial of intellectual freedom in the Soviet Union. The Committee for Cultural Freedom was also designed to oppose the American League for Peace and Democracy, the League of American Writers, the National Committee for People's Rights, and similar Red-front groups.

The Dewey committee pledged itself "to expose repression of intellectual freedom under whatever pretext, to defend individuals and groups victimized by totalitarian practices anywhere, to propagate courageously the ideal of untrammeled intellectual activity."

The Boas committee enlisted the support of Secretary of Agriculture Henry A. Wallace and Secretary of the Interior Harold L. Ickes, which was not suprising; but it could not win the endorsement of the council of the American Association of University Professors for its manifesto to educators because that statement, like a companion statement signed by 1200 scientists, hit only at German and Italian totalitarianism, whereas the Committee on Cultural Freedom hit at all dictatorships, including the Russian.

The signers of the call included many people who, it was later revealed, did not wholeheartedly believe in "untrammeled intellectual activity" but here is the complete list and the reader can decide for himself:

Louis Adamic, Van Meter Ames, Sherwood Anderson, Robert O. Ballou, Ernest Sutherland Bates, W. M. Baumgardner, Arthur F. Bentley, David Bernstein, George Boas, Boyd H. Bode, S. L. Boothroyd, P. W. Bridgman, Paul F. Brissenden, Dorothy Dunbar Bromley, Robert C. Brooks, Edmund de S. Brunner, E. A. Burtt, Witter Bynner, V. F. Calverton, W. B. Cannon, Rudolf Carnap, John Chamberlain, John N. Childs, L. S. Cottrell, George S. Counts, Philip W. L. Cox, Countee Cullen, Merle Curti, Walter Damrosch, John Dewey, Elmer Davis, Ned H. Dearborn, Arthur Dresden.

Max Eastman, Irwin Edman, Edwin R. Embree, Abraham Epstein, Morris L. Ernst, Edna Ferber, Herbert E. Harris, George W. Hartmann, Henry Hazlitt, Milton P. Hermann, Philip M. Hicks, Jesse H. Holmes, John Haynes Holmes, Sidney Hook, B. W. Huebsch, Inez Haynes Irwin, James W. Ivy, Horace M. Kallen, William H. Kilpatrick, Suzanne LaFollette, George W. Lee, Arthur O. Lovejoy, Robert H. Lowie, Ferdinand Lundberg, Eugene Lyons, Benjamin C. Marsh, Milton S. Mayer, Nelson P. Mead, Marston Morse, Philip E. Moseley, David S. Muzzey.

Henry Neumann, Jesse H. Newton, H. A. Overstreet, Walter Pach, Saul K. Padover, John Dos Passos, Frederick L. Redefer, Victor Riesel, James Rorty, Leonard Q. Ross, Morrie Ryskind, J. Salwyn Schapiro, Willi Schlamm, George S. Schuyler, John Sloan, Joseph Hilton Smyth, Clara G. Stillman, Benjamin Stolberg, V. T. Thayer,

Norman Thomas, Dorothy Thompson, Frank N. Trager, Howard M. Trueblood, Frederick F. Van de Water, M. R. Warner, William Carlos Williams, and Helen Woodward.

There was, I seem to recall, a large gathering somewhere in Greenwich Village of these people who were as concerned about totalitarianism in the Soviet Union as in Germany and Italy. The committee began publishing *Cultural Freedom,* a mimeographed bulletin to which I contributed in June, 1940, an essay "Cultural Freedom and the American Negro." On the editorial board of the bulletin were Isabel Lundberg, Victor Riesel, Clara G. Stillman, and Helen Woodward. I don't know when it passed away but I don't think it lasted long.

In view of what has happened in the world, especially since World War II, I think the most significant article I wrote during this entire period was in *The Crisis* for August, 1938, on "The Rise of the Black Internationale." It was the leading article in that issue, and a lengthy one, which predicted much that has happened in the developing color conflict, including the worldwide liberation of the colored peoples from white rule, which I referred to as the White Internationale. This was exactly a year before the Nazi invasion of Poland. It was a factual summary and an analysis which led logically to the inevitability of World War II and the awakening of the nonwhite people everywhere.

On February 11, 1939, I added my voice to those who saw the war clouds gathering. In that issue of the *Courier* I wrote:

In practice there is no difference between Communism and Fascism. Both are anti-democratic, both are dictatorial and ruthless regardless of the alleged reasons, both brutally suppress minorities. It is a cruel jest to say there is any basic difference between them or any fundamental antagonism. There is privately more in common between Hitler and Stalin than there is between Roosevelt and Chamberlain. *I should not be at all surprised to hear shortly of a Moscow-Berlin alliance.* [Emphasis added.]

248

And indeed, six months later on August 23, 1939, the Nazi-Soviet non-aggression pact was signed in Moscow, with Communist and National Socialist leaders grinning around the council table like big gamblers at Monte Carlo or Las Vegas.

In a front page story immediately after the invasion of Poland, I discussed the probable impact of World War II on the colonial world and indicated that the result would be the eventual liberation of the colonies.

A few days later, in our issue of September 9, 1939, I wrote:

> The sudden waltzing together of Hitler and Stalin has shocked the liberals and starry-eyed fellow travelers, and greatly embarrassed the naive majority of Communists, but it left me quite calm and chuckling.
>
> I have been saying all along that there is no difference between Fascism and Communism, and this position has brought shrill and frothy protestations from the Comrades and their stooges, especially from the black Reds parked on the Communist payroll. And yet nothing has been more obvious to an impartial and sensible observer.
>
> That so many people have been fooled about the Russian regime is a tribute to the effectiveness of the Red propaganda and the strange power of words. It proves the contention of Hitler that any lie will be believed if repeated often and loudly enough.
>
> It was apparent from the very beginning of the Communist revolution that it had nothing to do with Communism, nothing to do with democracy, nothing to do with freedom. Twenty years ago any sage fellow could predict the inevitable course of the regime that won its way to power in Russia. Very early in its history it "liquidated" all opposition, both radical and conservative.
>
> It concentrated all power in the hands of a small oligarchy, and as the years passed that oligarchy grew

smaller, until today it is an autocracy presided over by Stalin, the ex-bandit and police informer. All the usual standards of public morality have been tossed into the trash barrel and in its lust for power "anything goes." It slaughtered the Social Revolutionaries, slaughtered millions of the farmers and workers, and finally killed off many of the founders of the regime and heads of the army. A more apt symbol of the regime would have been the Double Cross rather than the Scythe and Hammer. It has long been nothing more than an Asiatic dictatorship, similar in every respect to the regimes of Fascism in Italy and Nazism in Germany which copied from it.

Like the Nazis and Fascists, the Russian dictatorship has had its agents in every country where they have organized "Communist" parties and sought by every means to spread disruption and undermine existing regimes. These stooge groups have done more to destroy working class solidarity and the development of organized labor than all the capitalist groups put together. From the very beginning they have "bored from within" or attacked from without every liberal force they couldn't control.

In the United States a valiant effort was made to "capture" the Negro group and the organizations serving its cause. They used the social equality device, the Scottsboro Case and the unbelievably stupid "Self-Determination for the Black Belt" bait to little effect, thanks to the basic common sense of the bulk of Negroes. They took in a few mis-educated Negro intellectuals and a few of the more thoughtless and gullible workers of color, but otherwise made little headway. Masters of duplicity, the various Communist parties throughout the world have expediently thrown overboard every principle they once espoused, just like the Nazis and Fascists. They ditched their "revolutionary" work among the black serfs, sold oil to Italy to help defeat Ethiopia, staged the *Black and*

White film fiasco, in an effort to make up to the Western powers.

It seems to me to be worthy of comment that my daughter Philippa played an important part in shaping my own development. The three of us had joyous times together, reading to each other, playing cards and games, putting together jigsaw maps of the nation and the world, holding parties where she not only played the piano but displayed her enormous versatility. Strangers were amazed at her diverse attainments and great promise. She had a prodigious memory which we learned about often by accident, as when we discovered that she had committed to memory the child's book *Little Black Sambo* and Blaise Cedrar's African stories. These ran to forty or fifty pages. She had an amazing vocabulary, and a tirelessness that often wore us out.

At the age of five she entered a notebook in the Philharmonic children's concert series and won first prize. Thereafter she won various prizes, including medals, from the Philharmonic until she was requested not to enter any more notebooks. She did all the necessary research herself and some of the drawings under the guidance of Josephine, who was both writer and artist. As noted earlier, when still five years old, she entered a class in music at the Manhattanville College of the Sacred Heart's Pope Pius School of Liturgical Music under Mother Stevens, a distinguished musician who taught her all the basic things. She appeared on the radio, entered several musical contests for pianists, and gave several recitals under the direction of her expert teacher. She was awarded a certificate and medallion by the New York World's Fair of 1939, and gave two recitals in the Education Building at the New York World's Fair of 1940. She was awarded a gold medal by the City of New York for a performance in Central Park.

She was a child who never had to be pushed either to study or to perform. She loved it and we took joy in opening the great wide world to her. Josephine kept her on a strict, vitamin-rich diet as soon as she was weaned after a year at the breast, and she was never ill. To this day she has never eaten sugar, commercial candy or pastry, or white flour, and has not eaten meat in fifteen years.

Philippa went through the eight grades of grammar school at Manhattanville in three years. Her associates towered over her when she graduated second in her class. The Mothers suggested that for psychological reasons she take second place even though she had surpassed everyone in all studies. Incidentally, she was the first colored child to attend the school. It was during this time that the president of Manhattanville College, Mother Dammann, was instrumental in breaking down the barrier that had excluded Negro undergraduates. The Roman Catholic Church has come a long way since that time.

Philippa's experience seems to indicate that with care and attention by loving parents, any physically normal child can perform impressively in almost any field, if stimulated and encouraged. So-called race has nothing to do with it, nor has nationality. The racial complexes are too often built in by parents and relatives. Individualism is the important thing. Philippa participated in all of our conversations to the extent of her knowledge and ability, and we tried as best we could to explain everything that aroused her interest. When we could not explain something, we went with her to the encyclopedia and dictionary, or to our rather large library. At the age of four she received her first library card at the 114th Street branch of the New York Public Library, and soon needed another because she read almost every book in the children's room, taking out five and six at a time. And yet she was physically the most active child of her age in the Morningside Park playground across from our apartment house.

So, although we had little money and did not have many of the material things others enjoy, we were happy and content. Outstanding people from all over the United States and from many foreign countries visited us, and this, too, was a big part of our daughter's education. Through a private tutor, Melva Price, she learned Latin, Spanish and French, later acquiring Italian, Portuguese, and Swahili. This stood her in good stead in her musical travels all over the world and when she covered the Katanga War for the United Press feature service. When she went to Mexico City at the age of twelve, she could converse easily with residents. She even found time there to compose her *Manhattan Nocturne*. Upon returning she orchestrated it herself. It was played two years later by the New York Philharmonic Orchestra, and subsequently by many others.

This has been not only her development but a part of my own. I do not think it is sufficiently stressed that children bring up parents to a large extent. With a safe base at home, one can go out more freely and have confidence to contend with society. This is a conservative view which I held from the beginning, but it was enormously strengthened by my life with Josephine and Philippa. I was elated when The Chaperons of Harlem gave Josephine a plaque on Mother's Day, 1959, inscribed "Love to a Worthy Mother." She is indeed worthy and her imprint is all over her daughter. On December 27, 1959, the 46th Grand Conclave of the Omega Psi Phi Fraternity's National Talent Hunt Committee gave its Achievement Award to Philippa "For Her Inspiration and Encouragement to Young People." She treasured that plaque as much as the medals and decorations she has received in so many parts of the world.

The decade from 1940–1950 was one of great importance. I wrote a variety of articles but aimed my shafts most often at the Communist conspiracy, devoting at least fifty full-length columns to the subject in the *Pittsburgh Courier* alone, to say nothing of many unsigned, restrained editorials supposedly expressing the policy of the paper. Actually there was never any conference on editorial policy with Robert L. Vann, who passed away in 1940, nor with Ira F. Lewis, who was stricken in New York in 1948, just after my return from a tour of South America. Once in a while a letter would come from one or the other of them suggesting treatment of a certain subject; but there were not over a half-dozen of them. I instinctively knew where and how to tread, and there was never a reprimand for having overstepped the bounds. Nor were there many under William G. Nunn and P. L. Prattis who were successive managing editors and editors. At the same time, taking the whole world as my oyster, I discussed in both editorials and my columns a world viewpoint of which the color problem was but one aspect related to the whole. For this reason the *Courier* readers got a much more varied fare than the readers of other newspapers serving the Negro public. Along with being colored our readers were Americans and citizens of the world, and I never let them forget it. I think this was an important adjunct to their education, and what I wrote had a great impact judging from the more than 300,000 copies we were then selling each week from coast to coast and overseas.

The first direct editorial interference came after I had taken over the editorship of the New York Edition of the paper, a post I assumed in February 1944. We had a considerable staff there and I inaugurated a vigorous editorial policy designed to build circulation and prestige. I got John Welch, a Negro pianist who had just returned from internment in Germany, to write a series "My Twelve Years Under Adolf Hitler" which sold very well. I carried a series by Howard Day, a retired teacher, on "What's Wrong With Harlem's Schools?" However, the big series was the one written by George Hewitt, a Communist defector whose Party name was Tim Holmes. He had been an official of the Communist Party for fifteen years and had been sent to Russia where he studied in the Lenin School. He was to tell of the Red efforts to "capture" the Negroes and divide, disrupt, and indoctrinate Negro leadership. In his series he named dates and places. The first articles told of the machinations and intrigue that went on en route to Russia and within the country, and how the colored comrades were treated as boys by both American and Russian functionaries. It was fascinating, informative "inside" stuff. After two or three articles in the series, Hewitt reached the United States and began to reveal many secrets of the Communist conspiracy, giving the names and roles of the conspirators and fellow travelers.

The series was abruptly terminated by Bill Nunn, who was then managing editor. I never got an explanation, although I sought one as soon as the series was stopped. I never pressed the matter with Ira F. Lewis because I believe in always going through channels, and not over the heads of my immediate superiors. Somebody had gotten to Bill and persuaded him that the articles were now becoming dynamite. I imagine the Communist Party and its Red Uncle Toms were delighted over the discontinuance of the series at its juiciest part.

Poor George Hewitt was harried from pillar to post by the Reds. He could get no work until Alfred Kohlberg, the millionaire importer of Chinese goods and a militant anti-Communist, made a job for him. Hewitt later was stricken with paralysis and was a pitiful sight. I shall always believe that his disability was brought about by Communist harassment. There have been similar cases, and even murder. The cause of the death of Manning Johnson, another deep thorn in the Communist side, is still unknown, although attributed to an automobile accident. One reason the Communist Party always wants to select wives for their functionaries is that it is easier to keep track of their activities and opinions. This happened in the case of Ben Davis, Jr., and with other Party hacks. Since honesty, loyalty, and love are regarded as petty bourgeois prejudices, the lot of an occasional Doubting Thomas tied to a Party wife is a tough one.

At the beginning of the decade, it will be recalled, I was business manager of *The Crisis,* and during my seven years there I was successful finally in making it self-supporting by getting a larger volume of advertising of the type it had not previously obtained. I made several trips soliciting business from large insurance companies and other businesses. I was on one of these trips, in New Orleans, the day Pearl Harbor was bombed by the Japanese.

In June, 1940, I went to Uvalde, Texas, and Eagle Pass on the Mexican border to write a story on John Garner, the Vice-President, then seeking the Democratic presidential nomination. I interviewed him and many others. The story, "Garner At Home," appeared in *The Crisis.*

For *The Modern Quarterly*'s V. F. Calverton Memorial Issue, Fall, 1940, I wrote "The Negro in the New Order": the other contributors included S. L. Solon, Herbert Gorman, Russell Cowles, Max Eastman, Roger Baldwin, Harry Elmer Barnes, John Chamberlain, Fritz Wittels, Scott Nearing, Thomas Hart Benton, and McAlister Coleman.

After the Pearl Harbor disaster, I immediately began writing my column on it and the future of the war with Japan in a Negro hotel in New Orleans across the park from the Southern Pacific terminal. I had just heard President Roosevelt on "the day that will live in infamy." The column which came out the next week predicted quite accurately what would happen to the Japanese-Americans; that they would soon be in concentration camps. Six months later they were, with homes, farms, and other property taken from them. I was one of the first writers to later take up the cudgels for them. This was at a time when most writers failed to speak out. It is noteworthy that Italian- and German-Americans were *not* interned in camps. I pointed out that what had happened to Japanese-Americans could happen to black Americans if the majority was sufficiently provoked and subverted.

In June, 1942, I wrote "A Look at Negro Louisiana" for *The Sepia Socialite* of New Orleans. In May, 1943, I was invited to become associate editor of a monthly magazine, *The African*, edited by A. Balfour Linton. Other associate editors were J. A. Rogers, David A. Talbot, and later, S. W. Garlington. I contributed a page, monthly, entitled alternately "Things of No Importance" and "It Happened in Africa." This assignment required me to keep in very close touch with events in Africa and the colored world. I learned a lot which I was able to use later when I wrote "The Red Drive in the Colonies" for the Catholic Information Society of New York in 1947. This experience was especially valuable because I learned the background and activities of several persons who, in the fifties, became heads of states or high officials. The majority of them were Red, especially those close to the French CGT, some of whom I met later.

On June 26, 1943, I wrote for *The New Leader* on "The Negro Press" and in November of that year I did "A Long War Will Aid the Negro" for *The Crisis* which raised the hackles of the

Red Uncle Tom, Doxey Wilkerson, who had left the Howard University faculty to become a Party official. I was never able to fathom why Wilkerson thought he had to leave Howard when there were other Red professors who remained.

In 1944, the Modern Library brought out another *Anthology of American Negro Literature,* this time edited by Sylvestre C. Watkins of Chicago. Included was my piece formerly appearing in *Common Ground,* "Dr. Jekyll and Mr. Hyde and The Negro." In March, 1944, the *Negro Digest* used my original piece, "My Most Humiliating Jim Crow Experience." This followed by a month an invitational article for *Transatlantic,* a monthly publication by Penguin Books, Ltd., of London, entitled "Harlem: Half-Way to Heaven." There were other pieces by Turner Catledge of the *New York Times,* Kathleen McLaughlin, and Lloyd Lewis of Chicago.

The following June I participated in a round table in the *Negro Digest* under the title "Should Negroes in the South Migrate North?" In July I reviewed *An American Dilemma* for Dwight Macdonald's *Politics.* In the same year the University of North Carolina Press at Chapel Hill published the symposium *What The Negro Wants,* edited by Dr. Rayford Logan of Howard University. Some of the contributions were so harsh that W. T. Couch, the publisher, was loath to carry them, causing Logan to threaten a lawsuit. My contribution was "The Caucasian Problem" which aroused most of Mr. Couch's ire. My thesis was that there was not a Negro problem but a Caucasian problem, and what the Negroes over the world wanted was fair and human treatment.

I participated in another symposium in the December, 1944, *Negro Digest* on "Have the Communists Quit Fighting for Negro Rights?" along with William L. Patterson, Benjamin J. Davis, Jr., R. Cayton and James W. Ford (which was weighting it pretty heavily on the Red side). My contention was that they had not quit because they had never started; that Communists had fought for nobody's rights except their own; that their policy had been one of complete expediency unburdened by principle or scruple, and in their drive for power they had ruthlessly used, double-crossed, and destroyed people, including their own leading party members; that "the embrace of this conscienceless gang is truly the kiss of death."

Moving from city to city, especially in the Northern industrial areas, I had become alarmed by the growth of racial intolerance during the war. Labor leaders I knew in the Detroit area were gravely concerned by the growing tension which they attributed to the vast influx of colored and white Southern migrants who had changed their residence in pursuit of war jobs but had not changed their mind about race relations, or their ways. Many women had entered the war factories, particularly from the middle classes nearby, and they were shocked by the crude language and habits of many of the migrant war workers. So many cases came before the unions' grievance committees and shop stewards that labor officials urged me to do something about it. The trend was observable everywhere.

It is tempting to assess blame for such conditions. Some blamed it on the Negroes, some on the whites, but the point was that the prejudice and the resulting discrimination were there. It could not all be blamed on the scarcity of housing, although that contributed much to the growing antipathy between the colored and white people impinging upon each other. The vacillation of the Federal government in the area of housing had contributed much to the racial tension. Even then there had not been sufficient time to provide adequate housing for the vast army of migrant workers. Nor had there been time to re-educate them in urban attitudes and relations. It was an emergency which no one had anticipated, the war being only a year old and the need for speedy production of munitions, armaments, and material being primary. Something needed to be done to avert a racial war, and that was re-educating those who might participate in such a holocaust. Unfortunately little or nothing was being done, although some thoughtful people were aware of the dangers. The work of mass education was beyond the vision of the NAACP, the largest and most viable of the colored organizations, or the powerful Negro churches.

So then, perhaps quixotically, I decided to do something about it, especially in the re-education of white people who, because they made up nine-tenths of the population, dominated and controlled the situation. I sent out a mimeographed broadcast to the hundreds of thinking Negroes I knew for cooperation and assistance in launching the Association for Tolerance in America.

After analyzing the basis of race prejudice, pointing out that while "color prejudice is prevalent but not inherent," I argued that "the primary step in bettering race relations and lessening color prejudice is to re-condition the white masses by scientific propaganda. To the extent that their prejudices are lessened, the upper white minority is strengthened in whatever efforts it may be disposed to make to end color prejudice—or to help others to do so. The error in our past procedure has been our disposition to labor with the enlightened five per cent to the exclusion of the unenlightened 95 per cent."

I promised that this nationwide organization of men and women of good will would not engage in legal defense, nor directly fight racial discrimination, nor organize mass meetings, marches or picketings, nor attack any person or group, nor descend to the methods of charlatanism or demagoguery.

On the other hand it would employ the latest and most effective methods of mass education, such as large and scientifically prepared displays in weekly and daily publications reaching the masses; use the radio extensively; utilize attractive outdoor advertising wherever feasible, prepare small, simple, illustrated pamphlets calculated to alter the popular conception of the Negro. It would always stress the idea that national unity is dependent upon national brotherhood; that real democracy is impossible without fraternity; that liberty cannot be realized without equality of opportunity and freedom of choice. Those were my views then, in January, 1943, and they are substantially my views in January, 1966.

Needless to say, I had no money of my own to launch such an ambitious campaign, but I proceeded on the assumption that other like-minded colored people would help finance it. The first task was to mobilize them, and to that I vigorously addressed myself.

The letterhead of the Association for Tolerance in America,

with me as president, Corinne Dean as secretary, and consulting artists Elton C. Fax of Brooklyn, Constance Bradley of Chicago, and Louise E. Jefferson of New York, describing the Association as "a group dedicated to the task of eliminating color prejudice through mass education," went out by the hundreds.

In a press release dated February 19, 1943, it was announced that "over 100 colored and white citizens" had organized the group which would "supplement and facilitate the work of existing organizations by preparing the way psychologically. Its job will be 'selling' the colored American to the white masses who have hitherto been neglected by Negro propagandists who concentrated on the enlightened minority of whites."

Elton C. Fax and I worked closely together on the six-page illustrated nine-by-seven-inch folder on beige-colored book paper with numerous small sketches illustrating the text. It read:

How will America treat him when he returns [illustration of colored soldier in battle dress]? He is fighting for democracy in Egypt, India, Liberia, Morocco, Algeria, Tunis, Australia, New Guinea and the Libyan desert. Will he enjoy democracy when he returns? It is up to YOU to decide. A little of your time and money spent NOW will help make America a better place for him to live in, and for you, too. When this war is over and the soldiers return . . . will we see this [illustration of returning colored soldier being offered a job, in contrast to another looking at a sign, "No Negroes Hired Here"]?

Let us not 'kid' ourselves. We cannot win full citizenship rights for colored Americans until we have changed the minds of white Americans. What *they* think about you determines your status. They will not agree to a change of your status until you change their minds. The minds of these people constituting 90 per cent of the American population can be changed, and this can be done by using the same means through which their minds were made up. With your financial and spiritual help we plan to use billboards and pamphlets, postcards and car cards, newspapers and magazines, the radio and films.

We will reach the white masses in their unions, churches, clubs and homes, in factories and on the streets. We will tell them about your past and about your present, and about your hopes for the future. We will reach the ordinary white American with the story of your service in all wars since the Revolution, of the excellence of your poets, the cleverness of your inventions, of the achievements of your scholars and business men; of the rise of the Negro church and your contribution as farmers, artisans and professional workers.

This statement was interspersed with twenty-two very small sketches. On the back page was a large sketch of a bust of a white worker scratching his head sceptically, with the legend: "You've got to convince him! Unless this ordinary white American believes you deserve a fair deal, you cannot win it. Let's change his mind!"

Thousands of these attractive folders went out across the country to educators, professional people, labor leaders and others. The response was very encouraging.

Mr. Fax and I then designed a car card for display in buses and street cars. It showed the head and shoulders of a Negro soldier in battle dress, with the text: "500,000 of these lads are fighting for *you. . . . Let* Them and Theirs Share in Our Democracy, ASSOCIATION FOR TOLERANCE IN AMERICA." This was reproduced on 10,000 postcards used for further solicitation, and recipients were asked to contribute at least three dollars to "put these red and black cards in a street car or bus in *some* American city for three months. . . . This is *one* way to do something constructive—NOW!"

In a Report to Associates for July-August, 1943, we were able to announce that:

Cards were carried in 120 buses and street cars in Gary, Indiana. . . . Mrs. Inez B. Brewer, our associate there, reported: 'The posters are on display in both buses and street cars throughout the city. . . . I belong to two mixed organizations of town people (interracial). . . . These white

261

members have seen the posters and are well pleased. They hope that the less tolerant members of our race will be inclined to *look* and *think* and *act*. . . . Two other organizations of which I am a member have asked for a poster to hang in their club room."

This had required a tremendous amount of work, and at the same time I was doing my work at *The Crisis,* writing editorials, columns and book reviews for the *Pittsburgh Courier,* and occasionally lecturing.

The difficulties in carrying on the promotion were great for a very limited treasury. There was, for instance, considerable correspondence with transit card companies. Sometimes space was not available in the vehicles in the cities we might have otherwise entered. A city with 500 or 1,000 vehicles would require the expenditure of $1,500 or $3,000, aside from the cost of the cards.

Matrices of postcard size were sent to 100 Negro newspapers with the request that they make a contribution of space to further the campaign. The only ones that did so were the *Ohio State Express,* the *Carolina Times,* the *Arkansas World, The Union* (Cincinnati), the *Michigan Chronicle,* the *Palmetto Leader,* the *Minneapolis Spokesman,* the *Chicago Bee* and the *Louisiana Weekly.* The others were not heard from. Better results might have been obtained from white dailies and weeklies.

I reminded the Associates that "Much intolerance is caused or increased among white Americans by the bad conduct of many Negroes with whom they come in contact. So any improvement in the conduct of Negroes will lessen ignorance and misunderstanding among whites—and that is our great aim."

We asked hundreds of colored ministers to buy the large card and we charged them only one dollar. The results were not pleasing to us.

In order that our cards could appear simultaneously in many cities, we considered asking the financial assistance of large industrial and commercial enterprises, and asked the Associates to provide us with lists of big employers in their immediate vicinities, preferably those with large numbers of Negro employees. I was able to place a full-page advertisement of the Association on the back cover of the July and August, 1943, issues of *The African* in two colors, mainly because I was an associate editor. I also wrote a piece on "The Education of White Folks" which appeared in the July, 1943, issue of the *Interracial Review*, a Catholic monthly.

We had an ambitious plan to carry on a campaign in Mobile, Alabama, using cards in 106 buses, one-minute recordings over the two radio stations, advertising in local newspapers, and wide distribution of a small pamphlet "What Every White American Should Know." The campaign was to last three months. Whereas in 1940 Mobile had a total of 78,720 people at the time of the census, the influx of industries and workers had swollen it to 200,000 of all colors. Inadequate housing and transportation facilities were increasing racial tension and friction, and there already had been clashes. Miss Bradley of Chicago was working on a car card for that city.

Nothing came of the tentative Mobile campaign, not because of lack of money but because the bus and car companies reneged. It seemed that the time was not propitious for work there. In August, 1943, I warned in a release that

> race relations are being worsened by public discourtesy, boorishness, uncleanliness, obscene language, garish display and drunkenness of a small minority of Negroes— and the whole group is judged by the uncivilized behavior of the few. It is felt that tolerance is not only furthered by educating the white masses, as the Association does with its bus and car cards, but by educating the colored masses also.

Elton Fax by that time had created another poster, using the familiar helmeted soldier's head, and the legend: "600,000 Warriors for Democracy" with the text: "You Can Help Make America Better For Them By Your Conduct. You are judged by your talk, your looks, your actions. Be neat, sober, clean, steady, thrifty, healthy, punctual, courteous, industrious." These posters were sold at 15 for one dollar or 100 for five dollars. A simple primer was prepared for distribution among whites to give even the least educated the major facts about the history and progress of Afro-Americans. We sold Tolerance Seals for letters.

By November of that year we had nearly 300 Associates and 19 business and fraternal organizations. This was the eleventh month of activity. On December 20, 1943, we were able to report the distribution of more than 30,000 pieces of propaganda of various kinds on a meager income of $1664.82, all duly accounted for. There was no charge for office rental or equipment, and I took nothing for myself.

The June 19, 1943, race riot in Detroit, following closely upon the NAACP national conference (I was one of the speakers there), and the rising tension and conflict in other cities, were discouraging factors. Equally discouraging was the lack of response for such a national undertaking. We needed a vast amount of money to do even a part of the job, and the money was not forthcoming. We could not go on, although I think the objective was a worthy one; and many of the things we did were forerunners of what has been done in subsequent years.

This was my second and last effort in group organization for betterment by self-help. I believed then, and still believe, that this approach to improvement of race relations is far better than agitation by self-serving Negroes who demand immediate solutions to age-old problems which have not been so solved anywhere on earth.

CHAPTER 15

IN FEBRUARY, 1944, Ira F. Lewis, the *Courier* president, asked me to take over the editorship of the New York Edition of the paper and attempt to expand its news coverage, and in that connection I have already related what was done. Until June, I also continued as business manager of *The Crisis* and as editor of the monthly NAACP bulletin which went to the membership. I expanded the New York *Courier* staff to about a dozen and we made quite a big splash, which alarmed our rivals, the *New York Amsterdam News* and the *New York Age.* I was also doing my usual editorial chores for the main office, which was a full-time job in itself; since 1937 I had been reviewing books and doing an illustrated, inspirational editorial as well.

During the remainder of the 1940's I was as busy as ever, perhaps busier. In May, 1945, I published in the *Negro Digest* "What the Negro Thinks of the South" and a piece in *The American Mercury* on the possibility of coming race riots. In April, 1946, the *Interracial Review* carried "The Negro and

Communism"; in October, the *Negro Book Club News* used "What's Wrong With Negro Writers," and in December, I did "The Future of the Negro in Northern Politics" which anticipated what has since occurred.

In 1946, Alfred Kohlberg began publication of the important anti-Communist monthly magazine, *Plain Talk,* with Isaac Don Levine as editor, Ralph de Toledano as managing editor, and as contributing editors, Christopher Emmett, Jr. and Karl Baarslag. It was the first post-war magazine to ruthlessly expose the Communist conspiracy in America and abroad. Mabel Travis Wood succeeded de Toledano, and Eugene Lyons, Suzanne LaFollette, and I became contributing editors in September, 1947, after I had written a scathing exposé of the Communist conspiracy against Negroes. I remained a contributing editor until well into 1950 when the magazine folded. The files of *Plain Talk* make extremely valuable reading today for those seeking background material on the Red conspiracy in the United States and all over the world.

Plain Talk attracted a galaxy of some of the best writers on Red subversion, and I met and talked with many of them. They included such as Leon Dennen, Joseph Zack, Alfred Kohlberg, Rebecca West, Julius Epstein, General Patrick J. Hurley, Ann Su Cardwell, E. von Hofmannsthal, Kurt Singer, Senator Jack B. Tenney, Freda Utley, Leopold Schwarzschild, Edna Lonigan, Eugen Richter, Bogdan Raditsa, John Chamberlain, Howard Rushmore, Robert Buchanan, Victor Lasky, Henry Hazlitt, H. R. Knickerbocker, Suzanne LaFollette, James H. R. Cromwell, Ruth Fischer, James Rorty, George Hamilton Combs, J. Anthony Marcus, Stanislaus Mikolajczyk, Guenther Reinhardt, Frank Chodorov, Siegfried Wagener, Ludwig von Mises, Helen Woodward, Alexander Kerensky, Zygmund Dobbs, Max Eastman, Martin Ebon, and others less well-known.

A fascinating man with whom Isaac Don Levine and I lunched one day was Leopold Schwarzschild, who wrote the devastating biography of Karl Marx, *The Red Prussian.* Another was Alexander Kerensky with whom I had a chance to talk at length one Sunday at Levine's place on Long Island. I had considerable association with Eugene Lyons, Howard Rushmore, Victor Lasky, Edna Lonigan, John Chamberlain, and Suzanne LaFollette.

I wrote several pieces for *Plain Talk* but the one I treasure most was the lampoon, "The Witch Hunt," in the issue of January, 1948. The collectivists are deadly solemn folk who never allow wit and humor to penetrate their work, but the anti-Communists are scarcely less so. I wish there were more pieces like this in anti-Red literature. It follows:

SCENE: *A gloomy basement off Union Square, New York City. In the center a cauldron boils over a blaze made with bundles of International Labor Defense letterheads and old American Peace Mobilization leaflets denouncing Roosevelt as a warmonger. The backdrop is red mesh woven from abandoned party lines. Three witches in long red tunics spangled with stars and sickles enter from the left and march around the cauldron.*

> ALL: Hark unto the Kremlin swindle
> Engineered by Narkomindel
> Fair is foul and foul is fair
> When we work in Union Square.

> FIRST WITCH: 'Tis clear the fire's hot enough.

> SECOND WITCH: 'Tis time for us to strut our stuff.

> THIRD WITCH: The Party's future's pretty tough.

> FIRST WITCH: (Heaving into the fire a bundle of old *Daily Workers*)

> Round about the cauldron go,
> In the Baltic treaties throw;
> Bones of Liths and blood of Letts,
> And Finns erased without regrets;
> Bulgar, Croat, Rumanian
> Traded off at Teheran,

267

Toss them in and feed the flame,
Boil them down in Stalin's name!

ALL: Double, double, plots and trouble,
Freedom burn and boil and bubble.

THIRD WITCH: Heave in an Old Bolshevik,
Stir in all the Trotsky clique,
Then the union leaders who
Scoffed at WFTU
Throw in every Anarchist
Accompanied by a Socialist,
Then the heart of financier
With a liberal's eye and ear;
Mongol, Negro, Jap and Jew,
Indonesian and Manchu,
Toss them in and stir them up
To make a brew for Stalin's cup
And then to crown the evil act,
Add the hapless Potsdam Pact!

(Offstage an American Youth for Democracy chorus chants The
Internationale. *The witches pause and give the Communist
clenched-fist salute. Enter Comrades Foster, Dennis, Winston
and Flynn, as Browder holds open the door on the right and
bows low.)*

FIRST WITCH: Sit down, Foster, without fuss
And tell us why you come to us.

FOSTER: Because we are assailed with doubt
We had to hunt you witches out;
The Kremlin doesn't issue books,
So find out, Mother, just what cooks.

THE WITCHES: 'Tis well, 'tis well!

(They circle the cauldron, replenishing the flames with bundles

*of old United Front pamphlets. The First Witch tosses a copy
of the American Authors Authority plan into the cauldron, and
a great smoke arises. Out of the cloud steps the shade of a Stalintern agent dressed as an honest man with a large button in his
lapel reading "Anti-Fascist Refugee." He materializes and
descends among them, waving a fake passport.)*

FIRST WITCH: Tell us, Voice of Uncle Joe,
What Bill Foster wants to know.
Is it true that he is bound
To take the Party underground?
With the "fronts" all on the bum,
Where's the money coming from?
And tell him, Master, if you can,
Do we get gold from Magadan?

STALINTERN AGENT: The situation's getting tense,
We're losing all the innocents.
But we must stall a little more,
Until we're ready for the war.
While we breed ten trillion germs,
All of us must work for terms,
With the hated bourgeoisie
Who dream of world security.
Keep them off with due aplomb
Until we get the atom bomb.
And then, according to our maps,
Democracy will just collapse.

FOSTER: We understand, and that is fine,
But what's the current party line—
The revolutionary norm
As doped out by the Cominform?

STALINTERN AGENT: Here's the course we must pursue
To put the Kremlin program through:
Cause disruption everywhere

And keep ourselves in Truman's hair;
Infiltrate among the dubs
In unions, schools and social clubs;
From Washington to worker's bench
Toss in the party's monkey-wrench;
And by pen and word of mouth
Play up the horrors of the South,
To strengthen colored folks' belief
That we alone can bring relief.
Battle sternly to a man
To undermine the Marshall Plan
And never once let facts get out
That Russia's ruled by gun and knout
That Stalin's corps of bloody knaves
Has shackled twenty million slaves.
And all the while we must not cease
To clamor loudly for world peace.
Carry out this party line,
And all our prospects will be fine.
So now I bid you all adieu
And leave the dirty work to you.

(The witches hurl copies of the U.S. Constitution into the cauldron, and in the resulting cloud of steam the Stalintern agent disappears. Exit Foster and Comrades singing "There's a Great Day Comin'.")

FIRST WITCH: When shall we three meet again,
In cellar, bus or subway train?

SECOND WITCH: When the coin's from Moscow sent
To overthrow the Government.

THIRD WITCH: To undermine and smear the while
And infiltrate in Kremlin style,
Calling all who balk our line
Dirty, filthy Fascist swine.

FIRST WITCH: Come the orders from above
To execute the jobs we love.

SECOND WITCH: We pass them on to comrades who
Are eager to know what to do.

THIRD WITCH: Grab the unions, smash the church,
Friends and foes leave in the lurch.
Lie and murder, steal and rat
To gull the proletariat.

ALL: Fair is foul and foul is fair.
As we plot in Union Square.

(They dance around the cauldron waiving red flags, and exit.)

At the end of World War II, Norman Thomas had asked me,
along with many others, to join a new group he was forming
called the Post-War World Council to help influence the course
of events during the period following the conflict. As I recall,
three or four other Negroes were asked to become members, but
I was the only one that regularly attended the meetings, and
in course of time I was elected vice-president. The association
was pleasant, even though liberal-socialistic in a Fabian sort of
way. The board had important guests to lunch on several
occasions, and that is how I first came to meet Governor
Luis Muñoz Marin, the Puerto Rican Socialist, and Syngman
Rhee, the Korean leader who was soon to become president of
his restored country, only to be later deposed.

One of the most daringly ambitious plans of the Communists
was to control and direct the literary output of American writers
under the guise of protecting their financial interests. There were
too many "misled" intellectuals in Hollywood and across the
country who were willing to go along with the plan. But a large
number of writers who were not taken in by Communist propaganda formed the American Writers Association. I can recall
offhand such people as John Erskine, Suzanne LaFollette, John

T. Flynn, Richard Romanecy, Edna Lonigan, Louis Waldman, Alfred Kohlberg, Zora Neale Hurston, Norman Thomas, and scores of others. We met periodically at the New Weston, the Waldorf-Astoria, the Roosevelt, or some other hotel in midtown Manhattan, and as a member of the executive board and finally as vice-president, I attended all of the meetings.

We so successfully aroused the literary community of the country that the various authors' and writers' leagues rejected the plan and it was defeated overwhelmingly. If it had succeeded, every author and dramatist would have submitted his writings to a central pool where it would have been passed upon, selected or rejected, by a board which the Communists would have made sure to control. Thus, an anti-Communist or non-Communist writer would have been out of luck even if he had the genius of Shakespeare or Flaubert.

When we had completed the interment, we had a considerable sum of money left; and it was voted to employ some young man to make a survey of the *New York Times* Book Review section. The result was as we had suspected. There was a singular absence of anti-Communists among the reviewers over a period of years. Pro-Communist books were given to Communists or fellow travelers to review, and so were anti-Red books! In either case the tenor of the review was as predictable as a solar eclipse. Thus, a whole generation of readers had been brainwashed, since most of the intellectuals who religiously read the *Times* Book Review section believed what they read.

Somewhat prior to this time, there was an interesting private dinner meeting held in the home of Forrest Davis of the Scripps-Howard papers and Mrs. Davis in Washington, D.C. to discuss the mounting menace of Communist subversion. Representative Carrol B. Reece (Republican) of Tennessee (a veteran legislator who was seeking controls over the tax-free funds and foundations which had given and were giving vast sums to subversive purposes) presided over the discussion. Others present were Mr. and Mrs. John Chamberlain, Suzanne LaFollette, John Dos Passos, myself, and two or three others. There was no correspondence or written account made of this gathering, but the conversation was stimulating and revealing, and what Representative Reece told us about the Red influence and activity in Washington, especially in the State Department, was electrifying.

During 1947 I wrote two pamphlets for the Catholic Information Society, an anti-Communist group (as distinct from the Catholic collectivists) that put out a whole series of fifteen or twenty-page publications with lurid red covers with an illustration on each. The ones I wrote were number nineteen, *The Red Drive in the Colonies*, and number four, *The Communist Conspiracy Against the Negroes*. They sold in a set of 26 for one dollar, and they had a wide circulation. Among the authors published were Eugene Lyons, Wm. H. Chamberlin, Rev. Richard Ginder, Dr. Hermann Borchard, Oliver Carlson, Alice Leone-Moats, Liston M. Oak, Archbishop Aloysius Stepinac, Isaac Don Levine, Ralph de Toledano, Freda Utley, and Suzanne LaFollette.

My years of gathering material for my chores as associate editor of *The African* helped me a lot in writing *The Red Drive in the Colonies*. I pointed out in the prefatory paragraphs that:

Since March 1919 when the Bolshevik conspiracy against Christian civilization got under way with the founding of the Third Internationale, a new, sinister kind of underground imperialism has labored diligently to capture the world for Communism. Failing in their efforts to fasten Red totalitarianism on other war-weary countries of Europe after several bloody attempts, the Communist founding fathers around 1924 turned to the more fertile field of the capitalist colonies and semi-colonial regions where living standards and literacy were low and grievances serious.

I then discussed in turn the massive Red efforts to conquer China, Mongolia, Sinkiang, Indo-China, Indonesia, the Philippines, and Manchuria; the several African colonies such as Algeria, Nigeria, Sierra Leone, Senegal, Liberia, Morocco, and Madagascar; and all of Latin America. Years later when the African and Asian lands gained their independence, I noted that many of the delegates to the United Nations who had once been high in the Communist-controlled *Rassemblement Démocratique Africain*, the Moroccan Istiqlal Party and the Malgache Rénovation Party of Madagascar even today make no bones about their adherence to collectivism.

The Communist Conspiracy Against the Negroes was simply a truncated version of an article previously printed in *Plain Talk*.

I have a suspicion that Alfred Kohlberg had a hand in subsidizing this fruitful effort of the Catholics, albeit he was a Jew. The sales of these pamphlets continued briskly for years, and I received letters about mine from many parts of the country.

During this year I also wrote "Was Booker T. Wrong?", and "What's Wrong With the NAACP" for *The Negro Digest*. During the 1940's I wrote 44 columns in the *Courier* which were anti-Communist in theme.

When the Party line on the Negroes was gradually altered following the Hitler attack on Stalin, I wrote:

> The time has come when the black brother must be sacrificed to the larger interest: i.e., Russia's interest. The Party Line has changed on the Negro, my dearly beloved, and Comrade Mose must look elsewhere for succor.

That was in April, 1942.

In January, 1944, when Earl Browder, speaking in Madison Square Garden, announced that "Socialism and the class struggle is being postponed," I commented that "It is not surprising that after this statement the Comrades began to walk out of the meeting thoroughly disillusioned. One can understand their feelings."

I attacked the myth of economic security in the USSR, expounded on the cruel jest of Russian "labor unions" and pointed up the astronomic cost of living there. I dwelt on the hapless role of minorities and quoted Anton Ciliga, author of *The Russian Enigma:* "There is no equality in Russia, even inside prisons." I cited horrible tales of the misery of

274

the Jews. These things I wrote while the USSR was our so-called ally.

When Russia renounced its neutrality pact with Japan toward the end of the war, I scathingly exposed the economic collaboration between Russia and Japan which had been to America's disadvantage. I told how Sidney Hillman of the Amalgamated Clothing Workers had betrayed the African workers at the World Labor Conference in Paris in October, 1945 (in order not to embarrass Britain's white Labor Party) and carried not a single Negro CIO delegate to the Paris conference which ended with most of the world's labor unions inside the Communist-controlled World Federation of Trade Unions.

In May, 1946, *The New Masses,* weekly American mouthpiece of the Communist world conspiracy, announced the addition to its contributing editors of Dr. W. E. B. DuBois who had recently returned to the NAACP staff after a thirteen-year connection with Atlanta University. On the Red magazine all of his colleagues were Communists. He had been nudging closer to the Comrades by joining CIO picket lines in disastrous strikes that dissipated war bonds and bank deposits of millions of workers.

I commented, reviewing his career:

It is singular that Dr. DuBois should now join the staff of white revolutionists in interracial association when back in April, 1934, issue of *The Crisis* he urged Negroes to fight segregation with segregation and to cut their association with white people to a minimum. It will be recalled that at the time Dr. DuBois ridiculed Walter White for his inability to feel the hurts of segregation and discrimination because he was a "white man." . . . DuBois quarreled with the NAACP board of directors over the segregation issue and shortly afterward severed his twenty-five-year connection with the Association.

Agitation is the food and fuel of Communism and all

of its organs of propaganda, so when Dr. DuBois joins *The New Masses* he is more definitely than ever committed to that policy. . . . After all, perhaps it is appropriate that DuBois should join Stalin's literary gendarmerie where inconsistency, backbiting and charlatanism are crowning virtues and political irregularity is the only vice.

I repeatedly criticized Negroes of the middle class for their gullibility in permitting themselves to be sucked into the Soviet orbit, pointing out the dangers of such affiliation, but the bandwagon was packed with them, and many of them were known as leaders. Naturally I was roundly denounced for harping on this subject. On October 19, 1946, I quoted both Doxey Wilkerson and Benjamin J. Davis, Jr., in their admissions that the Reds had abandoned the Negroes' interests by not pushing the struggle to protect Negro war-time gains during the period of conversion cutbacks.

My 1000-word column reviewed *The Report of the Royal Commission* of Canada which had exposed the sell-out by well-paid, well-fed, well-clothed intellectuals to the Russian apparatus; the same type as many American Negroes on Communist letterheads.

Shortly afterward I devoted a column to the return of Dr. Robert C. Weaver, director of the Community Services Division of the American Council of Race Relations, from a six-month jaunt with UNRRA, studying the "economic rehabilitation of the Ukraine." Weaver had leaped off the boat chanting, "If I ever had any doubts that minority problems can be solved, my recent trip to Russia dispelled them." Despite anti-Semitism and national hatreds before the revolution, Weaver claimed that Russia was "today relatively free from inter-group tensions," and that the average Russian "cannot understand how the United States can claim to be a democratic nation and still persecute its darker citizens."

I wrote:

It is passing strange, if there is no anti-Semitism in

Russia, that the Jews are so eager to leave there! When the Communists in the collaboration with the Nazis partitioned Poland, they shanghaied hundreds of thousands of Jews to the frigidity of Siberia. About 150,000 of the Jews torn from their ancestral homes on an hour's notice actually survived. After the war the Soviet Government which had automatically made them Soviet citizens without asking the Jews' permission or application, offered to let them return to anti-Semitic Poland and assume their old Polish citizenship. Did these 150,000 Jews elect to remain in the Soviet Paradise? They did not! The whole 150,000 grabbed the opportunity to leave what they unanimously called "Povertyland." . . . Actually hundreds of leading Jews have been exterminated by the Russian Reds, the principal ones being Ehrlich and Alter, the Jewish labor leaders. . . .

Of course there is no discrimination against Negroes in Russia because there are fewer in that vast country, twice as big as the United States, than there are in Rochester, N. Y. There has never been any discrimination against Negroes anywhere in Europe, except in Nazi Germany, as scores of American Negro travelers will testify, nor was there any in Fascist Japan. Are we to conclude therefore, that nazism and fascism are good? . . .

The astute doctor attributes the "happy" racial state of affairs in Russia to existence of full employment and an elaborate system of social security which removed causes of intergroup tensions and rivalries. What a laugh! In Russia it is the full employment of the prison and the most insecure existence known anywhere on the globe. Weaver must have been wearing blinders during his six-month stay where the standard of living is lower than in South Africa.

However, to Dr. Weaver's credit, he was smart enough not to repeat this fiction, unlike so many other Negro leaders, and remained silent on the subject. A brilliant man, he went on to become New York State Rent Commissioner, chairman of the NAACP board, Administrator of the Housing and Home Finance Agency, and finally Secretary of Housing and Urban Development. Had he persisted in mouthing the Moscow line, he would have never gone so far.

I exposed the United Negro and Allied Veterans of America which in nine months had established chapters in thirty-nine states in a drive to corral the one million Negro veterans. It was one of the seventy nationwide organizations and national committees under Communist discipline, and listed also were the Council on African Affairs, National Negro Congress, Southern Conference for Human Welfare, American Crusade Against Lynching, Civil Rights Congress, American Youth for Democracy, League of Women Shoppers, all of which corraled some Negroes.

Another target of my typewriter was the colored and white fellow-travelers who rushed to defend the notorious Stalinist agent, Gerhard Eisler, whom the House Committee on Un-American Activities arranged to have nabbed on the eve of his departure from America to become propaganda chief of Communist East Germany. He had been cited in contempt by a 370-to-one vote in the House of Representatives, with Representative Vito Marcantonio voting against this action and Representative Adam Clayton Powell cravenly voting "Present" after denouncing the procedure.

Ruth Fischer, Eisler's sister, and Louis Budenz, ex-editor of the *Daily Worker,* said Eisler had been sent to the United States to disrupt and undermine American institutions preparatory to Red destruction of the country. There was no excuse for any literate citizen not knowing about Eisler because his activities had been widely noted in the press. He had done his dirty work all over Europe, in China and the United States. And yet the House Committee on Un-American Activities was denounced for its action by such Negro leaders as Dr. W. E. B. DuBois, director of NAACP research; Dr. D. V. Jemison, president of the National Baptist Convention, Inc. (the largest church group in colored America); Dr. David D. Jones, president of

Bennett College; Professors Luther P. Jackson and Harry W. Roberts of Virginia State College; Earl B. Dickerson, president of the National Bar Association, and a long-time NAACP director; Frank Marshall Davis, executive editor of the Associated Negro Press, and Mrs. Christine S. Smith of the National Association of Colored Women, to name just a few.

They condemned "the shameful persecution of the German anti-fascist refugee" and the "hysterical atmosphere contrived around this case on a nationwide scale."

I pointed out that:

> Eisler is no anti-fascist because he is an admitted Communist, and *all* Communists are as much fascist as the followers of Hitler, Mussolini, or Franco. Indeed, they are *more* dangerous because they represent and work for a much more sinister organization which has been working longer and is much better organized.

But these people would not quit, or could not. Next they were taking the position not to outlaw the Communist Party. I dubbed them "lame-brains" and was denounced by some fellow *Pittsburgh Courier* columnists. I said in reply:

> They rendered no public service when they let their names be used in big advertisements paid for by fellow travelers and crypto-Communists. They revealed themselves as politically adolescent, and regardless of their disavowal of Communist sympathies and their concern only with protection of so-called minority rights, the impression given by the display was that they had foolishly been trapped by clever Red Uncle Toms who spiced the petition with sufficient references to anti-lynching and anti-poll tax legislation, pleas for an FEPC act and a national code of civil rights, to snare the educated suckers . . .
>
> The Communist Party is in truth a minority, just as Hitler's, Al Capone's and Imperial Wizard Evans' gangs

were a minority, and as inmates of Alcatraz, San Quentin and Sing Sing prisons are a minority . . . The Reds have made no headway with the colored masses but seem to be having no difficulty in corraling the Talented Tenth.

The Communists and fellow travelers became increasingly bitter and hysterical in their denunciations of me, and their letters were gems of smearing and billingsgate which I shall long cherish and preserve. I was virtually the only person writing in the Negro press regularly who understood what they were up to and felt obliged to criticize and expose them. After all, the *Pittsburgh Courier* circulation was around 300,000 weekly, exceeding that of any other such newspaper, and the Reds would have been delighted to silence me, but could not.

My views were as those expressed at the time by Lewis Schwellenbach, the Secretary of Labor; by several congressmen who introduced bills to suppress the Communist Party; by Admiral Thomas C. Kinkaid, commander of the Eastern sea frontier; by William C. Bullitt, former ambassador to Russia, who told a Congressional committee that the Red movement was "composed of potential traitors" dedicated to a "conspiracy to commit murder" through mass liquidation; by the heads of the American Legion and the American Federation of Labor; by J. Edgar Hoover, director of the FBI; and inferentially by President Truman. But the fellow travelers continued to sign petitions and their names appeared in full-page advertisements for which the signers did not pay.

I had to take my colleague, P. L. Prattis, to task for defending a Russian-born woman, Mrs. Shura Lewis, who regaled a Washington, D.C. high school assembly on the "glories" of education in the Soviet Union. He was mad because three of the students walked out on her pro-Communist speech. I rebutted by quoting extensively from House Document 574, entitled, "Communism in Action," prepared under the direction of Representative Everett M. Dirksen (R., Illinois) by the Legislative Reference Service of the Library of Congress, and sold by the Government

Printing Office. My colleague was madder than a wet hen but the redaers were delighted.

Representatives Adam Clayton Powell and Vito Marcantonio again stood alone in the House citation of contempt against another of Stalin's agents, one Leon Josephson, brother of Barney Josephson of Café Society in New York. Barney had won over several Negro "artists" to the Party line by giving them jobs, and probably Powell could not forget that Barney let him hold his wedding party on a Sunday in Café Society Uptown where the liquor was reportedly "on the house." Powell is pastor of the Abyssinian Baptist Church in Harlem, largest Baptist Church in the nation.

Shirley Graham (later wife of Dr. W. E. B. DuBois) held that Eisler and Josephson were being "persecuted." Paul Robeson, long a darling of the Reds, who sang from the Communist trenches in Spain, agreed with Miss Graham, adding a denunciation of capitalism. There was something ironic about that, for I can think of no one who received more favors from the hands of the rich and powerful despite mediocre talents, as any capable and honest music or drama critic would admit. Naturally he received the Stalin Prize for services rendered, as, indeed, did Dr. DuBois.

I observed at the time (May 10, 1947) that:

> The Communist Party not only has nothing to do with democracy, but everywhere despises and seeks to destroy it. Fascism came to power in Germany because it was helped to power by Communists. Indeed, the Communists helped build the German war machine and for nearly two years was allied with it. The Luftwaffe was trained on Russian soil with the approval of Stalin.

The above-mentioned Shirley Graham shared the platform with Eisler at a meeting at Webster Hall in New York City after he was released on bail from Federal confinement. Mary Lou Williams, the jazz pianist, whipped the keyboard on that memorable occasion.

Walter Garland, the national adjutant of the United Negro and Allied Veterans of America (whose honorary president was Joe Louis, the heavyweight boxing champion) was one of the witnesses for Gerhard Eisler at his trial for passport fraud.

Although middle- and upper-class white people were being similarly caught up in the post-war Communist web as their non-white opposite numbers were, I felt that the danger was greater for Negroes because they already had trouble enough being black without going Red. While the generality of Negroes had no interest in Communism and paid scant attention to the Red propaganda, the danger lay in the control the black bourgeoisie exercised over the various organizations and institutions that were the backbone of the national Negro community, thus enabling them to speak for the masses, whether or not they were authorized to do so. As I pointed out:

> It is curious and somewhat alarming that some of the same leading Negroes whose names appear on letterheads of the Urban League and the NAACP also appear on those of the National Negro Congress, the Council on African Affairs, the American Youth for Democracy, the Southern Conference for Human Welfare and kindred smearbunds.

There was but one other writer in the Negro press who was outspokenly opposing the Communist conspiracy against Negroes. That was Willard S. Townsend, college-trained and able president of the United Transport Service Employees Union, who wrote a column for the *Courier*. Late in 1947 he was bitterly attacked by Earl Conrad, white leftist editor of the Negro-owned newspaper, the *Chicago Defender,* which by that time, in my judgment, had become almost as Red as the *Daily Worker.* Conrad called Townsend a Red-baiter, which the latter admitted with relish, and of course I joined him. It was quite a fray. I extract a few lines from one of my columns:

> Like all of his ilk, Comrade Conrad strives to confuse

the readers' minds by identifying communism with the Russians. These people use Russia and Communist and the Soviet Union as synonyms. The bulk of Russians loathe communism which has forced them to the lowest level of degradation. The so-called Soviet Union is neither Soviet nor union because there are tolerated no opinions contrary to the glorified goons in the Kremlin and no voice whatever in the Government, nor dare anyone try in any way to influence it.

I was delighted when in May, 1947, my friend Leopold Schwarzschild had published by Scribner's his *The Red Prussian: The Life and Legend of Karl Marx*. Many of the reviewers being, at bottom, Marxists ducked it as if it were radioactive, but I reviewed it at length and with relish. Working from such original sources as the voluminous correspondence between Marx and Engels, Schwarzschild had brilliantly assembled the facts of Marx's life. The founder of "Scientific Socialism" emerges as a lazy, envious, vicious pamphleteer whose few books were so unreadable that they have long been regarded as profound. Actually, they were either nonsense or barefaced distortions of the obvious. As I said:

His dictum of the ever-increasing misery of the workers, the inevitably decreasing number of capitalists, the increasing recurrence of catastrophic economic depressions leading unswervingly to final stalemate, world-wide starvation and overthrow of the capitalist system by proletarian revolution—all of this bilge has been disproven again and again during and since his time. Nevertheless, so gullible are the "intellectuals" that they not only continue to believe in the Marxian twaddle, but most of them actually hope for world-wide catastrophe so that their master can be proven right at last.

On the basis of this meagre knowledge and fantastic "science," Marx and his stooge, Engels (a life-long beneficiary of capitalist profits), annually prophesied the revolution from 1850 onwards. He double-crossed everybody who ever befriended him, including his own father, who almost went broke trying to get him educated while the young Marx squandered his money and time in aimless argument and roistering in coffee houses.

He did not graduate from Berlin University because he refused to attend classes. He finally got a degree by mail from Jena. . . . Before he foisted his bastardized Hegelianism upon the gullible world, the "Father of Socialism" was opposed to it. His Socialist ideas, such as they were, were stolen from Proudhon and Fouricr, while the terms Socialist and Communist were coined by Robert Owen, a wealthy English Utopian.

Marx attributed all the social difficulties of the Jews to themselves and their alleged mania for bargaining. He cried, "What is the worldly cult of the Jews? Bargaining. What is their worldly God? Money." Naturally Hitler and Goebbels would have agreed with this.

He referred to the peasants as "the class which represents barbarism within the confines of civilization." His letters were full of references to "the European emigrant swine" and "the rotten emigrant swine who wallow in the filth of newspapers."

I have never disputed the Communists when they have boasted of being the authentic Marxians. Their leaders, their careers and their institutions are cut from the same cloth as Karl Marx.

In December, 1947, the Department of Justice listed as Communist fronts the Council on African Affairs, the National Negro Congress, the Civil Rights Congress, the American Youth for Democracy, the Southern Negro Youth Congress, the United Negro and Allied Veterans of America, the Joint Anti-Fascist Refugee Committee, and a host of kindred outfits with which numerous supposedly intelligent and educated Negroes were identified. I warned that "all government workers who are in any way identified with the organizations listed above are in grave danger of losing their jobs because the Government views these organizations as anti-American." Civil service jobs have always been the backbone employment of the Negro middle class.

William G. Nunn, the *Courier* managing editor, had an idea for a series of articles on the civil rights picture in the state capitals as contrasted with the situation in the federal capital, which was rather bad at the time and had been for years. Aside from a couple of fairly good restaurants operated by Negroes, two or three very mediocre hotels also owned and operated by them, and a few lunch counters in Negro drug stores, there was virtually no public accommodation for people of color in Washington, D.C. The situation there had actually worsened since Reconstruction times. This was especially true after the Supreme Court's "separate-but-equal" decision of 1896 and the return to power of the Democrats in 1913.

Nunn asked me to journey to all of the state capitals during the winter of 1947–1948. Ira F. Lewis, the company's president, approved. Nunn, an outgoing and imaginative man, and Lewis, a shrewd and capable administrator, were usually in accord. Lewis had been Mr. Vann's right-hand man since the paper's founding in 1910, and Nunn had come to it in 1924 as a boy just out of school, at about the time I joined the staff. We had confidence in each other and worked well together.

Although the assignment was a difficult and arduous one, since I had to continue my other writing at the same time, I willingly accepted it. I started at Augusta, Maine, and traveling mostly by airplane, I visited in turn every state capital, interviewing colored and white people about the existing freedoms of accommodations, work, and schooling. As usual I worked fast, returning to New York City each weekend. Because I or somebody on the *Courier* editorial staff knew at least one key person in almost every one of the capitals, I was able to cover about four a week.

It was no more difficult an assignment than had been my eight-month social survey of the South twenty-three years before, but there was the same problem of getting a night's lodging. Unless there was a colored-owned or -operated hotel or rooming house, I was out of luck. There was no use wiring ahead for reservations. Fortunately, by this time there was a small registry of hotels that would accommodate colored people, and this proved a boon. At that time the vast area from the Missouri River to the Pacific Coast was a veritable no-man's-land for the Negro traveler whether he journeyed by train, automobile, or airplane. Many dark motorists had to sleep in their cars because all tourist camps turned them down. In one instance, in New Mexico, a kindly camp operator let a friend of mine stay the night in the last cabin—on condition that he leave at dawn. Another friend who was sleeping in his car (which was against the local law) was offered accommodation in the local jail by a considerate white policeman. When Joe Louis, the heavyweight boxing champion, and his entourage went to Salt Lake City for an exhibition, they had to fly back to Los Angeles that night because no local hotel would accept them. A colored theatrical group working Olympia, Washington, had a similar experience. This could be duplicated elsewhere in the region. It was the rule, of course, throughout the South; but there, at least, Negro accommodations of a sort were available.

When I had finished that assignment I started almost immediately on another right in New York City. This was an in-depth survey of actual conditions in the Harlem area, the most maligned community in the United States. For this job I hired a very capable young woman as assistant. She was not only well educated but also a "voluntary" Negro: that is, blonde and blue-eyed, she could "pass" for white. She was married to a dark-skinned man and was well-known in upper-class Negro social circles. Consequently she could use her color (or lack of it) to great advantage in getting information I could not secure easily.

Aside from interviews, we consulted the U.S. Census reports from 1910, when colored people first arrived in numbers in the area, and more important, the reports of the Consolidated Edison Company, which were even more accurate and revealing as to occupancy, rentals, and home ownership. We also used data from the Departments of Education, Housing, Police, Fire, Sanitation, and Hospitals, along with whatever studies were relevant.

The data we uncovered were most interesting. We found, for instance, that far from being *more* congested, Harlem, in 1948, was less congested (by 100,000) than in 1910 when it was largely populated by whites. The ill-famed central Harlem area had only 10,000 more inhabitants than it had forty years before, but there were now thousands more dwelling units and more schools. There were more owner-occupied dwellings than in any other district in Manhattan, not excluding the midtown East and West sides. There were several libraries in the Harlem area and they were well patronized. Building inspection was very lax, either through inattention, dereliction, or graft, and this at a time when migrants from areas of lower culture were pouring into the community, who would for long be socially difficult to assimilate.

The series, "The Truth About Harlem," ran for a couple of months and was very well received. The research I had done for the *Transatlantic* magazine four years previously, "Harlem: Half-Way to Heaven" and for my *New South* piece on "The Future of the Northern Negro in Politics" plus my own observations of Harlem life since World War I served me well. We received requests for clippings of the articles from many parts of the country and Western Europe.

Since Harlem was clearly less congested than it had ever been when its inhabitants were overwhelmingly white people, I wondered how the fiction of overcrowding came into being despite all statistics to the contrary. Its genesis arose partly from a picture in *Look* showing buildings on the west side of Lenox Avenue between West 135th and West 136th Street with the windows and even the roofs crowded with Negroes. There was no mention of the fact that the photograph was taken in 1919 when the 369th Infantry, the first allied unit to cross the Rhine, returned triumphantly from France, after having been in the trenches longer than any other American regiment. The photograph was used endlessly as "proof" of Harlem's congestion. Similar pictures could have been taken on midtown Fifth Avenue during great military parades, proving the "congestion" of that silk stocking, high rental area. When the swarm of sociologists and anthropologists descended on Harlem to find "proof" of degeneration and deterioration, they sought out and photographed the worst blocks and alleys to be found; something they rarely did for the Lower East Side of Manhattan, Hell's Kitchen on the midtown West Side or the slums of Greenwich Village. This has been a not-too-subtle anti-Negro campaign.

If any district or city on earth depicted only its seamier side and failed to show anything else, the tourist business would rapidly decline and the city's reputation would greatly suffer. This has been the case with Harlem. I have had on several occasions to take newspaper and magazine editors to task for carrying whole pages of pictorial displays of a Harlem which most of its residents do not recognize because they live on blocks comparable to the best in Manhattan, attend some of the largest churches on earth, maintain all sorts of charities, and have never run afoul of the law.

CHAPTER 16

NO SOONER was the Harlem assignment completed than Ira F. Lewis decided to let me make the tour of Latin America that I had suggested a decade before. Advertising was good and circulation was booming. The previous year we had distributed a survey made by an economics professor at Duquesne University entitled *The Negro Market,* the burden of which was that advertisers had neglected a market of great potentiality by ignoring the Negro newspapers. We had set up an office at 545 Fifth Avenue for our Interstate United Newspapers as foreign advertising representative for a large number of newspapers published by Negroes for Negroes. These efforts were paying off, and the *Courier* was blossoming out with commercial displays previously not seen in our pages.

We could afford this new tour. I left in mid-June, 1948, and for the next six weeks I visited Cuba, Venezuela, Colombia, Panama, Ecuador, Peru, Chile, Argentina, Uruguay, and Brazil, traveling always by airplane and with an "open" ticket all of the way. Armed with portable typewriter, Ciroflex camera, a trunkful of clothing, and a long list of contacts supplied by various friends, I made the trip without untoward incident, despite my lack of knowledge of Spanish or Portuguese. I surprised myself by making excellent headway without either. My reporting experience in every part of the United States and in Liberia and England had helped me to master the system of getting facts swiftly through key people in many walks of life, and the curbstone view from informed non-whites, a view usually far different from that of white people. I had expected to find color prejudice and discrimination in Latin America, and I did, everywhere. There were traces even in Argentina for whose independence black Brazilian soldiers had fought valiantly.

Although the commander of Havana's garrison, General Gregory Querejeta Valdes, was a mulatto and the chief of the national police was a dark Negro, neither could belong to any of the clubs which dominated Cuban life in the capital and elsewhere. To fill the gap upper-class non-whites had established the rather swank Club Atenas. The other city clubs were as lily-white as those in the States.

Half of the Havana population was what Americans would call Negroes but one would never think so by looking at the workers in stores, shops, hotels, and restaurants. They were widely employed on newspapers as reporters and editors, but none worked in telephone or telegraph offices. The non-whites did not have one grocery store, restaurant, or hotel; exclusive beaches were barred to them. There were colored nurses in public (but not private) hospitals, and Negro physicians were on the staff of one government hospital. Unlike in the States, there were Negro firemen and engineers on the railroad. There were many in skilled crafts. A colored woman was a professor of education at the University of Havana, and 35 per cent of the 10,000 students there were Negroes. Tuition in private schools was so high that it virtually excluded Negroes. There were on this overwhelmingly Catholic island only two Negro priests. It was amazing to note that with a non-white population one-third the total, Negroes had so little power and influence.

I learned that there were four Negro senators out of 54, and the representatives, numbering 154, had six Negroes. Most of these Negro legislators were Communists. One of the senators was a lawyer who owned three pharmacies and was reputedly a millionaire. One of the more flagrant Communists, Senator Lazaro Pena, was removed by the government from his union leadership. Pena was Stalin's right-hand man in Cuba. The government also closed down the Communist radio station and the Red publication *Hoy*. Of two women representatives, one was a Negro Communist. The elected governor of Oriente province was a Negro, as was the Senate president.

At the time I was there the General Confederation of Cuban Workers was torn by the struggle between Communist and anti-Communist workers. The workers were better off financially than most of the middle-class and white-collar workers.

The slums of Havana I found to be the worst I had yet seen. People slept eight and ten to a room and in relays. Rentals were $5 to $10 a room monthly; malnutrition and tuberculosis were rampant on the rice-bread-beans diet. The three-way color caste system was endemic. There were two carnivals, one white and one colored, as in the New Orleans Mardi Gras.

I was fortunate in finding in Havana an English-speaking native, a dark-skinned newspaper reporter who had assisted our sports editor, Wendell Smith, the previous year when Smith was in Cuba for the winter baseball season. This native was William Portuondo, now in the States and employed by the Voice of America.

In Caracas, Venezuela, I had difficulty finding suitable quarters, although I had wired ahead for a reservation at the National Hotel which was reputedly owned in part by Fulgencio Batista. The considerate mulatto taxicab driver who had brought me from the La Guaira airport carried me to several hotels until I finally secured lodging at the Gran Ambassador. It was the only hotel in the city where there were a couple of Negro waiters and a black Trinidadian nightclerk. The latter had been in Caracas for twenty years and he filled me in on the inside of politics and social life in the Venezuelan capital.

I was extremely fortunate in having a white American contact,

Michael Lever, who was employed by an American public relations firm working with the Department de Fomento. He introduced me to the United Press man and to several prominent people in government. He also arranged for me to speak at the Episcopal church on the very night of my arrival, and the following day took me to the American Embassy and introduced me to Ambassador Walter Donnelly. The latter, an affable, amiable man, agreed to give me a fifteen-minute audience which was extended to more than an hour.

Ambassador Donnelly, a graduate of the University of Venezuela, gave me a great deal of information about the history of the country: how it was run; the facts of integration (there had never been a president who was not tarbrushed); the usual Latin American addiction to revolutions; and the wealth that had come to the country through American enterprise in oil and iron ore.

I had been unable to get a visa to Colombia, which a couple of months earlier had had its capital, Bogota, gutted by a Communist uprising during which mobs came out of the slums armed with Molotov cocktails and burned the Palacio Municipal and other public buildings. Mr. Donnelly had been there at the time and knew the facts. He telephoned the Colombian consul and then gave me a letter to him requesting the courtesy of a visa. The next morning I went to the Colombia consulate and secured a visa to stay in Colombia for ten days instead of the usual four days then being granted, when any were granted at all.

I also met Valmore Rodriguez, president of the Senate, who had served in the U.S. Navy and spoke English well. Like so many others he was definitely of Negro-Indian descent. There were many Negro representatives and senators, as I noted when I sat through a session of the House.

Michael Lever took me to the Salon Elliptical, the Venezuelan Pantheon, where the gallery of paintings of national heroes showed conclusively the multi-racial character of the population. There was even a vivid portrait of President Petion of Haiti who had twice given Bolivar asylum, staked him with arms, food, and money, and, after the revolution was finally won, asked only that the victor free the slaves. Several huge paintings showed Negro heroes. Bolivar had said, "We do not know to what race we belong because we are all races."

The Commissioner of Education was a dark-skinned man of culture and charm. There were colored officers in the Army and Navy, the schools were completely integrated racially, but the class system obtained, and sons and daughters of the rich were favored, as elsewhere. Negroes suffered no job discrimination and indeed held high positions—a fact, Mr. Donnelly said, that made some whites show color prejudice. But they could do nothing about it, being in the minority. The non-whites would "take nothing off them" and did not cringe.

The race mixture had created some very handsome men and women and the people were well-dressed. The capital was very clean and orderly. There was a huge modern housing project, but there were also some pretty bad slums, and the jails were crowded from dungeons to roof, thanks to the most recent (1946) revolution which had brought Romulo Betancourt to power. At the time the President was a famous poet, Gallegos, a mulatto. I was informed that Betancourt was a long-time Communist who had helped organize the Communist parties of both Costa Rico and Colombia.

I was surprised to learn that there was a rigid regulation against any black immigrants, and that this was the case throughout Latin America. Venezuela permitted visiting blacks to stay in the country only 24 or 48 hours, which explained why my stay was so limited. This was true even in the case of an invited artist, Dorothy Maynor, who had difficulty getting hotel accommodations. This incident enraged the Caracas press.

Caracas was just a showpiece, very unrepresentative of the country, which was largely roadless and backward despite the great wealth, derived from oil and iron ore, which did not seem to trickle down.

Thanks to an old friend, George Westerman, managing editor of the *Panama Tribune*, I got through customs quickly in Panama and was given quarters at the Roosevelt Hotel without cavil. Many American Negroes at that time were being turned down by Panamanian hotels, even though they had made reservations in advance. Sidney A. Young, publisher of the *Panama Tribune,* and a powerful force in the large West Indian community, had for long fought all color and cultural discrimination and some visible headway had been made both in the Republic and in the Canal Zone.

West Indians in large numbers had come to Panama to help build and maintain the big canal. They settled and in time established some of the biggest businesses there. However, they were regarded socially as aliens by the people of Spanish culture. The relations between the two peoples were similar to those between Negroes and Puerto Ricans in New York. It was clear that the West Indian Negroes were the more enterprising, energetic and militant. A high official told me: "There are no racial hatreds in Panama. An effort is being made by men of goodwill toward assimilation of all foreign groups in the national life."

A brave effort was being made by the more enlightened, but it had a long way to go, and the presence of the white Americans did not help. There was a rigid color caste system in the Canal Zone, indistinguishable from that in, say, Alabama. With the coming of the CIO and its agitational and organizational work, the "gold" and "silver" signs (euphemisms for black and white) had come down all over the Zone. There remained, however, the separate racial housing, club houses, stores, and schools. Negro teachers received a minimum pay of $80 and a maximum of $100, while whites received $280 minimum and $350 maximum, monthly. However, at the time, changes were being made on the basis of training and the wages were being brought closer together.

The number of "silver" workers in the Zone was about 20,000, and their pay, along with that of the United States military personnel, was the backbone of the Republic's economy. A Negro worker who started at nine cents an hour in 1907 was then getting sixty-four cents an hour, while a "gold" employee (white) averaged from $1.75 to $2.00 an hour. The "gold" quarters of three bedrooms, living room, kitchen, and bath rented for $20 to $25 monthly, while a "silver" apartment, with two porches, community toilets and bath, rented for $14 monthly. The grounds surrounding the "gold" quarters were well kept by the Zone government, and the buildings were fireproof. The surroundings of the "silver" houses had to be maintained by the occupants and the houses themselves were firetraps and vermin-infested. There were "gold" and "silver" YMCAs and YWCAs. The "gold" manager received $375 monthly; the "silver" manager received $185 a month.

In the hospitals the two groups found the food entirely different: superior for the "gold" and inferior for the "silver," with the latter having to sign for knives and forks. The administration of justice was similarly discriminatory. I noted, also, a Jim-Crow section of the cemetery, with "silver" employees being buried between noon and 1:30 daily, and "gold" employees buried in early morning and late afternoon. The "silver" gravediggers had to leave the cemetery after interring their people. There was even color discrimination in the care of the graves!

Understandably, all Panamanians resented the arrogance of the whites very deeply, and they turned easily to Communist propaganda. There were numerous Reds, colored and white, in Panama City and Colon. It was fertile ground because the poverty of most of the people was staggering and the slums were about as bad as could be found anywhere.

I had fruitful interviews with the Foreign Minister, Ernesto Jaen Guardia, and President Enrique Jiminez. Both stressed the importance of agricultural development and both criticized the United States for not building a bridge over or a tunnel under the Canal to connect the two parts of the Republic. And of course they insisted that the treaty should be liberalized so that the government could get more money annually out of the operation.

The Spanish Negro Panamanians had always played a prominent role in political life. Basically, however, a few white families dominated the country even though they were a little island in a sea of Negroes, mulattoes, and Indians. Darien province and Colon were almost entirely Negro. Indeed, Balboa found Negroes on the Isthmus when he discovered the Pacific Ocean.

One Spanish Negro, Carlos Mendoza, had been president, and

his son, Santo Thomas Mendoza, was at the time superintendent of the capital's hospital. Another Spanish Negro, Tomas Gabriel Duque, owner of the *Star and Herald,* was president of the Duque Company (real estate, stocks and bonds, and the biggest printing shop) and also owned the largest of the nation's businesses, the National Brewing Company. He had been Vice-President, once had been President for a month during the incumbent's absence, and had headed the Ministries of Public Works and Finance.

A West Indian, C. W. Omphrey, held the exclusive agency for many makes of automobiles and electric refrigerators in a $200,000 building, housing some thirty employees. He started his business with a one-room bicycle shop. Another, Cecil Sterling of Colon, owned a thriving business handling auto parts, repairs, and accessories.

Panama was severely handicapped in its development by an almost total lack of industry and manufacture to absorb the agricultural migrants. Farm mechanization and the many mouths to feed drove them to the fetid slums of the two cities where they vegetated, ready for the call of any agitator, nationalistic or communistic. In this it was similar to the other Latin American countries and the basic cause of their backwardness.

When I was ready to get a reservation to fly to Colombia, the haughty Pan-American Airways clerk abruptly informed me that I could not have a reservation to that country as no visas were being given because of the insurrectionary Bogotazo of the preceding April. He said, "Why, there are big white people here, representing powerful American companies, who have been here for weeks awaiting visas." I toyed with him for a little, and then opening my passport, I replied: "Look, I already have the visa, all I want is a reservation on that plane leaving tomorrow."

He gazed incredulously at the ten-day visa and gasped, "How did *you* get this?"

"Well," I casually replied, "I know people that those white American salesmen don't know." I got the reservation.

Bogota, nearly 9,000 feet above the sea and producing tires and beer, and having several boiler factories (in contrast to seashore Medellin which makes textiles and clothing), reminded me strongly of Washington, D.C. Buena Ventura, the seaport on the Pacific, seemed to produce nothing but a swarm of impoverished, malnourished Negroes; while racially mixed Cali, the orchid capital, was in an agricultural area, producing mostly coffee.

Aside from the gutted public buildings and the steel-helmeted soldiers, replacements for the regular police (who had gone over to the Communist mob), downtown Bogota and its rich near-suburbs was a beautiful city, nearly twice as high as Denver, Colorado. The city, in fact the entire country, was under martial law, with soldiers at all strategic points, directing traffic and carrying bayonetted rifles and hand grenades. They were an ill-kempt, faceless, largely Indian crew, apparently ready for anything and capable of doing it. The dismissed police force had had quite a few Negroes in it.

The city was completely modern with tall buildings, automatic elevators, shoals of American automobiles, stores full of American goods, and many English-speaking clerks and attendants. In Colombia, as in Venezuela, and in most Latin American lands, the masses were short in stature, thanks to their rice-bread-coffee diet. The better nourished bourgeoisie and people from the cattle country are so much taller and better proportioned that they seem to be of another race.

There was no discrimination in the rank-and-file of the army, except that a draftee could buy off for one hundred pesos, which left mainly the poor and ignorant to serve. In the officer corps, however, the color bias was readily apparent. Very few colored officers were above subaltern rank. Colombia generally dotes on its whiteness, especially in high Bogota. There at 8,700 feet the temperature is an equable sixty degrees during the day and colder at night. Although at latitude four degrees North, it is chilling to the bone if one arrives in a summer suit. Most of the habitations have no heating system.

At the time, women did not vote, and cafés were for men only. There they sat like conspirators, whispering over their coffee and rum. One informant said that with a handful of Indian soldiers, a few pesos, and a big jug of rum, he could start a revolution at any time. Probably an exaggeration but not difficult to believe.

There were at the time fifteen Negro representatives and ten Negro senators in the Congress, mostly Communists. The Minister of Labor, until recently Governor of the newly-created Department of Choco, was a Negro who had authored all of the liberal labor legislation and had been Dean of Law in the National University. Choco was the gold-mining state of Colombia adjacent to Darien department in Panama, and heavily Negro.

I was very much interested to learn that Communists led many of the labor syndicates, especially in the oil fields. In this, Colombia was by no means unique. Indeed, the same was true of most CIO unions in the United States at that time. In 1949 the CIO ousted eleven of its unions because of Communist leadership.

While there is no mention of race and though the population is mixed, Colombia's immigration laws are as rigidly anti-Negro as are those of Australia. In both Venezuela and Colombia, officials excuse this racial exclusion on the ground that people not of Hispanic culture would not assimilate easily into their society. When I asked about the blacks from the impoverished Spanish and French Caribbean, my informants clammed up.

I was fortunate enough to meet John M. Vebber, the public affairs officer at the American Embassy when I made the customary visit there, and he took me up to see our Ambassador, Willard L. Beaulac, a career man who had served all over Latin America. He was intrigued by the fact that we were both born in Providence, Rhode Island. I had dinner with him, Mrs. Beaulac, their children, and Mr. Vebber, at their palatial residence on the outskirts of town. It was all very lovely. Perhaps I appreciated most the fact that they had a fireplace with huge logs sending out heat. I had been shivering since my arrival and the radiator in my room at the Bolivar had never been warm.

Because of our acquaintanceship, when my daughter played in Havana some years later, and Beaulac had been transferred there, he gave a garden party for her; something that just "wasn't done" in white Havana society, and the Ambassador saw to it that there were guests of all shades of color.

Dr. Louis Cordero of the U.S. Office of Information in Bogota was also most helpful in collecting information. My stops in Buena Ventura and Cali were brief. Guayaquil was more colorful and interesting. The latter, once having the reputation of being a plague town, was a mixture of Negroes, Indians, Zamboes, and mulattoes with a slight leavening of whites. This was initially indicated by the colored customs official at the airport. The downtown area was clean and generally attractive, with a few fair hotels and German restaurants, many nice apartments, and several colleges and schools. Negro traffic policemen abounded. The mixture of population produced many very handsome women but few over five feet tall. Guayaquil had above-ground cemeteries as in New Orleans, and the worst sort of thatch-hut slums surrounded the city like some evil fringe. However, Guayaquil was a bustling place in the day.

For all its brave show of palaces, cathedrals, monuments, and hotels, Lima, Peru, had been oversold by the travel agents. The horrible slums of this ancient, largely Indian metropolis had to be seen for it to be believed that such habitations existed and that human beings actually lived in them. Here the Indians rather than the Negroes were on the bottom. They were a malnourished, stunted, mostly unemployed, diseased people, as much enslaved under their mestizo bosses as they had been under the Spaniards, and yet they performed labors that would have staggered the average North American.

Peru's Negroes, once rather plentiful but now almost lost in the sea of Indians, constituted about three per cent of the total population, and lived in recognizable groups in the cotton producing area in the south around Canete. In Lima, the hometown of Saint Martin de Porres, a mulatto, there were only 11,000 Negroes in the city proper amid 562,885 inhabitants. At the end of the colonial period there had been 96,000 slaves. Now the Negroes worked as chauffeurs, maids, and servants. There was but one at the Hotel Gran Bolivar, and he was a giant black man with the trappings of a field marshal.

My visit to the ancient University of San Marcos, the oldest in the Western hemisphere, was very rewarding. Both the rector,

Dr. Louis Alberto Sanchez, and the secretary, Roberto McLean, were most gracious. Fortunately Señor McLean had held seminars on the Negro and written a monograph on the Negro in Peru. He took me to several of the classrooms which had remained unchanged since the sixteenth century and resembled small theaters with hand-carved, high-backed chairs, and deep wells for the lecturers. A meeting with the deans was arranged for me in the ancient board room. A suprising number spoke and understood English. One of these was a Dr. Quiroz, a colored man.

There were but two Negro students, both poor. McLean told me that until the end of the eighteenth century Negroes were barred from attending the university. The first one to matriculate there was by order of the Spanish king, so strong were colonial color prejudices. At the time I was there a French chemistry professor on the faculty had a Negro wife and two children. One of the most important physicians in Lima, Dr. Julio Gaseiaboru, a colored men, taught bacteriology at the university. There were several colored lawyers and physicians.

Although a small minority, the Negroes possessed such leadership qualities, unlike the Indians, that one, Samuel Vasquez, was a labor leader, a member of the executive committee of the APRISTA party, and a city councilman. In the Congress as deputy was a colored man, Augustine Vallejos, a labor leader from the north where he headed a sugar workers union. The Negroes were reported to be good speakers and quite active in politics, according to Andres Townsend, editor of the APRISTA daily newspaper, *La Tribuna*.

The Army's officer corps contained a few Negro and negroid types, but there were none in the naval or air forces. Most of the rank and file were Indians of the most ignorant kind, but I noted some blacks in uniform. There was conscription but one could buy out for a small sum; however, any sum was too large for most of the Indians, so they dominated in the ranks, with whites and mestizos scarce.

In most of the countries there either had been a revolution, or one was threatening. While I was in Peru there was an outbreak in the southern province, and immediately martial law was declared and a midnight curfew established. I remember how the American vice-consul with whom I was dining in his cozy apartment overlooking the vast, packed prison, suddenly jumped up and remarked that he had to rush me to the Gran Bolivar and put his car away before the curfew sounded. We made it.

I had an enormous room in the British style, with a wide balcony and wrought iron balustrade, and after donning my pajamas, I went out on it for fresh air. Across the street were offices of Helena Rubinstein and the International Business Machines. Down the street thundered an army truck packed with armed soldiers, their bayonets glistening in the street lights. They spotted me standing on the balcony and, as if by command, all rifles were trained on me. I promptly hit the floor and stayed there until the troop convoy passed.

Considering my assignment, there was no point in tarrying in Santiago, Chile, although I would have liked to be able to pause in Valparaiso where my father had had such good times in his youth when he was ship's cook, but there was not time. Santiago had the usual facade of central modernity surrounded by fetid slums and people sleeping in streets and alleys at night. Negroes were scarce in that white city, with the sun setting behind the snow-swirling peak of 23,097-foot Aconcagua, the jumping off place for the perilous trip across the high Andes.

There was no more reason to pause in Buenos Aires than there had been in Santiago for there, also, Negroes were scarce. My series was entitled, "Racial Democracy in Latin America," and for that Buenos Aires was not the place. The Indians were mostly killed or caged on reservations and there were fewer than 300 Negroes in the Republic, although thousands of them had fought and died for its independence.

Fortunately, I had had correspondence with Calvin Respress, a Georgia Negro who had come to South America with the entourage of Jack Johnson. He had stayed on to become heavyweight champion of South America (no great distinction in that world of pugilistic stumblebums), and later became physical director of the famed Jockey Club in La Plata, a suburb of Buenos Aires, a position he held until he retired. He married a Swiss woman and sent three children through the university.

We met at the La Cabana restaurant, famed for its fabulous four-inch beef filets, and had a long talk. In his position at the Jockey Club, Respress knew everybody of importance from Peron to the legislators, the big businessmen, the diplomatic corps and the social leaders. He won great repute from having trained the heavyweight boxer Luis Angel Firpo, who almost dethroned Jack Dempsey. He wanted to arrange an audience for me with President Peron, his personal friend, but I could not wait long enough.

Buenos Aires with its tall buildings, tree-shaded streets and avenues and mosaic sidewalks was truly a majestic city, but there, too, were some truly awful slums rivaling those of Havana, Caracas, Panama City, Buena Ventura, Lima, and Santiago, and worse than any in the United States. In that continent of immense wealth, progress was retarded by sharp lines of class and caste. The paucity of industry and manufacture almost assured a continuance of the status quo, regardless of political upheavals.

Uruguay promised to be the exception to the rule. A Texas-sized cattle country with a beef aristocracy on 100 *estancias* employing an average of thirty or forty hands each; great packing plants (British and American) and shipping firms; brick and cement factories; a fabricated steel plant and thriving vegetable farms; it suffered from lack of coal and oil.

It also suffered from socialism, which in later years was to bankrupt it. Uruguay, with a population then of 2,700,000 of which 800,000 lived in Montevideo, had had a Socialist government for almost fifty years, and followed the pattern of the Scandinavian countries, with free enterprise carrying the collectivist programs, thus obscuring the weaknesses of socialism. Because the unions were strong, wages were the highest on the Continent, with carpenters and plumbers getting $120 or more monthly, while good stenographers got $70. The government owned and controlled many enterprises operating in competition with private concerns. For instance, its tire factory made 25 per cent profit; but since there were only about 600,000 motor vehicles, this modern tire factory could produce in a few months more tires than could be sold. Then it was closed down for some months. In order to hold the skilled workers pending reopening, they had to provide them with homes and gardens, and this wiped out the profits. Thus the built-in bureaucracy burgeoned and became a burden; taxes had to be increased and the cost of living rose. To my astonishment, there were slums in this Socialist paradise rivaling the worst. It was the vast tourist trade from Buenos Aires that lent the appearance of prosperity.

There were about 50,000 Negroes in Uruguay, and they were not enjoying a bountiful life. They were sharply restricted in employment and none was to be seen behind a counter. An indication of their progress was the fact that only four Negroes had ever attended the tuition-free University of Montevideo, and none had ever graduated. The only Negro of prominence was Mario Lequiszamon Montero, one of the editors of *Colectividad Negro,* the Marxist oriented mouthpiece of a small NAACP-like organization which held occasional dances. I saw many of the Negro colony when I went to a local theater to see the Louis-Walcott heavyweight fight picture. They looked and dressed well. Many of the Negroes, I learned, were seamen and also worked in the packing plants. The armed forces were integrated, but all officers were white, since there were no qualified blacks or mulattoes.

The Communists controlled the General Labor Union through a Deputy Secretary General, and there was one Red senator and three representatives. They made a pitch for colored adherents, but there being no Negro middle class, the Reds had little success corralling the colored workers. The white middle class sought to make up for that lack.

Rio de Janeiro was a surprise, delight, and disappointment. It was a fantastic fairyland setting of green chocolate-drop mountains and scalloped valleys rising from the meandering Guanabara Bay in the most incongruous manner. Right away there was a Negro customs official and a multi-colored police force, leaving no doubt as to what kind of country one was in. I was fortunate enough to get a spacious taxicab driven by an English-speaking mulatto who had once driven a cab in New York City! No novelist would have used such a coincidence in a story; but here it was, 4,970 miles from Manhattan!

When I directed him to the Hotel Gloria, he looked somewhat surprised but said nothing. I had heard about color discrimination at hotels in Brazil and elsewhere in Latin America but, except in Caracas, I had encountered none. However, to be on the safe side I had written to the Gloria air mail six or seven days before from Lima, Peru, asking for a room-and-bath reservation.

When we arrived at the hotel and slowed to a stop at the foot of a very wide staircase of about a half dozen broad steps and I started to get out, two bellhops rushed down the steps crying, "Got reservation? Got reservation?" Assuming that I had, I said yes, but suspecting that I was getting what American Negroes dubbed the old "okey dokey."

The bellhops reluctantly took my suitcase and typewriter into the lobby and I went immediately to the desk. The clerk was apologetic and courteous, but diligent search disclosed no evidence of the reservation request air mailed from Lima. A little disconcerted, I sat down to await a call I was expecting from Joe Band, a wealthy Belgian Jewish jeweler, a contact to whom I had written from New York. I explained my dilemma. He was astonished and indignant, told me to wait there while he telephoned the Copacabana Hotel. I intended to wait anyway because the cabbie had asked me to do so while he contacted a nice, new hotel he knew about. Joe Band called back to report his failure. He had made the error of telling them at the Copacabana that I was a noted American Negro editor. That did it! Suddenly, in off season, the hotel was crowded.

The upshot was that I was soon ensconced in a suite at the Hotel Grande on the tree-lined Rua Barreto in the Botofogo district where many diplomats and upper-class people lived. I telephoned Joe Band about my good fortune and he was much relieved. The suite consisted of dining room, pantry, bedroom, and bath, with a small balcony which, by virtue of foreign exchange, cost me about five dollars a day. The official exchange rate was eighteen cruzeiros to a dollar. At the cambio it was thirty cruzeiros to the dollar. Since breakfast was served in the suite, this made for an even better bargain.

At the American Express Company office next day I hired a guide and interpreter, a Belgian Jew, who had lived in Rio for some time and not only knew the city well but was "right" on the color question. We visited about three of the 119 horrible squatter colonies, called *favelas*—primitive villages constructed of packing cases and hammered out gasoline tins where there was no running water, no lights, no sewers and nothing but meandering paths between the shacks. These *favelas* were perched at the base of the lovely sugar loaf mountains on land so steep that one could stand in front of one hut and step on the roof of the one below. At noon the hot sun beating down brought out all the odors from ground saturated with urine and feces. Water was brought up in gasoline tins from a hydrant a half mile below by women carrying their burden on their heads. From the *favelas* one could see the roof gardens of skyscraper apartments fringing Guanabara Bay. I took several pictures for the record. This was the slum proletariat with a vengeance. Most of them were *pretos* (blacks) and *pardos* (browns) but there was a sprinkling of whites.

Some years previously I had met, in the office of *The Crisis,* the famed Brazilian anthropologist and author of *The Negro in Brazil,* Dr. Arthur Ramos. I had written to him from New York telling him of my mission and soliciting his assistance when I arrived in Rio. I called him when I got in town, and he told me that a reception was arranged for the following evening in his penthouse apartment atop a 35-story house on the Avenida Atlantico which fringes the famed Copacabana Beach. I knew many professors in the States but had encountered none living so luxuriously.

As was to be expected, there were many Negroes present at the party, including leading members of the *Teatro Experimental do Negro,* a writer or two, a black and intense Communist poet, a major of the General Staff and other prominent whites of a liberal and radical bent. It reminded me of similar gatherings at Carl Van Vechten's or Pearl Buck's.

A greenhorn in Brazil, I did not expect to find a General Staff officer at such a party. I knew that the Communist Party was outlawed. Later I was to learn that the Reds had thoroughly infected the officer corps.

The major, who spoke excellent English, told me much about the color question in the armed forces. This was one of my major concerns, so I listened intensely and made many notes. Basically the Army was colored, the Navy much whiter, and the Air Corps almost completely so. In 1910 there had been an insurrection in the Navy led by a black sailor, and it was not forgotten. Because of the vast illiteracy, few blacks and browns could qualify as officers.

There were a number of Negro colonels and nine black generals, but one *preto* colonel had recently been retired when he was on the point of being promoted. There were no Negro officers in the Navy or Marine Corps or Air Corps. However, there were always a handful of dark cadets in the military training school.

Later, with the assistance of the major, Dr. Ramos, and the War Department I was privileged to visit the Regimento Sampaio at the Vila Militar twenty miles outside the city, commanded by the gracious Lieutenant Colonel Syseno Sarmento, who had fought in World War II with the regiment in Italy. I spent one afternoon at this brigade post for infantry, cavalry, and artillery. From a color viewpoint, the outfits I saw were well mixed, with whites, browns, and blacks, but I saw only one Negro officer, a second lieutenant. But I noticed great camaraderie among the men regardless of color.

It would be erroneous to assume, however, that there was no discrimination because of color. Undoubtedly much of what existed could be attributed to the lack of literacy in the lower class, which means the blacks and browns. When I was in Rio, 75 per cent of the people could not read and write. There is no class mobility as in the United States, and one stays in the class into which one was born.

This helps to perpetuate the color caste system whose impact is not to be exaggerated. I learned that tolerance was making some headway. For example, in 1937 a secret order was issued against Jews and blacks in the officer corps, and also in the foreign office. Since then the directive had been much modified. But I was truly surprised to run across anti-Jewish attitudes, especially toward European refugees whose money and uppishness on the part of some did not help in the cause of tolerance. They were the bulk of the guests at the swank Regente, Copacabana and Serrador hotels. At one time the Copacabana turned down Joe Louis and his entourage after reservations had already been made by the U.S. Embassy. Some of the Jewish refugee guests had made the objection and the proprietor went along.

I went to dinner one night in Bahia with Marshall Levins, who was in charge of the music program in the secretariat of education. The next morning, a high official who had been squiring me about town and introducing me to officialdom, asked me how I had spent the evening, and I told him that Marshall Levins had taken me to dinner at the Bahia Yacht Club. "Oh!" he exploded, "that damned Jew!" Levins was an American, a war veteran, an all-around good fellow, but one would never have guessed it from the intensity of the high official's bitterness.

A story was related to me with malicious relish about a white Brazilian who befriended a Jewish refugee for two years, giving him employment and keeping him in his home. When the Jew's son fell ill, the Brazilian arranged for his hospitalization and medical care. The Jew's only complaint was that his son was "in there with all those niggers." His highly indignant host upbraided him, saying, "Why, I have some Negro blood myself!"

The story may not have been entirely apocryphal. I recall how casually the Foreign Minister of Uruguay told me that his grandmother was colored.

There are more color contradictions in Brazil than in the American South, and it would be tedious to list all of them.

307

Many non-whites are in high position but they do not want their color mentioned. When I was given an audience by the Commanding General of the Bahia garrison, my guide and interpreter cautioned me beforehand: "Don't use the expression, 'we Negroes,' whatever you say." This puzzled me until I met the man, who was the color of Roy Wilkins of the NAACP.

Similarly, the contemporary governor of the rich state of Sao Paulo was clearly of Negro descent, but wisely I in no way intimated that we were racially identified. I had been warned that he was touchy on the topic. He was puzzled that there should be a newspaper like the *Pittsburgh Courier,* owned and published by and for Negroes, and I tried to explain the situation with as much finesse as I could summon.

There is so much evidence of race mixing in Bahia, the former Black Belt of Brazil, that many prominent citizens traveling elsewhere are derisively dubbed "Bahia brancos" by Brazilians. The meaning is that they are white only in Bahia, once Brazil's capital and hotbed of chattel slavery. Appropriately, Sao Salvador de Bahia is where Brazil's anti-slavery movement was launched.

It was much the same in Belem, at the mouth of the Amazon, where Indian-Negro mixture predominates, with just a sprinkling of whites. The Commanding General of the military district was a black colonel with an attractive Italian wife, but he made no pretense of being white. It would have been ludicrous.

Society everywhere in Brazil is white-oriented. It is the universal desire to lighten or whiten families, and this process is called "improving the race," a description which hypersensitive U.S. Negroes would be ashamed to use, even though it also voices their sentiments on the process. Paradoxically, there are more Negro-white marriages in the United States than in the Republic of Brazil.

The position of the Negro in Brazil I found to be economically and actually socially inferior to that of his counterpart in the United States. People were astonished to learn that I had flown there and that there were thousands of American Negroes financially able to do so. The thought of Negroes driving Cadillacs was beyond them, for such a car even second hand cost a fortune in Rio. Most Brazilian blacks were relegated to the cheapest jobs but had a wider selection of them. No unions barred them from membership, and Negroes were seen working at the highest levels, such as electric locomotive engineers.

There were twice as many of what we call Negroes in Brazil as in the United States but they seemed to have no businesses at all, relatively few professions, and nowhere near the available educational facilities. Only a small minority lives as well as Chicago Negroes on pubic welfare. They are nowhere near as race conscious as American colored folk, because whereas they are divided into many shades and classes, all American Negroes are lumped together by virtue of the one-drop theory of race (which is so unscientific: it works only one way).

CHAPTER 17

RETURNING TO New York, I plunged into another assignment, a series of articles on "What's Good About the South?" This involved visiting fourteen Southern states and in each visiting one urban and one rural Negro family, and interviewing them in depth about their lives and what they thought of their surroundings.

When Thomas E. Dewey won the Republican nomination for President, a group of outstanding anti-Communists arranged to confer with him in Albany, New York, in the hope that we might be able to prevail upon him to make two or three speeches dealing exclusively with the Communist menace in government. The Truman Administration was very vulnerable on this point and we felt that if Dewey made a head-on attack on the Red issue, he would win the election.

The delegation was led by Senator Styles Bridges of New Hampshire, and included Alfred Kohlberg, William Loeb, publisher of the *Manchester Union Leader*, Isaac Don Levine, Louis

Waldman, and myself. We first met for lunch, and afterward went to the Governor's office.

Mr. Dewey seemed super-confident about being elected. We conversed for some time but we were unable to bring him around to our viewpoint. He would only say that he would touch upon the subject of Communism in some of his speeches but not devote any speech exclusively to the subject. We felt that this would be a mistake, and said so. And indeed, Dewey lost by a narrow margin.

During the winter of 1948–1949, I stepped up my newspaper attacks on every aspect of the Communist conspiracy such as: a comparison of the penal system under the Romanovs and the Communists; the services of Paul Robeson and Dr. W. E. B. Du-Bois to the Red cause; the fate of the Jews in the USSR; the conspiracy against the NAACP; the conviction of the Communist leaders; and the ouster of eleven unions from the CIO because they were Communist-led. I regularly received baleful letters from Red correspondents, along with commendatory letters from my adherents. It made life very interesting.

In the spring when I learned from Rio that a conference was to be held in early May on the problems of the Negroes in contemporary Brazil, I suggested that I be sent to cover it and write in greater depth about life in the Brazilian capital. Mrs. Vann (who was now president of the company after the death of Ira F. Lewis) was in agreement, and William G. Nunn, the managing editor, thought well of it, too. Then we agreed that I cover the entire Guiana and West Indies region afterward. This latter series was to be "The New West Indies," exclusive of Cuba which I had covered the preceding year. It was to cover a longer period than the Latin American tour, and in fact I was gone from early May until mid-August. Before leaving I wrote "Color Lines in Latin America" for the *Negro Digest* and "Jim Crow in the North" for *The American Mercury*. Mencken's former assistant, Charles Angoff, was then managing editor and Lawrence Spivak was editor and publisher.

There was some hitch about publishing it and I went to the office to discuss the matter with Spivak and Angoff. I found that the trouble centered around my castigation of the Metropolitan Life Insurance Company for its Jim-Crow housing policy; of New York's Mayor LaGuardia for permitting Manhattan's Stuyvesant Town development to bar Negroes after having been given many concessions as to closing streets, and the like; and of the various FHA-subsidized Levittowns where no Negro family could be found residing. Mr. Spivak, hiding in the smoke screen of free enterprise, contended that the discriminators had a right to their policies of barring Negroes. The argument grew pretty hot and heavy. When I finally saw the June, 1949, issue, it had been so heavily cut that there was no mention of Metropolitan Life, Stuyvesant Town, or doughty Mayor LaGuardia.

In Rio I attended the sessions of the Negro conference in the modernistic Education Building, and the conditions disclosed by various speakers were reminiscent of the worst of America. The speakers were welfare workers, teachers, professors and journalists. A white American friend, C. A. Gauld, sat beside me and translated it all from the Portuguese. The economic discrimination was shocking and the speakers were caustic.

Several of the speakers were apparently Communists, of which Rio had a generous supply, but the disclosures could not be discounted entirely for that reason. There were most damaging charges of discrimination against darker colored people made by people in the labor exchange and the welfare department, such as sending back to the office all the black workers sent to a factory while accepting those of lighter hue.

One day I walked the entire length of both sides of the Avenida Rio Branco, the Fifth Avenue of Rio, casually looking into business places of all kinds. I discerned one brown bank clerk and one mulatto in a telegraph office. Otherwise all employees were white, including the girls working in lunch counters, the waiters in restaurants, and hotel employees. As in Havana, black workers, if there were any, were behind the scenes in kitchens. It was the same in the stores, large and small. Later, when I was in Sao Salvador de Bahia, the acknowledged Black Belt, I made an extensive foot journey of the many commercial thoroughfares and did not see a half dozen blacks in stores, shops, restaurants, and hotels. Certainly there were none in the hotel in which I stayed. My friend James E. Hill, Negro refrigeration engineer and importer, hailing originally from Evanston, Illinois, confirmed this, and he had lived in the state of Bahia for twenty years. The same sort of color discrimination in employment was also apparent in the big city of Belem at the mouth of the Amazon. Miss Lucy Lucas, an amiable black missionary from Philadelphia, fluent in Portuguese and resident five years in the country, confirmed this.

I concluded that the picture of Brazil as a land without a color line had been painted by white rather than black Brazilians. To be sure there was more camaraderie among people of various colors in Brazil than in the United States, and in the neighborhood dance halls they danced freely together. However, I was somewhat surprised to learn that there were at least four organizations in the country similar to the NAACP, although by no means as prominent and effective. One earnest, dark brown-skinned man, editor of a paper called *Homen de Cor,* came to my hotel one night after dinner bringing an interpreter with him to tell me some things he did not think I was likely to find out. In effect, he confirmed what I had already learned.

After leaving Brazil I proceeded to Cayenne, Paramaribo, and Georgetown in French, Dutch, and British Guianas respectively; to Trinidad, Curaçao, all of the Lesser Antilles, Puerto Rico, the Dominican Republic, Haiti, and Jamaica. I saw much and made many acquaintances and friends. Surinam (Dutch Guiana, now independent) came nearest to that racial democracy one would expect in such a multiracial country. British Guiana was a hive of prejudice, suspicion, and contention, and it was not surprising that the East Indian-Negro conflict later came into the open and British troops had to be sent there to restore order. The less said about French Guiana, the better; and while Martinique and Guadeloupe were quaint and attractive, the poverty and backwardness, mixed with rabid Communism, left little to commend them. All were outrageously overcrowded, just like the neighboring British Islands, and the most bitter color and class prejudice prevailed. These were less marked in Puerto Rico, the Virgin Islands, Haiti, and Jamaica, but they were and are still there. This may not be readily apparent to rollicking tourists spending a few days under the palms and then moving on, but more experienced travelers duly note it.

The social club, so great a part of the life of every community in the area, is everywhere characterized by color discrimination. The colored had their clubs, the whites had their clubs, and the blacks had nothing but their evangelical churches and Friendly Societies. Of the twelve clubs in Trinidad's Port of Spain, none accepted black membership although the blacks could come as guests. The same was true in the French islands, and to a considerable extent in all of the islands. A middle-aged mulatto lawyer in Fort de France, Martinique, could not recall in his lifetime there a single non-white being invited to a home of the minuscule minority of whites. Nor was it different in Guadeloupe. In Haiti the color-class lines are, if anything, stronger than in Santo Domingo.

All of this seems quite ridiculous, even pathetic. There is not an economically viable island in the whole area which, as President Herbert Hoover truthfully said of the Virgin Islands, is "a poorhouse." Conditions would be worse than they are if it were not for the subsidies received from the several "mother" governments. Were the other Caribbean islands as fortunate as Puerto Rico in being "enslaved" by Uncle Sam, most of the impoverished inhabitants would be in the United States. Sir Grantley Adams, the distinguished Barbados leader, was pessimistic about the future of his island, where there were 1400 people per square mile in an agricultural enclave which produced, aside from sugar, only flying fish. Other leaders voiced the same doubts. There seemed to be a considerable agreement on the futility of political uprisings, save among the large Communist element.

One dividend derived from my long May–August tour was the large number of "stringers" I accumulated. They airmailed weekly news stories to me which, considerably condensed, appeared in our New York edition and attracted many more readers, since the area we covered had the most foreign-born and -related nonwhites in the country. They could get this news from no other source than their island newspapers which required several weeks to get to the States. During the fifties we carried at least a page of news covering the area from Brazil to Jamaica.

The year 1949 was notable in that the Communist conspiracy reached its lowest ebb of effectiveness. The CIO and the British trades unions and their satellites quit the Red-controlled World Federation of Trade Unions, eleven Communist-controlled labor unions were thrown out of the CIO, there were all sorts of exposures of fellow travelers and of the machinations of crypto-Communists, and the Marxists were bemoaning their trials and tribulations. This was also the year in which world Communism chose to stage a big "peace" conference at the Waldorf-Astoria Hotel in New York City attended by Reds, fellow travelers, and dupes from all over. Several prominent American Negroes were present, led by Dr. W. E. B. DuBois and Charles S. Johnson, first Negro president of Fisk University.

At the end of the year, Radio Station WLIB, which had been on Flatbush Avenue in Brooklyn, moved to Manhattan's East 30th Street and decided to change policy and make a sustained effort to cultivate the growing Negro market. I had spoken on the station several times since 1946, and now Harry Novik, the manager, asked me to do a weekly program, "The Negro World," which would deal with the nonwhites who were beginning to come in as United Nations delegates from Africa and the Caribbean, and in general with news of those areas. With the largest number of foreign "stringers" of any Negro newspaper (and most white ones), I had the information and contacts to do this. The program began at the end of December, 1949, and dealt mainly on that first show with Communist activities in the Caribbean area.

From thence onward, through collaboration with the British Information Service, the French Press Service, the Jamaicans, and other West Indian groups, I presented as guests many notable Negroes from abroad, such as Senator Jane Vialle of Equatorial Africa, Norman Manley of Jamaica, actress Ruth da Souza of Brazil, Nnamdi Azikiwe of Nigeria, and outstanding persons from Haiti, Sierra Leone, Ethiopia, and Liberia. This was the first program of its kind in the United States, and of course it has been widely copied since delegations have come from an increasing number of newly independent countries.

From that time to the present I have been associated with station WLIB in one capacity or the other, principally on the weekly program, "The Editors Speak," consisting of a panel of local Negro editors, usually one other editor besides myself and the program director. We have in the past fifteen years interviewed many outstanding persons of all races and colors on a multiplicity of important matters and institutions. It has been quite an education for me.

I was busily at work in my office one spring day in 1950 when Melvin J. Lasky, editor of *Der Monat,* the intellectual monthly published in Berlin, telephoned at the suggestion of Sidney Hook, philosophy head at the New York University, to ask if I would like to attend as delegate from the United States a Congress of Cultural Freedom in Berlin in June. This was a logical outgrowth of our Committee for Cultural Freedom founded in 1939. I immediately accepted. (Incidentally, all expenses were to be paid.) This conference was to be the largest and most important of its kind in the long history of anti-Communism, and would be held one hundred miles inside the Iron Curtain.

It was not easy for me to go because I was extremely busy with my editorial work, and the usual writing and radio, but I arranged it. The American delegates to the gathering were Irving Brown, James Burnham, Elliott Cohen, James T. Farrell, Louis Fischer, Sidney Hook, S. M. Levitas, Robert Montgomery, Herman Muller, Nikolas Nabokov, Boris Nicolaevsky, A. M. Schlesinger, Jr., George S. Schuyler, Solomon Schwarz, Sterling Spero, Ethel Vance, David C. Williams, Tennessee Williams, and Max Yergan. Some of the other delegates among the total of 100 were Julian Amery, German Arceniegas, G. A. Borgese,

317

Margaret Buber-Neumann, R. H. S. Crossman, Arthur Koestler, Eugen Kogon, Elinor Lipper, Richard Loewenthal, Herbert Read, Jules Romains, David Rousset, Carlo Schmid, H. R. Trevor-Roper and Boris Yakowlew. It was probably subsidized by the Central Intelligence Agency.

The headquarters office of the Kongress Für Kulturelle Freiheit, extending from June 26th to 30th, 1950, was the Hotel am Steinplatz, Berlin-Charlottenburg 2, on Uhlandstrasse. It was a pistol shot from East Berlin. The sessions were held at the Studentenhaus am Steinplatz. Several of the delegates, including me, stayed in the headquarters hotel, an excellent hostelry where all of us dined. As a precautionary measure two plain clothes detectives were stationed at the head of the stairway on all floors and others mingled with the guests in the lobby. City uniformed police were stationed outside the front entrance night and day. The great fear was kidnaping. Several of the delegates had prices on their heads. Once overpowered, they could be thrown into a truck and taken through the Brandenburg Gate in four or five minutes to the isolation of an East Berlin jail.

It was an exhilarating atmosphere amidst the great and near-great of the intellectual world, establishing the first international front against the Communist intellectual drive. I soon discovered, however, that most of these delegates were socialists of varying kinds and consequently their basic goal was identical with that of the Reds: that is to say, collectivism.

I reflected this in my contribution to the second discussion panel on Tuesday, June 27th, at the Studentenhaus am Steinplatz, where the chairman was Robert Montgomery. The other speakers were G. A. Borgese, James T. Farrell, Carlo Levi, Nikolas Nabokov, Charles Plisnier, Herbert Read, Denis de Rougement, Ignazio Silone, Renee Sintenis and Ethel Vance.

Like the others, my talk was brief, but I think it was effective.

Art reaches its highest expression only in an atmosphere which permits choice, experimentation and, if necessary, error.

Whenever a society becomes regimented, regulated and

rigidly ordered, art becomes static, stolid and unimaginative, timid and fearful. The artists are the most economically and socially vulnerable element in society.

Their contributions to the social order are not absolutely essential to sustain life although art is the prerequisite of any type of civilization above the primitive. When society resorts even temporarily to barbarism, it is the most fragile elements which suffer first and most devastatingly.

It is for this reason that the artist, the writer, the painter, the sculptor, the musician, have the greatest stake in the preservation of a free society. When the artist attempts to compromise, he jeopardizes his future and very often his present.

Fashionable to Quibble

It unfortunately has become fashionable for the artist in modern society to quibble over this issue of freedom. He says on the one hand that he prefers a society which emphasizes physical security for all (which necessitates in technological civilization a degree of regimentation which endangers freedom). At the same time he properly wants a society where he is free to write, paint and compose as he wills. He fails to recognize that the artist is so influenced by the society of which he is part, that he cannot remain free when all else is controlled.

The error of the intellectuals of the West for the past two centuries has been advocating a society actually slavish but paraded as freedom. This means, then, that along with free art (and indeed the very basis for it) must be free political institutions, free economic enterprises and a society free of onerous restrictions.

The tragedy of so many intellectuals in the contemporary world is that while opposing extreme forms of totalitarianism, they are themselves half-totalitarians; that is to say, they express a desire for a society which is half-controlled, half-regimented, half-planned, part capitalist

319

and part Socialist. This strange hybrid they will find (indeed, have found) to be a Frankenstein monster which, ironically, they have a great responsibility for creating.

When Men Revolt

Thus, the Fabian of yesteryear becomes inexorably the totalitarian of tomorrow, and ultimately the victim of his own creation. Horrified by some evils and excesses in a free society (which will always be imperfect) he turns hopefully to the blueprint of a controlled society which promises a heaven on earth in the very near future. But since the individual must always be imperfect this side of paradise, his society must also be imperfect, and the more absolutely it is controlled by single committees or groups of imperfect men with unlimited power, the more imperfect it is likely to be.

And when men revolt against this leviathan, terror is invoked by the frightened men who hold power. The press, the church, the labor unions, the cooperatives and the schools are systematically controlled, regimented and goose-stepped behind some Fuehrer calling himself a democrat. Has this not happened? And where it has, how fare the arts?

To the keen student of history, it is manifest that the first victim of this combination of unlimited knowledge and morality must inevitably be freedom, resulting in the crushing of all difference of opinion, all divergences, and all intellectual pioneering, and thus lead to the complete imprisonment or death of those who dare to think and differ. This stagnation of the intellect leads to barbarism and destruction.

Thus, there is no middle road, no choice for the artists who want to live and grow, except the support of a completely free society, economically, socially and intellectually. It is as dangerous to go half way down the crocodile's throat as to go all the way into his belly. Too many artists, even today, are stuck in this alimentary track.

I had typed this just the night before after three days of observing the scene, and it reflected my pessimism about most of those who were participating in this alleged anti-Communist intellectual campaign.

Prior to leaving New York, I had sent Melvin J. Lasky, the Congress secretary, the copy of my main address "The Negro Question Without Propaganda," an eight and one-half page, single-spaced manuscript which became Congress-Paper No. 23. It was delivered before a large audience at Amerika Haus, Berlin, on June 29, 1950.

It was an analysis of the Negro experience in capitalist America and a spirited defense of the free enterprise system against the attacks of the Soviet prostitute press and radio. In an early paragraph I wrote that:

> Actually, the progressive improvement of interracial relations in the United States is the most flattering of the many examples of the superiority of the free American civilization over the soul-shackling reactionism of totalitarian regimes. It is this capacity for change and adjustment inherent in the system of individual initiative and decentralized authority to which we must attribute the unprecedented economic, social and educational progress of the Negroes of the United States.

I gave examples of interracial cooperation, the philanthropic contributions of middle- and upper-class whites to Negro education and welfare, and cited the impressive statistics on Negro income, ownership and integration without at all minimizing the remaining racial segregation and discrimination, while contrasting these with the evils behind the Iron Curtain. I summed up by saying that:

> The cumulative effect of these broad, continued and statesmanlike efforts has been improvement of racial relations in geometrical progression. Thus the gains in the past ten years have far surpassed those made in the previous thirty. This explains not only the social, economic

321

and educational well-being of the colored minority, but the latter's continued and unsurpassed loyalty. American Negroes understand, far better than Soviet propagandists, that in the American system lies the hope of all submerged peoples who have the ability and determination to rise to the full stature of free men.

This presentation was regarded as so impressive that I was requested by Philip M. Kaiser, Assistant Secretary of Labor, to permit its circulation by his department. Mimeographed copies were sent to every United States embassy and consulate in the world for distribution. Mrs. Frances Bolton, the Congresswoman from Ohio, inserted the entire contents in the Congressional Record for August 30, 1950.

At the suggestion of my friend Suzanne LaFollette, who was then editing *The Freeman* with John Chamberlain and Henry Hazlitt, I condensed considerably "The Negro Question Without Propaganda" and rewrote it as "The Phantom American Negro," a strong fact-packed piece taking to task the large writing clique which had systematically presented a false and dire picture of the position of the Negro in the United States and thus aided and comforted the Red propagandists. The Negro thus presented, I insisted, was a phantom.

The article evoked an overwhelmingly favorable response following its publication in June, 1951. The *Christian Science Monitor* immediately requested permission to reprint. A clergyman requested and was granted permission to translate the story into Gaelic for a publication in the United Kingdom. In all, seventeen publications in the United States and abroad asked for permission to reprint the article. *The Freeman* was so flooded with requests for copies of it that thousands of reprints were distributed to individuals and groups all over the country. *Life* did a short editorial on it.

The *Reader's Digest* requested permission to reprint "The Phantom American Negro." On January 25, 1952, DeWitt Wallace, editor (with Lila Acheson Wallace) of the magazine, wrote to me:

Dear Mr. Schuyler:

It is no news to you that your article, "The Phantom American Negro," was read by the largest magazine audience in the United States. But I know you will be gratified to learn that, in addition, this excellent piece was reprinted in nine of our International Editions. Thus you have reached millions of other readers in many lands.

The selection of your article for this wider distribution was a tribute to both the fundamental and general interest of its appeal. A number of articles are used in few or none of our foreign editions because their flavor and factual content are of special appeal only to our United States audience.

So that you may have permanent proof of how many foreign friends you have made, we are sending you copies of the International Editions in which your story appeared.

Sincerely yours,
DeWitt Wallace

The American edition carried the article in July, 1951, and it appeared contemporaneously or subsequently in the Danish, Finnish, Swedish, British, Canadian (French and English), Norwegian, Belgian, French, and Australian editions.

The *Pittsburgh Courier* had at that time a lively promotional department under Clyde Page which reprinted the article from *The Freeman* and circulated it widely among the Negro masses.

Thus a point of view was advanced and circled the globe which disputed the anti-Negro, anti-American propaganda wave of the Soviets and their American intellectual prostitutes.

After attending the Congress for Cultural Freedom, with its many artistic and social highlights and amenities, including a tour of East Berlin, a special performance of Beethoven's *Fidelio* at the Städtische Oper, the European premiere of Orson Welles' *Macbeth* and a reception for guests, observers and Allied and German officials, I flew to Paris.

There I remained for the better part of the week. I renewed my acquaintance with the President of the Senate, Gaston Monnerville, the shrewd Cayenne-born mulatto who had visited our home in 1947, and now was ensconced in the Luxembourg Palace. I had had my old *Courier* colleague Lemuel Graves, who was then connected with the U.S. Embassy, make a reservation for me at the small Trianon Palace Hotel which was only a few doors from Monnerville's quarters. One evening I dined with Senator Jane Vialle of Equatorial Africa, whom I had had on my radio program a few months previously, and we enjoyed the cuisine at the Eiffel Tower restaurant. The next evening Max and Lena Yergan took me to dinner at the venerable La Reine Pédauque restaurant immortalized by Anatole France. I went to the Louvre, the Pantheon, the Rue Pigalle and enjoyed other sights. I lunched one day with a Martinique native who had lived in Paris for twenty years and had an above-average job in a bank. He also had invited an American Negro student who was a rabid Communist, albeit the American government was paying for his tuition. In a surprisingly short space of time I discovered that there was a hotbed of U.S. Negro expatriates in Paris who seemed mainly concerned with running down their country and praising Russia. However, none had given up U.S. citizenship.

Senator Vialle, a staunch anti-Communist, had been busily occupied in trying to keep the French colonial students out of the Red clutches by persuading French families of the middle and upper class to take them into their homes. Otherwise they would have had to stay in small hotels and pensions where the Communists swarmed. I was not too sure about the effectiveness of this because, as elsewhere, some of the most convinced Communists were in these very intellectual classes. Be that as it may, Jane Vialle was an ardent, efficient, bustling brown-skinned woman, one of the seventeen colored women in the French Senate.

The following November an organizational meeting of the Congress for Cultural Freedom was held in Brussels, Belgium, and again Max Yergan and I were among the delegates representing the United States. The sessions were held by this much smaller group at the offices of the International Confederation of Free Trade Unions and at the Hotel Atlanta. The terrific London fog delayed me a day in arriving because no planes could get as close as 100 miles of London and we had to come from Hearn by train. I had to leave in the same manner the next morning, arriving in Brussels late in the afternoon, where I was to stay at the swank Hotel Metropole.

I acted as the reporter for each session, with the help of James Burnham, and when we had finished, the news stories were wired to the press in New York and elsewhere. The sessions were routine but I enjoyed seeing Brussels. I was fortunate in meeting a plump, jovial black man from Dahomey, Paul Fabo, editor of a small weekly, *L'Afrique et le Monde*, who was most helpful in increasing my knowledge of the more than 700 Africans then resident in Belgium, about 90 per cent of whom were from the Belgian Congo. I found that they were mostly farm workers, although some worked in industry. There was one mulatto lawyer but no doctors or businessmen.

Most of these Congolese were married to Belgian women or had them as common-law wives. Many had children who were well cared for, as I noted. Most of these men dreamed of returning home but it was mostly only a dream. They could not carry their wives back with them since this would be discouraged by the Belgians and disliked by the tribal Africans. I met many of these persons at a reception given for the delegates by the *Union Africaine Artes et Lettres*.

Most of the Africans were dissatisfied with their life in Brussels and their lowly status as porters and laborers. Some older ones had been there since World War I and could not get back home because of low pay, incapacity or color discrimination. Nor did the Belgians encourage their return.

A white man, M. Maurice, who was engaged in establishing liaison between Africa and the Continent, and had lived in the Congo many years, was most helpful. He said he had fought there for better relations between blacks and whites, and held conferences at Belgian universities on the subject. Interestingly, nine years later Philippa met him in Elisabethville. Some people thought he was a Communist, which would not have been surprising since Brussels crawled with them.

I had met George Padmore when I passed the night at the Park Lane in London where he served as the *Courier's* correspondent. When the conference was over, I went back to London for a couple of days for a prearranged recording session with the young Bechuanaland chief, Seretse Khama, his very attractive young British wife, Ruth, and George Padmore. I had brought several blank records with me to Europe for that purpose. We all met in the lobby of the Park Lane Hotel and then went to the studio where the record was cut. It was later broadcast over Radio Station WLIB in New York, as were the other recordings I made on the Continent.

Seretse Khama was a bright, knowledgeable young law student who had experienced difficulties with both the British Government and his Regent because he married a white girl, a really charming young secretary, for whom he renounced his right to the rulership of his people. The recording was the first of its kind and most successful.

In the recording we discussed the current political situation in Bechuanaland, the influence of South Africa's racist policies on the colony, the reaction of his people, the Bamangwato, to his marriage, and whether he planned to return against the wishes of the British. I introduced his wife to our audience in New York and had her say a few words. George Padmore summarized the situation in Bechuanaland.

Through Padmore I came to know Mrs. Nola Hatterman in Amsterdam, an artist interested in drawing and painting colored people. When I went to her home there was a party in progress, where I met many Negroes from Surinam, or Dutch Guiana. This recalled to my mind that Otto Huiswoud, whom I had debated on Communism twenty-seven years before, was also from Surinam. I suspected that many persons at the party were also Reds, but this did not disturb me; it was an opportunity. Mrs. Hatterman lectured widely on Negro art. She later took up residence in Paramaribo.

I learned from them and also from the colonial office at The

Hague where I spent a day that there were about 3,000 Negroes in Holland, and 1,000 in Amsterdam. They were mainly seamen, doctors, musicians, and students. There were some artisans, nursemaids, and import-and-export agents. One man, Eugene A. Gessel, was principal of a public school. There were a few teachers in the public schools and a couple of professors at the University of Leyden. One man was a wealthy importer-exporter and another operated a small iron shop and boasted twenty years residence in the city. I also met a black dentist and an ophthalmologist. I made a recording with Mr. Gessel for WLIB.

J. A. Rogers had visited Copenhagen and told me about some of the things to see but I had no contacts there. I dislike hitting any city "cold" but I did not have long to wait for acquaintanceship in that lovely, friendly metropolis. I was staying at the Palace Hotel in the center of things. After a very economical evening at the National Scala, I met next morning on the street the two Negroes whose very entertaining song-and-dance act I had seen the night before. They were Harry Williams and Dolores Flemming, both Danish-born. They had been in show business for twelve years, performing all over Western Europe. Dolores Flemming was married to a Danish musician and Williams' wife was a ravishingly beautiful blonde with violet eyes and strawberry cheeks. They had two lovely children. Williams' father came from the Virgin Islands, and had moved to Denmark when the United States purchased the archipelago. Miss Flemming's father was from Philadelphia, and had come to Denmark when dancing with Josephine Baker.

There were only about 300 Negroes in Denmark. Among them were three school teachers and a high school principal, a dentist, a manager of a restaurant unoriginally called Uncle Tom's Cabin, and others in clerical and business employment. All were bilingual, speaking Danish and English. They were charming, cultivated people, and all interracially married. In 1958 when I revisited Copenhagen, coming straight from Bamako in the French Sudan, I spent a pleasant evening in the Williams' home.

I was on my way to Oslo, Norway, to cover the Nobel Peace

Prize ceremonies for Dr. Ralph J. Bunche of the United Nations. I had contact with my old friend, Ann Brown, the famous singer, who was living there and married to Thor Schielderup, the ski champion, son of the Chief Justice of Norway. It was a week of festivities and ceremonies, tours and repetitious talks on peace. This was the time when the Communists' Stockholm peace appeal was being signed all over the world, especially by so-called intellectuals. One could scarcely turn without hearing about peace while Moscow was frantically trying to perfect the atomic bomb from data stolen in America.

I was fortunate to meet many journalists, some of whom interviewed me; people of the diplomatic corps, high Norwegian government officials, and all the local brass. In meeting Philip Boardman of Oslo University, who had been there since 1947, I learned the part he had played in bringing six or seven American Negro students to study there. One girl was elected president of the student body. Through his contacts with Oslo businessmen, and in cooperation with the Nobel Peace Prize winner, Boardman and I arranged the Ralph J. Bunche scholarship for an American Negro student.

I met many members of the American Embassy. The Chargé d'Affaires, Mr. William P. Snow, expressed his deep gratification that I had come. He told me that he regarded my contribution as great as Bunche's. Just about that time all of the U.S. embassies and legations throughout the world had received bundles of the mimeographed copies of my Berlin speech, "The Negro Question Without Propaganda." What intrigued Mr. Snow was the surprise of the Embassy people when they saw an interview with me in *Dagbladet* and so learned that I was in Oslo. He said a dozen people had called the Embassy about the contribution I had made.

Dr. Bunche made a very good impression on the officials and people of Norway. Careful, correct, but amiable and outgoing, he gave the appearance of a perfect representative of the United States, the United Nations and Negro America. An interesting sidelight on the occasion was the arrival of a considerable contingent of Negro military personnel, male and female, from their posts in Germany. It greatly impressed the public.

Even in frigid Norway, I learned, there were some 400 Negroes, many of them born there. They lived mostly in the seaports of Bergen and Stavanger. I met two or three of them on the street but unhappily they spoke nothing but Norwegian, and I had no interpreter with me at the time.

I made recordings with Dr. Bunche and Ann Brown, and these were later broadcast over Station WLIB.

The American Committee for Cultural Freedom began its activities shortly after the Brussels organizational meeting. Yergan and I were on the executive committee along with Arnold Beichman, Daniel Bell, James Burnham, Elliot E. Cohen, George S. Counts, James T. Farrell, Sidney Hook, Hans Kohn, Milton R. Konvitz, S. M. Levitas, Norbert Muhlen, William Phillips, Merlyn S. Pitzele, David Riesman, Irwin Ross, Richard Rovere, and Peter Viereck. The chairman was Robert Gorham Davis, the vice-chairmen were German Arciniegas, Charles S. Johnson, H. J. Muller, and Arthur Schlesinger, Jr. Norman Thomas was chairman of the administrative committee, C. Dickerman Williams was chairman of the legal commission, and Sol Stein was one of the several successive executive directors.

We met in various places about town periodically and the association was pleasant. But my differences with the Committee crystalized early. In the first place, there were too many Socialists in it who were anti-Stalinists rather than anti-Communists, as I had noted in Berlin. In the second place, these people were primarily concerned with maintaining a small clique rather than reaching out to the wide intellectual community. They wanted, as Sidney Hook explained, to keep it small so that it could be more easily controlled; and that was not my idea at all. I wanted to see branches in every college and university in the United States, and even among high school faculties. I wanted to see among its membership many business executives and politicians, so that it would have a national influence and not remain just a sect. I was virtually alone in that ambition. The excuse that it had no funds for such expansion was a lame one. There were thousands of intellectuals who would have joined immediately once they knew our aims. In the beginning we had immense prestige.

My dissatisfaction grew with the Committee's actions which

I felt reflected the policies of the American Civil Liberties Union, the Anti-Defamation League and the Americans for Democratic Action, which are and were socialistic agencies, rather than those of an organization dedicated to cultural freedom and therefore anti-Communism. I did not like its speed in rushing to the defense of Arthur Miller and Charlie Chaplin over the travel issue. Nor did I agree with its position on the J. Carroll Reece Committee's investigation of tax-exempt foundations to determine whether any of these foundations had furthered the Communist conspiracy. The Committee's position was that the hearings were improperly held.

More serious was the clumsy attempt to frame James Burnham, an executive committee member and a founder of the international body, because he wrote the foreword to Medford Evans' *Secret War for the A-Bomb*. The plan was to castigate and reprimand, perhaps expel Burnham for having approved the book which exposed the machinations and conspiracies of the Communist clique at Las Alamos. I got wind of the plot and at the next meeting of the executive committee at some midtown restaurant I got up and blasted the whole thing. That blast killed it.

I could see that the majority panted to get into the fight on Senator Joseph R. McCarthy, a well-intentioned politician who was appalled by what he learned of the wide ramifications of the Communist conspiracy against America and wanted to do something about it, despite the frightened opposition of everybody from the White House down. So the Committee which had been pleading poverty suddenly found or was given sufficient money to hire a hack to write a book, *McCarthy and the Communists*, which was just another attack on a great American.

This coupled with the official ACCF soft line on Dr. Oppenheimer, the atomic scientist, as shown by its intervention with two alleged facts for the consideration of the Gray Board (which ultimately condemned him) filled me up, and I resigned with a blast at the Committee. This was in October 1954, and the Committee has long since gone down the drain. It could have been a great force for freedom in America.

CHAPTER 18

LONG PRIOR to all of this, on November 27, 1951, I participated in a television symposium, "Are We Close to Solving Our Race Problem?" presented by the New York City Clubs of Barnard, Bennington, Bryn Mawr, Connecticut, Mount Holyoke, Radcliffe, Smith, Vassar, and Wellesley Colleges and the American Association of University Women, New York City Branch, and the United Negro College Fund, in cooperation with "America's Town Meeting of the Air" at Hunter College Assembly Hall, 69th Street and Park Avenue, New York City.

The other participants were Edward Weeks, editor of the *Atlantic Monthly*; Frederick D. Patterson, president of Tuskegee Institute and of the United Negro College Fund; Dr. Sadie T. M. Alexander, legal advisor of the National Council of Negro Women, and a director of the National Conference of Christians and Jews and the National Urban League; George V. Denny, Jr., founder of "America's Town Meeting of the Air"; and James Jackson Kilpatrick, Jr., editor of the *Richmond News Leader*.

The estimated audience over 280 stations of the American Broadcasting Company network was ten million throughout the United States, Hawaii and Alaska. A recording of the program was later made available to the "Voice of America."

The United Negro College Fund, Inc. represents 32 Negro private colleges and every year seeks to help the member colleges augment their budgets. I had supported this effort from its beginning.

The Hunter College auditorium was packed with a very distinguished audience drawn from the cream of liberal elements in and around New York City.

I did not particularly relish opposing Dr. Alexander, an old friend from Philadelphia and one of the most distinguished women of our nation with a keen mind and a remarkable scholastic background. However, a debate is a debate, and I have always delighted in debates. I took the affirmative and she took the negative view. We were the stars of the occasion and the exchange was spirited. She stressed the long way the Negroes had to go before achieving full citizenship and I pointed out the gains that had been and were being made, and what it was reasonable to expect in a multiracial society.

One of the interesting and significant reactions of Negroes was their commiseration of me for having to take the affirmative position. They did not want an intellectual exercise of logic, wit, and opposing facts but a champion. One must never appear to take any position that seemed to gloss over or explain America's dealing with the racial problem, as if America were not dealing better with it than any other multiracial nation. It was all well and good to expect more of America than any other country, but what was an American problem was also a global one from which no country was free. Indeed, it is in a way indicative of the superior position of the Negro in America that he has such rising expectations, elsewhere chiefly nonexistent, save among a tiny minority of the better circumstanced.

In 1953, James V. Spadea of the Spadea Syndicate in New York City launched Spadea Columns, a news feature with a notable group of contributors of the anti-Communist, free enterprise persuasion, and it was introduced with considerable fanfare. My friend Victor Lasky, the editor, asked me to become one of the contributors and I gladly accepted. I was the only Negro journalist invited and it afforded me the largest audience I had had since the series on Liberia in 1931.

The Spadea Syndicate started off with 48 American and two Italian daily newspapers. My "For the Record" columns reached a subscribers' audience of more than 6,000,000, and among some of the larger metropolitan subscribers were the *Boston Traveler, Chicago Tribune, Detroit Free Press, Kansas City Star, Long Island Press, Minneapolis Tribune, Newark Evening News, Richmond News Leader, St. Louis Globe-Democrat, Daily Oklahoman* and *Mobile Register.*

By no means did I confine myself to commenting as a Negro. Most of my Spadea columns were devoted to subjects only remotely related to matters of color. I was one of the first to point out in 1953 that the Caribbean with its heavy Communist infiltration was the "Soft Under-Belly of the USA." Immediately after Castro's capture of Havana, and while he was being congratulated in Caracas by his old Communist mentor, Romulo Betancourt, I wrote "Cuba Swaps the Devil for a Witch," giving the lifelong Red background of the Red dictator at a time when most U.S. newspapers were ecstatic about the "liberator."

When Castro's subsequent killings shocked American opinion, I pointed out that "Castro's Butcheries Follow Leftist Pattern." A few weeks earlier in November, 1958, I reported that "Mao Tse-tung Exports Brainwashing to Latin America." The previous September I asked, "Should We Abandon Formosa?" In August, 1957, I presented the readers with the "Unique Soviet Contribution to Government" which was government by traitors, since all those governing Russia from Lenin onward were traitors, according to the denunciations of them.

Late in January, 1959, I warned that "U.S. May Regret Emergence of Castro" and in April I described "The Communist Conquest of Cuba," which took so long for our State Department and much of the American press to find out.

Back in June, 1953, I had written on "Bolivia's Red Bosses

Love U.S. Generosity," and a few months later I was pointing out the danger of an atomic raid from within the United States and also that "Hawaii Statehood Means Power for Harry Bridges."

So far as I know, I was the first U.S. reporter to dig up the facts about what had happened to the 15,000 Red Chinese prisoners who elected to go to Formosa rather than return to the Chinese Communist paradise. As president of the American China Policy Association I had many sources of information on both sides of the Bamboo Curtain.

In between I was commenting on "Socialism Strangling Our Cities," which has become increasingly apparent in our current urban dilemmas; on high taxes, campaign gifts, the bankruptcy of the post office, and other domestic matters.

Nor did I ignore the Negro. There was "Negro Education Pays Dividends," "Why Negroes Shun Reds," "Tribute to Booker T. Washington," "Growing Southern Negro Votes," (1957); "The Negroes Wouldn't Play" (in Korea when they resisted Communist brainwashing), "Africa Winning Spot Light," (1957) and "South Africa's Agonizing Reappraisal."

Newspapers in all parts of the country carried these columns and they, along with their readers, knew I was a Negro. Often my picture appeared. I think the contribution was educational in several ways. It exposed the Communist conspiracy here and abroad, in Asia as in Latin America; presented the Negro in a light rarely seen by a mass white audience, and without the usual nauseating special pleading.

In the fifties I wrote at least fifty columns in the *Courier* on almost every facet of the Communist conspiracy, especially as it touched Negroes, and I also wrote about it in other publications. For *The Freeman,* in addition to some book reviews, I wrote "The Pro-Slavery Propagandists," "New Masks for Old," "FEPC Is a Fraud," "Will the South Secede?" and "The Case for the Private School."

For *Phylon,* Fourth Quarter, 1950, I wrote a long piece on "The Van Vechten Revolution," dealing with the influence of the noted novelist on the general recognition of Negro talent. It was widely reprinted.

334

For the *Negro Digest* I wrote "What's Wrong With Negro Authors?" (1950); "Why I Want To Stay in America" (1951); and "Are Negroes More Prejudiced Than Whites?" In March, 1951, I summarized "Forty Years of *The Crisis*" for an anniversary issue of that magazine for which I had worked seven years.

An article that attracted widespread attention appeared in *Human Events* for April 22, 1959, entitled, "Where Communists Fear to Tread." It dealt with the Dominican Republic of Generalissimo Rafael Leonidas Trujillo, the *bête noir* and despair of Red conspirators. The late Frank Hanighen, then editor, was delighted with it, and thousands of reprints were sold across the country. It would have been good if the U.S. State Department had shared this view instead of conspiring to bring about El Jefe's assassination. Trujillo was a dictator (like most Asian, African, and Latin American rulers) but he was "our" dictator. So was Cuba's Fulgencio Batista, another strong man let down by his "friends." It is a grim commentary that the man Uncle Sam later backed as president of the Dominican Republic was Juan Bosch (a protégé of the Russian Communists, Kohaz and Biolostosky) who was magnanimously pardoned by Trujillo, after the Red gangs he commanded were rounded up, tried and sentenced!

In the late fifties some of my contacts paid off for the *Pittsburgh Courier*. I sold a special supplement to the Haitian Government, to the French Information Service ("The New Look in Black Africa"), the Government of Jamaica and the Portuguese Government ("The Portuguese Way"). The special supplements were completely written and edited by me, and in connection with them I traveled extensively in Haiti, French West Africa (Senegal, Sudan, Guinea, and Ivory Coast), and in Portugal, Angola, and Mozambique. No Negro weekly had ever been able to get such special advertising. Six months before the Portuguese trip, I was invited by my old friend Nnamdi Azikiwe of Nigeria to attend his inauguration as the first African Governor-General of that vast country, along with several of his New York friends. I had known him when he was attending the University of Pennsylvania and teaching at Lincoln University. In 1950 I had him on my "Negro World" program on

335

Station WLIB and later advised one of his representatives on the purchase of some printing machinery for his powerful *West African Pilot*. Upon my return from the week-long festivities and ceremonies, I wrote a series of four articles on Nigeria for the *Courier*'s magazine section.

On leaving French West Africa in 1958, I flew directly to Copenhagen to see my friend Harry Williams, and then took a leisurely train trip to Hamburg where I did the first articles in a series, "In Brightest Africa," and then went on to the International Fair at Brussels and renewal of acquaintance with Paul Fabo, editor of *L'Afrique et le Monde,* and to contact the Belgian Information Service looking toward a special supplement on the Belgian Congo. This latter never materialized and I think Belgium was the loser, as well as the Congolese people. What subsequently happened would have been better understood if the Belgians had run a special supplement as the French did; and they had a better argument to offer.

Again I went to Paris, this time by train, and renewed my acquaintance with Gaston Monnerville, president of the French Senate, a position comparable to our vice-presidency. I stayed in the quaint Trianon Palace Hotel, close to the Luxembourg Palace and hard by the Boulevard San Michel, the University of Paris, and the Pantheon. I learned a lot about De Gaulle and French politics from my conversations with M. Monnerville. He shared my conservative views on constitutional government and was alarmed at the growth of centralized power.

The new decade started with an article in my old love, *The American Mercury,* dealing with the dramatic changes that had taken place in French Guinea since I had visited it in April, 1958. It was entitled "Khrushchev Gets a Foothold in Africa" and explained the background of the Red influence there. I had spent several days in Conakry, interviewed Sékou Touré and others of the Communist-oriented African leaders, and French officials. Except for the Ivory Coast, what was politically true in Guinea was equally so throughout the French-controlled areas, although at first only Guinea opted for independence.

As stated before, I had for years been a close student of

336

African affairs as necessitated by my contributions in *The African* during the war period and my understandable interest in the literature on the subject. I saw Africa as a poorhouse except in natural resources which could only be exploited by foreign capital, there being none of native derivation. Its people were in the main ill and ignorant, ravaged by a multiplicity of diseases and by hundreds of prejudiced tribes who often looked upon the white "invaders" with more favor than they did upon their tribal neighbors. They seriously needed the services of the Christian missionaries who, with all of their faults (much exaggerated by propagandists), were providing spiritual training, schooling, medical care, and agricultural information, so necessary in a transitional society. When I wrote my views on these matters in the *Courier* my writings aroused the ill-will of many of my friends, domestic and African, who had fallen under the spell of "Negritude" and "the African Personality," neither of which was logically explainable.

The power of an idea or superstition is great. Through constant repetition of falsehoods and half-truths by superficial or malicious minds, it is easy for lies and distortions to gain wide currency. There was not a single one of these African countries prepared for independence, educationally, socially, economically, or spiritually. None of them was a nation in the sense of homogeneity, culture, language, or social organization, and practically all of them were not only broke but had often been a financial burden on the "mother" countries. Not one had a sensible border or a viable economy for survival in the modern world. For that matter the same thing was true of the newly emergent Asian states. To a lesser extent this also was true in Latin America where a form of mestizo-run colonialism has always been in force, with the untutored aborigines or transplanted Africans as the fall guys.

Take these hapless aggregations of people and permit them a leadership filled with the superficialities of European intellectualism, Fabian and Communist, and with a superiority complex toward its people whose long-developed culture they despise and would uproot, and it is easy to understand what has happened since the wave of freedom inundated the continent. The Communists, Russian and Chinese, have not made more headway only because of their ignorance and ineptitude. I did not make friends among the starry-eyed by pointing out repeatedly these unpleasant facts of life, but I think I performed a service for the *Courier* readers in my editorials and columns.

There was no point in going overboard on these matters just because the Africans and Asians were non-white. They were the victims of arrested development who, without European and American investment and direction, would have fallen farther behind each year until chaos and stagnation engulfed them. They were the international retardates, and there was no blinking at the fact, unless one were a True Believer. Mechanization, industrialization, and automation had simply given the industrialized nations such a headstart that, barring a miracle, no backward nation, not even such behemoths as Red China, Indonesia, India, and Pakistan, could overtake them. After nearly fifty years of planned misery, the Soviet Union is still trying to catch up with the West despite wholesale theft and espionage.

Many people wondered about my continued connection with the *Pittsburgh Courier* in view of the fact that for long periods it specifically disavowed over my columns any responsibility for their content. I was the only contributor who received this special attention, embarrassing though it would be to explain, if it had occurred to the editors to do so. As they say in the underworld, it was copping a plea.

Efforts were made to handicap me and lessen my effectiveness, short of discharge. Although from 1957 to 1961 inclusive, and through my own efforts and contacts alone, I brought almost $40,000 into the company's coffers, the company was so badly managed that most of this money was squandered in various adventures which were obviously unsound. Men were put in as publishers who did not have the slightest conception of newspaper economics, or knowledge or respect for the craft. In four years I was subjected to three pay cuts, until it was barely possible to make ends meet.

In September, 1960, after having been editor of the New York edition for seventeen years, I was succeeded by a former *Courier* colleague, George F. Brown, and without any notification whatever! I simply heard a rumor and had it confirmed by writing to Brown in Philadelphia where he was on the staff of the *Bulletin*. I never received any notification from the main office! However, those who occasionally communicated with me addressed me as associate editor, which I had been since 1942. I continued to write all of the editorials of the paper and tried to keep our readers on an even keel during the civil rights hysteria when the Negro press generally surrendered leadership to the professional agitators and their competing mobs vying for larger slices of the available civil rights dollar

CHAPTER 19

FROM THE beginning of the so-called Negro Revolution and the insane antics identified with it, I had taken the same position editorially and in my column that I had throughout the years. I had opposed all of the Marches on Washington and other mob demonstrations, recognizing them as part of the Red techniques of agitation, infiltration, and subversion. This was indicated by the fact that invariably they were proposed, incited, managed, and led by professional collectivist agitators, whose only interest in the workers was to exploit them; backed by the proliferation of "liberals" of position and influence who always run interference for them by "explaining" and defending their course.

I had consistently warned Negroes for forty years that their miseries could not be alleviated in any way by mob action, nuisance provocations, and civil disobedience. The waving of empty pistols, accompanied by insults, imprecations, and denunciations of white people, generally and specifically, was quite futile, and would simply create what Negroes could not afford: that is to say, more enemies. Week after week I pressed the point (as I had since 1923). But under the influence of their white (or Red) mentors, a contaminated Negro leadership snapped at the Communist bait, received the support of white "liberals" charting a course of disaster, and like pied pipers led the lunatic fringe astray.

During that hectic period when traffic was being disrupted and stalled, public works interrupted, city officials picketed and insulted, garbage tossed on streets and lawns, and when supposedly intelligent young Negroes were sprawling on court house steps yammering spirituals and the slogan, "We Shall Overcome," first popularized by the Castro forces, and people of worth were being obscenely traduced, I held to my position. Of course this made me an "Uncle Tom" to those people who had no answers to what I was writing and saying. It was ever thus.

What was especially galling to me was that practically all of the communications media—newspapers, magazines, radio, and television—not only surrendered to this hysteria, religiously and monotonously repeating all of the self-serving fictions of the civil rights agitators, but virtually excluded contrary comment. Negroes who had lived in various communities for a lifetime and were intelligent and informed were almost never asked to write or comment on this manufactured phenomenon. Only on two occasions did any of the swarm of reporters ever ask me anything. Nor did they bother to interview hundreds of outstanding Negroes about the merits of the tactics and strategies being used. Many of these, of course, might have feared to be frank and thus risk the resultant epithets and characterizations by which the mob sought to silence objections. Some of the most obscene and scurrilous letters I have ever received (all anonymous, of course) came during that period, and my wife and daughter were not spared.

How much validity is there to the civil rights agitation of the sixties? It is undeniable that through the methods of amelioration pursued by Negro organizations and associated whites, the Negro's lot since World War I had immeasurably improved, legally, socially, educationally, and economically (as I had pointed out in Berlin in 1950 at the Congress for Cultural Freedom). Because of this his position in the world of minorities was enviable, and he had more of everything that people desire on this earth than had any other non-whites, and most of the whites. The Negro and his white friends had beaten back the forces of obscurantism on every front and were driving them into retreat.

To be sure, there was, despite laws and regulations, de facto segregation in housing designed to keep Negroes in certain localities, but Negro ingenuity had enabled thousands and thousands of Negro families to move to the suburbs to the extent of their pocketbooks. Thanks to the efforts of the NAACP, the restrictive covenants were no longer valid in keeping property "white" so it was quite possible for resourceful Negroes to break down residential barriers, if they so chose. Apparently few of them so chose to organize for this effort. If they had, it could have been done quietly and without frightening ballyhoo.

When the "Revolution" began there were areas of bad housing occupied by Negroes for which the agitators popularized the term "ghetto." This led in turn to its synonymous use with the Negro residential area, and finally with the Negro himself as an ignorant, lowdown, retarded, drug-using, anti-social, criminal being, because he *was* non-white. Not in sixty years had there been such a wave of Negro defamation in high places and low; and respectable newspapers and magazines vied with each other in printing doleful articles of poorly concealed disparagement under the guise of Christian interest, and illustrated by the most unflattering photographs to be found in the morgue.

There is not a Negro community in the country today that does not have more areas of good, often new, housing than of bad. This is not due to any street demonstrations but to a sustained effort through the years by public and private interests to improve housing. Moreover, it is only the result of poor Negro leadership that many unsightly and unsanitary blocks

343

of houses have not been razed and replaced. A few enlightened colored leaders have achieved this in several parts of the country, notably some preachers who eschewed soapboxes and demonstrations. After all, the welfare of Negroes is primarily the responsibility of Negroes. Unfortunately, this responsibility has been too often avoided or ignored as men who should have known better "idealistically" chased butterflies.

The very real problem of illiteracy and cultural deprivation, while greatly exaggerated, is one which has long concerned leaders of all colors. Much of it is a product of social transition from well-rooted rural life to urban instability. If blame is to be attached to anybody, it should be the New Deal agricultural policies of crop restriction, which forced large numbers of farm workers into adjacent towns and cities and finally to Northern metropolises where there was insufficient industry and commerce to employ them, and where labor union Negro-exclusion policies discouraged or prevented job mobility and escalation.

This is all deplorable but is not to be solved by name-calling, the shouting of obscenities, and raising the racist bogey. It calls for statesmanship which, unfortunately, has been sadly lacking among Negroes, and also among whites. Thus we have had this craven acceptance and condoning of anti-social agitations and demonstrations which have too often led to arson, vandalism, and killings. My position was and is that none of these deplorable situations has been improved by attacks on "whitey," the "white power structure" (which often merely means the Government) and the suddenly obnoxious "white liberals." In defending (?) their position, the self-styled Negro spokesmen have done more to increase racial antagonism than has the Ku Klux Klan. I have frequently commented on their vested interest in disaster.

Not having any illusions about white people per se, I have long been fearful that this increasing racial animosity, exacerbated by the Communist-influenced policies of Negro racial agitation, might lead to actual civil war which would certainly lead to genocide. Nobody who knows history can discount this. Like the colored people, whites also have their callous and craven politicians, their professional agitators, and their swarms of the mentally deficient, and their number and influence is not decreased by calling them dirty names and figuratively tramping on their corns. I have not forgotten that an American administration put more than 100,000 Japanese-Americans in concentration camps only twenty-four years ago or that the Turks massacred 800,000 Armenians in 1915. Nor is the fate of the Amerindians of the eastern United States to be forgotten.

In the *Christian Herald* for September, 1963, which was published on the eve of the much-touted March on Washington, I discussed the background of the Communist planning and maneuvers since 1922, of the current uproars. The article, "The Road to Riot," spoke of violence to come. And indeed within less than a year, a half dozen cities were disgraced by a wave of rioting and vandalism. However spontaneous their beginnings may have been, they were obviously exploited by elements which J. Edgar Hoover regarded as Communist. It was grim confirmation of what I had been warning against, almost alone, for years.

At the time of the shameless and inexcusable vandalistic outrages in New York City, precipitated by the shooting of an armed schoolboy by Lieutenant Thomas Gilligan of the Police Department, I was sitting on the New York County Grand Jury, which finally absolved the officer of all blame. We heard about 47 witnesses through those hot days of July and August. Immediately after we had handed down our findings and they were made public by the District Attorney, the organized agitators yelled "whitewash." Leaflets quickly appeared with Lieutenant Gilligan's picture and the caption, "Wanted for Murder!", further inciting the mob and adding grist for the agitators' mill. The loudest of these agitators were known Communists. Others, less flagrant, led and addressed big street demonstrations which the police in their singular indulgence permitted to block traffic. Thanks to the news media, which had a field day over the saturnalia, news and pictures of the shambles were broadcast with the effect of alerting similar criminal elements elsewhere. If the Negro press did anything to allay this unrest,

I have yet to hear of it. Added investigations and reviews completely upheld my position.

People who should have known better, including supposedly responsible leaders of civil rights movements, repeated the made-to-order alibis that the Hunnish outrages were caused by "ghetto" congestion, job discrimination, de facto school segregation, cultural deprivation and "police brutality." The latter charge, which has the least validity of all, is a part of the technique used by the international Communist conspiracy against the police in capitalist countries, as detailed in U.S. government documents published a decade earlier. It is designed to undermine public faith and confidence in the police as preservers of the public peace and property.

With shameless and irresponsible abandon, those designated as Negro leaders and the various news media exaggerated every incident that could be construed as an exercise of excessive police force, without any regard to the provocation. The use of firehoses, tear gas, and dogs was cited with horror, as if these were not true and tried methods of mob control the world over. There was only the mildest criticism of the men like Dr. Martin Luther King and James Farmer who had organized these mobs to march to the city centers for confrontation with "the white power structure" in order to compel the authorities, through sheer physical force, to accede to their demands. This was nonviolence?

My own observation has been that there is a minimum use of excessive force by the police whose official duty it is to use force whenever necessary. That is what the police are paid to do everywhere and in some situations they are the only barrier against chaos. The objective of the civil rights activists is clearly to inhibit the police so severely that they will be over-tolerant toward nuisance demonstrations that can lead to open rebellion. In short, they want to handcuff the police. One of the devices toward that end is the so-called civilian review board which craven politicians have advocated in a shameless bid for votes. Wherever accepted or imposed, this constitutes another victory for international Communist strategy.

I observed the police handling of the most recent Harlem

rioting and I think the police restraint was admirable in the face of the harsh provocation, including even gunfire. I understand this was true in other cities. This must have been disappointing to the top agitators who needed some instances of police terrorism in order to strengthen their propaganda campaign against law and order. These elements can be understood on the ground of self-interest. But what are we to say of the respectable citizens who joined the outcry against the police, repeated all the tired canards, and swelled the chorus of those crying for control of the police? I know of a public-spirited white man who was seeking signatures on a petition supporting the police and opposing a civilian review board. He was unable to get more than a few Negroes of importance in Harlem to sign it! Thousands of New York whites signed it.

This is one of the many instances which serve to show how widespread has been the influence of the Communist conspiracy. It touches millions who do not recognize its touch and who derisively deny being dupes.

Back in November, 1961, I had joined with Frank S. Meyer, Thomas A. Bolan, Anthony Bouscaren, Daniel J. Buckley, Miss Taylor Caldwell, Earle T. Holsapple, Mrs. Alfred Kohlberg, Frederick G. Reinicke, William F. Rickenbacker, and Godfrey Schmidt in a provisional organizing committee for The New York State Conservative Political Association, Inc. It was keenly felt that with the me-tooism of the Republican Party, conservative Republicans really had no party, and that we should remedy that condition. The founders were Kieran O'Doherty, J. Daniel Mahoney, Robert M. Saunders, Richard R. Doll, Paul N. Cheney, and Paul Franklin.

If the socialistic Liberal Party, polling only about 300,000 votes, had grown so influential with the Democratic Party in New York State that it was able to bargain for political posts, there was no reason why a Conservative Party could not wield similar influence if it could get on the ballot and show sufficient following. It turned out that we were able to get on the ballot. The new party received sufficient signatures in every county of the state, and in the first election rolled up a respectable vote of 142,000.

In May, 1964, the Conservative Party nominated me to run for Congress in the Eighteenth Congressional District represented by Representative Adam Clayton Powell. The campaign attracted a lot of attention and gave added interest to a widely-published North American Newspaper Alliance interview in which I blamed the Harlem race riots on the incessant incitement of civil rights leaders.

A letter to that effect was written by me and carried prominently by the *New York Times,* and reprinted elsewhere. The *Times* identified me as "associate editor" of the *Pittsburgh Courier.* This apparently so incensed the publishers in Pittsburgh that the editor, P. L. Prattis, wrote a letter to the *Times* denying that I held such position. It was such an unusual disavowal that before publishing Prattis' letter they telephoned me about it. I had never heard about any demotion and was as surprised as anybody else. I had held the position since 1942.

The unprecedented Prattis letter warrants reprinting:

To the Editor:

George S. Schuyler is not the associate editor of *The Pittsburgh Courier* or any of its affiliates, as stated by the italic note above his letter published September 9. He is a columnist, like Arthur Krock, and what he writes and says has no more to do with *Courier* policy than what Mr. Krock writes has to do with *Times* policy.

Several years ago when *The Courier* was under different ownership, Mr. Schuyler was designated as associate editor. That is not true today.

We offer Mr. Schuyler the freedom of publishing his views in his column. They may or may not coincide with the policy of the paper. *The Pittsburgh Courier* does not agree with the opinions written in his letter in *The Times.*

P. L. Prattis

Editor, *The Pittsburgh Courier,* Pittsburgh
Sept. 9, 1964

The facts were well known to Mr. Prattis. From August, 1926, to November, 1964, I was editorial writer for the *Courier* and therefore shaped whatever editorial policy it had. I have never yet been notified verbally nor in writing that I am not associate editor of the paper. As late as December 30, 1963, the publisher in a letter addressed me as "Associate Editor" which indicates that if there had been any change in management's policy it occurred not "years ago" but between the time the publisher's letter was written and the date of the Prattis letter to the *New York Times,* eight months later.

Following a long interview over Radio Station KMOX in St. Louis, Missouri, in which questions are posed by the listeners, I was asked what I thought about Senator Goldwater. I replied that he was a fine man, a good conservative, and that as a Republican I would vote for him for President as I usually supported the Republican ticket. And in any case, I have never considered the individual as important as what the party stands for.

My reply stirred up a storm since all of the civil rights organizations were openly fighting Goldwater because of his opposition to the Civil Rights Act which he regarded as unconstitutional. Some people called the *Courier* cancelling their subscriptions. Others demanded that I be fired. But then other letters came in, and the odd thing about the letters was that out of about sixty, only two were from Negroes, and with the exception of these two all were congratulatory. The *Courier* knew this because the publisher opened all of them before forwarding them to me, something that had never happened before.

Twice thereafter, the *Courier* went out of its way to state editorially that I was nothing more than a columnist, that I was not any kind of editor, and that my writings and opinions "did not directly reflect the policies of the *Pittsburgh Courier* and other newspapers in the *Courier* chain." One editorial appeared on the front page of all editions.

This was extremely puzzling to me and to others concerned. During all this period I had been writing the *Courier* editorials. True, I was not reflecting the "policies" of the *Courier* because these had never been stated verbally or in writing. Apparently, however, my opinions were wanted, else my services would have been discontinued. This indicated that there was definitely a *Courier* market for my views.

When I devoted an entire column to the bestowal of the Nobel Peace Prize upon Dr. Martin Luther King, it was much too caustic for the *Courier* editor who, like many other Americans, had been fascinated by the man and actually thought he was performing some valuable service to the Negro and to the country. I offered it to my friend William Loeb of the Manchester, New Hampshire, *Union Leader,* who carried it prominently. It was reprinted in many parts of the country. I held that King was quite undeserving of any prize as an apostle of peace, either globally or domestically; that his entire activity was to the contrary.

Later that month I wrote my last editorial for the *Courier* and also ceased doing my weekly world news summary; but my other contributions, such as book reviews, column, and inspirational editorial, continued. How long this will go on I cannot say.

More and more conservative Republican groups, mostly white, asked me to speak to them during the winter and spring of 1965. Then through Sid Goldberg, the editor, I became associated with the North American Newspaper Alliance. It was the first time since the cessation of the Spadea columns that I had an opportunity to reach a wide audience. My first lengthy feature came right after the Watts riot which I attributed, like all similar outbursts, to the long campaign of incitement and dire predictions by the organized claque of the civil rights agitators. They were the intellectual authors of these outrages and would have to bear the blame.

This article, to my knowledge, appeared in more than 200 daily and weekly publications, some of which carried it long after its original appearance. The conservative weekly, *Human Events,* had a lively sale of reprints, and I personally received more than 250 letters, postcards, and telegrams of commendation. The various dailies that carried the piece published dozens of letters about it and in one instance, in the *Philadelphia Bulletin,* letters appeared for a month afterward.

There was a long, vast silence from the so-called civil rights forces. Finally, *The Crisis,* official magazine of the NAACP, devoted an editorial to me, putting me down as a mere iconoclast who had gone too far, adding that because of the wide coverage of NANA the article had harmful effects.

My own view is that the numerous articles I have written on this subject in the *Courier* and elsewhere, and my talks over radio and television, have been beneficial. They have to some extent cleared the foggy air of unreality by means of facts and logic which, by previous seeming collusion or negligence of the news media, had been largely kept from the general public.

A real unity of purpose and accomplishment on the racial front can only be brought about by a realistic appraisal of public events and personalities, and not by accepting what is said and done on face value. The issue is much too serious to permit a handful of dreamers and self-serving schemers to divide the country further, increase irritation, resentment and hatred, and thus hasten the likelihood of civil strife, which has been the goal of the international Communist conspiracy for more than forty years.

To elicit more sympathy for their cause, the radical Negro agitators operating on the white collar front have been engaging in a veritable compaign of Negro mass disparagement. They write theses on the "failure" of the Negro family, dwell on the "helplessness" of the colored community, emphasize the high incidence of crime, disease, narcotics addiction, and other social evils. The white sociologists and welfarists vie with them with a suspicious relish reminiscent of the Negrophobic propaganda of a half century before, when such hatemongers as Thomas Dixon held literary sway. The picture of Negro life that emerges is pessimistic and frightening, tending to make insistence on integration ridiculous. Thus, the proclaimed aims are defeated in advance. The prestige given to public nuisance and civil disobedience hurt rather than help the Negro future. Racial adjustment is delicate and difficult enough without the efforts of all the sorcerer's apprentices who for the past half decade have devoted themselves to performing miracles that became shambles.

Relegating spurious racism to limbo, in our future America we need to stress the importance of the individual of whatever color. At best, race is a superstition. There will be no color war here if we will and work not to have one, although some kind of color line there may always be, as there is elsewhere in the world. We do not need to share the wealth as much as we need to share our heritage so that all may proudly claim ownership in it. We need to strive to become one people in our resolution, determination, and achievement instead of two peoples, colored and white.

There are forces in the world that want us to fail, and conspire toward that failure, which means disunity and destruction. We are here blessed with the right of mobility, the right of ownership, the privilege of privacy and development of personality, and the precious machinery of peaceful change. These gifts and gains it is the purpose of the conservative to defend and extend, lest we perish in the fell clutch of collectivism. These gifts and gains I have been trying in my small way to preserve.

INDEX

353

Bentley, Arthur F., 247
Benton, Thomas Hart, 256
Bernstein, David, 247
Besant, Annie, 149
Betancourt, Romulo, 293, 333
Blaney, Sgt. William, 38, 39, 52
Blanshard, Paul, 149
Bledsoe, Jules, 143
Boardman, Helen, 198
Boardman, Philip, 328
Boas, Franz, 149, 246
Boas, George, 247
Bode, Boyd H., 247
Bohn, Dr. Frank, 149
Bolan, Thomas A., 347
Bolivar, Simon, 292-293
Bolton, Francis, 322
Bolton, Rollen, 115
Boothroyd, S. L., 247
Borchard, Dr. Hermann, 273
Borgese, G. A., 317, 318
Bosch, Juan, 335
Boudin, Louis B., 179
Bouscaren, Anthony, 347
Bousfield, Dr. M. O., 196
Bowman, Leroy, 149
Boyd, Ernest, 219
Bradford, Gamaliel, 170
Bradley, Constance, 260, 263
Brewer, Inez B., 261
Bridges, Harry, 334
Bridges, Sen. Styles, 311
Bridgman, P. W., 247
Briggs, Cyril V., 123, 145, 220
Brissenden, Paul F., 247
Bromley, Dorothy Dunbar, 247
Brooks, Robert C., 247
Broun, Heywood, 148
Browder, Earl, 189, 274
Browder, Raissa Berkman, 189
Brown, Ann, 328, 329
Brown, George F., 339
Brown, Irving, 317
Brown, Joseph E., 10
Brown, Oscar C., 214, 225
Bruce, Richard, 169
Bruere, Henry, 149
Brunner, Edmund de S., 247
Buber-Neumann, Margaret, 318
Buchanan, Robert, 266

354

Buchholz, H. E., 196
Buck, Pearl, 306
Buckley, Daniel J., 347
Budenz, Louis Francis, 222, 278
Bullitt, William C., 280
Bunche, Dr. Ralph J., 328, 329
Burleigh, Harry T., 213
Burley, Dan, 233
Burnham, James, 317, 325, 329, 330
Burtt, E. A., 247
Butts, Major, 38
Bynner, Witter, 247
Byrnes, Rep. James M., 136

C

Cabell, James Branch, 168
Caldwell, Taylor, 347
Calverton, V. F. (George Goetz), 170, 179, 213, 247, 255
Calvin, Floyd, 176
Campbell, D. N. E., 150
Canby, Henry Seidel, 179
Cannon, W. B., 247
Cardwell, Ann Su, 266
Carlson, Oliver, 273
Carnap, Rudolf, 247
Carter, Elmer A., 196
Castro, Fidel, 333
Catledge, Turner, 257
Cayton, Horace R., 239
Cayton, R., 257
Cedrar, Blaise, 251
Chamberlain, John, 170, 247, 256, 266, 267, 272, 322
Chamberlain, Mrs. John, 272
Chamberlain, Neville, 248
Chamberlin, William Henry, 273
Chaplin, Charlie, 330
Chase, Stuart, 147
Cheney, Paul N., 347
Childs, John N., 247
Chodorov, Frank, 266
Church, Robert R., 198
Church, Roberta, 199
Ciliga, Anton, 274
Claessens, August, 115
Clark, Evans, 149
Cleghorn, Sarah N., 141
Cohen, Elliott E., 317, 329

355

Hitler, Adolf, 147, 224, 241, 248, 249, 254, 274, 279, 284
Hofmannsthal, E. von, 266
Holloway, Wilbert L., 159
Holmes, Jesse H., 247
Holmes, John Haynes, 141, 179, 214, 247
Holmes, S. J., 196
Holsapple, Earle T., 347
Hook, Sidney, 247, 317, 329
Hooper, Chauncey, 171
Hoover, Herbert, 207, 315
Hoover, J. Edgar, 280, 345
Howe, Frederick C., 149
Hubert, James H., 213
Huddleston, Sisley, 239
Hudson, John, 51, 52, 72
Huebsch, B. W., 247
Hughes, Langston, 159, 168, 169, 205, 221
Hughes, Rev. T. J., 179
Huiswoud, Otto, 145, 146, 147, 150, 209, 326
Hunt, Capt. John E., 93
Hurley, Patrick J., 266
Hurston, Zora Neale, 159, 272
Hutchins, Grace, 141
Hyndman, H. M., 149

I

Ickes, Harold L., 246
Irwin, Inez Haynes, 247
Ivy, James W., 144, 247

J

Jack, Hulan, 166
Jackson, Luther P., 279
Jackson, "Reverend," 51
Jefferson, Louise E., 260
Jemison, Dr. D. V., 278
Jiminez, Enrique, 295
Johns, Vere, 215
Johnson, Charles S., 157, 161, 173, 196, 316, 329
Johnson, Georgia Douglas, 169
Johnson, Jack, 301
Johnson, James Weldon, 123, 150, 157

Johnson, the Rev. John H., 225
Johnson, Manning, 190, 191, 255
Jolas, Eugene, 170
Jones, "Broadway," 143
Jones, Dr. David D., 278
Jones, Eugene Kinckle, 212
Jones, J. Raymond, 167
Jones, Julia Bumbry, 234
Jones, Rufus M., 141
Jones, William N., 192, 196, 210, 211
Josephson, Barney, 281
Josephson, Leon, 281

K

Kahn, Otto, 160
Kaiser, Philip M., 322
Kallen, Horace M., 247
Kelly, J. Livert, 243-245
Kennon, Col. L. W. V., 38
Kerensky, Alexander, 266
Khama, Ruth, 326
Khama, Seretse, 326
Kilpatrick, James Jackson, Jr., 331
Kilpatrick, William H., 247
King, Leslie, 39
King, Dr. Lorenzo H., 213
King, Dr. Martin Luther, Jr., 346, 350
Kinkaid, Thomas C., 280
Kipling, Rudyard, 42, 43, 66, 90
Kirchwey, Freda, 157
Knickerbocker, H. K., 266
Koestler, Arthur, 318
Kogon, Eugen, 318
Kohlberg, Alfred, 255, 266, 272, 274, 311
Kohlberg, Mrs. Alfred, 347
Kohn, Hans, 329
Konvitz, Milton R., 329
Krock, Arthur, 348
Kun, Bela, 144

L

Laidler, Harry W., 148, 149
LaFarge, Fr. John, 143
LaFargue, Paul, 115

357

Monnerville, Gaston, 324, 336
Montero, Mario Lequiszamon, 303
Montgomery, Robert, 317, 318
Moon, Henry Lee, 205, 206
Moore, Richard B., 145, 150
Morand, Paul, 239
Morgan, J. P., 194
Morgan, Sgt. "Tush," 88-89
Morse, Marston, 247
Morton, Ferdinand Q., 171, 195
Moseley, Philip E., 247
Moton, Robert R., 88
Muenzenberg, Willi, 151-152, 169
Mugdal, H. G., 213
Muhlen, Norbert, 329
Muller, Herman J., 317, 329
Munson, Gorham B., 179
Murray, Mrs. Peter M., 213
Mussolini, Benito, 146, 241, 243, 279
Muste, A. J., 179, 192, 222
Muzzey, David S., 247

N

Nabokov, Nikolas, 317, 318
Nathan, George Jean, 142, 168, 219
Nation, Carrie, 7
Nearing, Scott, 256
Neill, James M., 150
Neumann, Henry, 247
Newton, Jesse H., 247
Newton, Ray, 141
Nichols, Franklin H., 213
Nickerson, Hoffman, 168, 196
Nicolaevsky, Boris, 317
Nkrumah, Kwame, 147, 209, 228
Nock, Albert Jay, 150, 165
Novik, Harry, 316
Nugent, Bruce, 142
Nunn, William G., 254, 255, 285, 312

O

Oak, Liston M., 273
O'Doherty, Kieran, 347
Odum, Howard W., 168
Olivier, Sidney, 149
Omphrey, C. W., 296

Oneal, James, 115, 179
O'Neill, Eugene, 160, 219
Oppenheimer, J. Robert, 330
Overstreet, H. A., 247
Owen, Chandler, 124, 133-134, 136-138, 144
Owen, Robert, 284

P

Pach, Walter, 247
Padmore, George, 146, 147, 208-209, 326
Padover, Saul K., 247
Page, Kirby, 141
Parnell, Charles Stewart, 216
Parsons, Alice, 141
Patterson, Frederick D., 331
Patterson, Jack, 89-91
Patterson, William L., 257
Pena, Lazaro, 291
Peron, Juan, 302
Perry, Edward W., 142
Phelps-Stokes, J. G., 148
Phillips, William, 329
Pickens, William, 142, 143
Pickens, Mrs William, 213
Pitzele, Merlyn S., 329
Plisnier, Charles, 318
Pogany, Joseph, 144
Porres, Saint Martin de, 299
Porter, Paul, 149
Portuondo, William, 291
Poston, Theodore, 205, 206
Pound, Ezra, 239
Powell, Adam Clayton, Jr., 225, 278, 281, 348
Prattis, P. L., 254, 280, 348
Price, Melva, 252
Price, Victoria, 219
Pringle, Henry F., 168
Prorok, Count Byron de, 239
Putnam, George Palmer, 173-174, 185

R

Raditsa, Bogdan, 266
Ramos, Dr. Arthur, 305, 306
Randolph, A. Philip, 124, 133-140, 144, 158, 159, 161, 176, 243

White, Stanford, 143
White, Walter, 169, 202, 204, 209, 228, 275
Whiteman, Lovett Fort, 153
Whitman, Walt, 132
Wilkins, Roy, 144, 198, 199, 204, 240, 308
Wilkerson, Doxey, 257, 276
Williams, C. Dickerman, 329
Williams, David C., 317
Williams, Harry, 327, 336
Williams, Mary Lou, 281
Williams, Tennessee, 317
Williams, William Carlos, 248
Wilshire, Gaylord, 148
Wilson, "Old Bill," 129, 130, 131, 132
Wilson, Woodrow, 137
Winchell, Walter, 234
Wittels, Fritz, 256
Wood, Hollingsworth, 141
Wood, Gen. Leonard, 84

Wood, Mabel Travis, 266
Woodward, Helen, 248, 266
Wooley, Johnny, 245, 246
Worré Mary Louise, 9, 24, 26, 48, 91, 111-112, 118
Wright Brothers, 20
Wright, Dr. Louis T., 171, 195, 210

Y

Yakowlew, Boris, 318
Yergan, Lena, 324
Yergan, Dr. Max, 209, 317, 324, 329
Young, Major (Lt. Col.) Charles D., 57, 86-87, 88, 143
Young, Sidney A., 294

Z

Zack, Joseph, 266
Ziff, William B., 165-167